"Deborah Madison refers to her cooking style as getting simpler and her tastes getting lighter. But it takes the particular 'simple and light' wisdom of Deborah Madison and her deep understanding of the beauty of the vegetable to know that this is a world that can sing for itself. With just a little bit of Madison magic to set it on its way."

—YOTAM OTTOLENGHI, author of *Plenty More* and *Jerusalem*

IN MY KITCHEN

IN MY KITCHEN

A collection of new and favorite vegetarian recipes

Deborah Madison

PHOTOGRAPHY BY ERIN SCOTT

TEN SPEED PRESS

California | New York

CONTENTS

Introduction 1

A Few Things I've Learned about Vegetarian Cooking 4

About the Ingredients 21

The Recipes

A

Artichoke and Scallion Sauté over Garlic-Rubbed Toast 29

Roasted Asparagus and Arugula with Hard-Cooked Eggs and Walnuts 33

Anise Seed Shortbread with Star Anise Impressions 37

B

Green, Yellow, or Purple Beans with Sun Gold Tomatoes and Opal Basil 38

Rio Zape Beans with Smoked Chile 42

Golden Beets with Mâche, Pickled Shallots, and Purple Orach 47

Berries Scented with Rose Geranium Leaves and Flowers 49

Black-Eyed Peas with Yogurt-Tahini Sauce and Three Green Herbs 53

Black Rice with Mixed Beets, Their Greens, Avocado, Feta, and Pomegranate Seeds 54

Breakfast Bread with Rosemary and Lemon 56

Broccoli with Roasted Peppers, Feta, Olives, and Herbs 59

Yeasted Buckwheat Waffles 62

Smoky-Spicy Butter for Three Orange Vegetables 64

Bulgur and Green Lentil Salad with Chickpeas and Preserved Lemon 67

C

Savoy Cabbage, Leek, and Mushroom Braise on Toast with Horseradish Cream 69

Warm Red Cabbage Salad with Togorashi Tofu Crisps 73

Carrot Soup with Zesty Relish or Smoky-Spicy Butter 76

Cauliflower and Sweet Peppers, Saffron, Parsley, and Olives 80

Roasted Cauliflower with Romesco Sauce and a Shower of Parsley 82

Celery Root and Potato Mash with Truffle Salt 85

Silky Braised Chard and Cilantro 86

Chard Stems with Lemon 87

Chard and Saffron Flan in an Almond Crust with Spring Greens 88

A Cheese Soufflé—My Go-To Recipe 92

Citrus and Avocado with Lime-Cumin Vinaigrette and Shredded Greens 95

Collards Simmered in Coconut Milk with Shallots 97

Corn, Shiitake Mushrooms, and Sage with Millet 98

Curry Mayonnaise for Roasted Cauliflower or Steamed Broccoli 100

Quick Cucumber Pickles 101

D

Three Winter Confections Using Dried Fruit 102

    Dried Fruits with Fennel, Sesame Seeds, and Orange Flower Water 102

    Figs with Toasted Almonds and Anise Seed 103

    Dates with Almond Paste or Marzipan 104

E

Egg Salad for Spring with Tarragon, Lovage, and Chives 105

Scrambled Eggs Smothered with Crispy Bread Crumbs 107

Eggplant Gratin with a Golden Dome of Saffron-Ricotta Custard 108

Roasted Eggplant, Two Ways 112

    Roasted Eggplant on the Stovetop 114

    Roasted Eggplant with Dill, Yogurt, and Walnuts 114

F

Mission Figs Roasted with Olive Oil, Honey, and Thyme 116

Warm Feta with Toasted Sesame Seeds 118

Shaved Fennel Salad with Fennel Blossoms, Fronds, and Pistachios 121

Trouchia: Failed-to-Catch-a-Trout Frittata 122

H

Herb (and Wild Green) Salad 124

Herb-Laced Fritters Made with Good Stale Bread and Ricotta 128

Hummus Worth Making 132

J

Roasted Jerusalem Artichoke Soup with Sunflower Sprouts and Seeds 134

K

Kale and Walnut Pesto with Roasted or Seared Winter Squash 138

Kale and Quinoa Gratin 140

L

Hearty Lentil Minestrone with Kale 144

Green Lentils with Yogurt, Sorrel, and Parsley Sauce 146

Red Lentil Soup with Berbere 149

M

Thick Marjoram Sauce for Beets
(and Other Vegetables) 152

Masa Crêpes with Chard, Black
Beans, Avocado, and Pickled Onions
156

Mushroom Soup for Company 161

Dried Porcini, Fresh Mushroom,
and Whole Tomato Ragout with
Seared Polenta 163

N

Stinging Nettle Soup with
Nigella Seeds 167

O

Rough-Cut Oats with Dried Cherries,
Raisins, and Toasted Almonds 170

Olive Oil, Almond, and Blood Orange
Cake 173

Easy Pink Onion Pickles 175

Caramelized Onions with Vinegar
and Cloves 176

Caramelized Onion Frittata with
Sherry Vinegar 178

P

Pasta with Caramelized Onions
and Crushed Roasted Walnuts 180

Pasta with Gorgonzola 181

White Peaches or Nectarines
in Lemon Verbena Syrup 184

Roasted Pepper and Tomato Salad
with Basil and Capers 186

Smoky Pimento Cheese
on Cucumbers 188

An Improvised Platter Salad 189

Potato and Chickpea Stew
with Sautéed Spinach 192

Potato and Green Chile Stew 195

Red Chile and Posole with Blue Corn
Tortilla Chips and Avocado 198

Q

Quince Braised in Honey
and Wine 202

Quinoa and Buttermilk Pancakes 203

Quinoa Soup with Spinach, Corn,
Feta, and Cilantro 204

R

Seared Radicchio Draped with
Mozzarella 206

Shredded Radicchio with a Garlicky
Dressing 208

Rhubarb-Raspberry Compote 211

Brown Rice Porridge with Nut Butter
and Chia Seeds 212

Yellow Coconut Rice with Scallions
and Black Sesame Seeds 213

Baked Ricotta Infused
with Thyme 215

Romesco Sauce 218

Roasted Fingerling Potatoes to
Serve with Romesco Sauce 219

S

Chopped Salad with Toasted Seeds and Marjoram-Mint Dressing 220

Sea Greens with Cucumbers, Ginger, and Sesame 222

Summer Squashes with Herb Blossoms, Basil, Pine Nuts, and Parmigiano-Reggiano 223

Japanese Sweet Potato Soup with Ginger, Smoked Salt, and Aged Balsamic Vinegar 228

Sweet Potato (or Pumpkin) Pudding with Silky Persimmon Purée 229

Sweet Potato and Coconut-Milk Curry with Paneer 234

Pan-Griddled Sweet Potatoes with Miso-Ginger Sauce 237

T

Tofu and Cilantro Salad with Roasted Peanuts 238

Tofu Triangles with Red Onions and Tender Greens 240

Golden Tofu with Orange and Yellow Peppers 242

Tomato and Red Pepper Tart in a Yeasted Crust 245

Sweet-Tart Sun Gold Tomato Soup with Avocado Relish 247

Three Tomato Sauces 250

   A Sauce Made with Canned Tomatoes 250

   A Sauce Made with Fresh Tomatoes 250

   An Oven-Roasted Tomato Sauce 251

Tomato and Roasted Cauliflower Curry with Paneer 252

Roasted Tomatoes and Fingerling Potatoes with Thyme, Olives, and Capers 255

A Rough-and-Ready Turnip Soup, Refined 258

V

Braised Summer Vegetables 260

W

Walnut Nugget Cookies 265

Winter Squash Braised in Pear or Apple Cider 266

Winter Squash and Caramelized Onion Soup with Eight Finishes 269

Native Wild Rice and Celery Root Soup 272

Y

Yogurt, Cumin, and Green Herb Sauce 273

Z

Zucchini Cake, Two Ways 275

   Zucchini Cakes with Cheddar, Oregano, and Tomatilla Salsa 276

   Zucchini Pancakes with Feta and Dill 277

Acknowledgments 278

Index 279

INTRODUCTION

I started cooking for others decades ago. I cooked at the San Francisco Zen Center, Tassajara Zen Mountain Center (and resort, come summer), Green Gulch Farm, Chez Panisse in Berkeley, Greens in San Francisco, Café Escalera in Santa Fe, and the American Academy in Rome. I began cooking when vegetarian food was weird—sincere, but stodgy—and when there were few resources available to help one learn about how to put vegetables in the center of the plate. Now I am cooking at a time when vegetarian food is part of a great mash-up of taste, values, and experiences. It is finally much more accepted and really not such a big deal. One doesn't have to defend one's position nearly as often or as fiercely as one used to; and in any case, one's position can be quite fluid—vegetarian one day, omnivore the next.

So much has changed in these decades, from values to ingredients, that it's sometimes hard for me to tell what people value when it comes to their own cooking. I look at a magazine that one week rates snacks at Trader Joe's and a few weeks later tells about the wonderful pastries you can make with brioche dough—a challenging dough to make—or how to butcher a lamb—something that's not easily within the reach or desire of most people. My guess is that one's cooking life can be very fluid, too, that many people go to the effort to make something by hand—to cook—and probably the same people do plenty of assembling from premade foods. There may be lots of people who make their own pizzas—I know one man who has made that his expertise—but pizza places have also gotten much better (not the chains, but small independent businesses) that perhaps it's not as compelling to make your own as it was when there were no alternatives and we were curious. Fresh pasta used to be so important to make at home; now many of us can buy good fresh pasta, and there are some really excellent dried pastas now available, too. Other prepared foods, from salsas to fermented foods, tortillas to breads, have also gotten better, so why not use them? Good food matters and so does being able to make it ourselves. But when my cooking is helped by some of the products that are now available—foods that are often made by people who care passionately about their craft—I'm happy to support their efforts just as their products support mine.

I cook every day, but when I recently looked at my notes, I realized that I hadn't made pasta by hand for some time, or pizza. I decided to revisit both, and it's been a pleasure, but it's also helped me realize that I prefer much simpler foods and preparations than I used to. We change as our culture changes, and I found I have been cooking in a more straightforward, less complicated fashion—one that is, for the most part, no less delicious. Fresh pastas, yeasted dough, pies and tarts both savory and sweet, or an involved dish that proudly takes the center of the plate—these still have their place. But some can be radically simplified without loss of flavor; or lightened, perhaps through the choice of one grain over another; or recast in light of the ingredients we have today that we didn't necessarily have in the past—coconut oil, berbere, freekeh, chia seeds, smoked paprika, truffle salt, real balsamic vinegar, and heirloom beans, to name but a few.

If you garden, even a little, there's a host of interesting plants to grow and cook with, and some of those that come up by the zillions in springtime can be a source of exotic greens and garnishes. I've also started to make use of some of the wild plants that are good to eat and are growing in my yard, and that has added to my kitchen vocabulary. Musk mustard in an herb, and wild green salad is a treat.

The one hundred or so dishes gathered here are those that have settled happily into my kitchen and my life, in one form or another. As a cook, I change things around in the kitchen all the time. I find it hard to follow a recipe, even my own. I learn from mistakes or inattention, and in the process I sometimes come up with something I like better. New ingredients, or new ways of putting ingredients together, also inspire me. So in a sense, these are all new albeit familiar dishes. Sometimes they're recipes that have been forgotten or overlooked but that deserve to be revisited and brought to light, like Warm Feta with Toasted Sesame Seeds (page 118)—so easy, so much simpler than when originally written, and so good!

And while I'm not vegan or gluten-free either, quite often my recipes are. They just turn out that way, and when they do, they are marked with a V (for vegan) or a GF (for gluten-free). Sometimes it just takes a small adjustment to make a recipe vegan or gluten-free, perhaps changing the fat or the grain used or leaving out the yogurt or cheese. For example, Rio Zape Beans with Smoked Chile (page 42) are finished with a dollop of sour cream—unless they're not. They're excellent either way.

Since I'm all for eating more lightly today, many of my old, rich favorites have a sleeker look. For example, a chard and saffron tart with pine nuts is as creamy as it once was, but the buttery crust is gone in favor of a baking dish lined with ground almonds (see page 88). It's a compromise I can happily live with, and, while not super-sleek, it's less rich by far. I'm still not about to give up my eggs and cheese entirely, but I can minimize them and, in some cases, leave them out. An eggplant gratin originally called for cheese "to make it more substantial," because in the early days of Greens I was very nervous that our food would seem too light. Now the cheese just seems excessive, so it's gone.

As I've delved more into the garden, and the growing of food, I've come to enjoy resources that are, at the moment, uniquely available to those who garden. (Though I can almost assure you that they're coming to a market near you.) Still, the foods you grow will always taste better than those shipped from afar. I think of Herb (and Wild Green) Salad (page 124), which uses the gorgeous purple orach leaves that arrive in spring and that eventually become the tall mountain spinach that will appear in dishes later in the season. My garden informs and beautifies my food as much as anything else, and when I mention it, my hope is that it will encourage your own attempt to grow something, even if it's just a pot of chives.

These recipes, then, are my favorites—changed or lightened a little or a lot, or utterly new, made several times over to make sure I'm presenting them clearly, and served to friends and family. Some of these are here because someone's told me it's a recipe they love, such as Citrus and Avocado with Lime-Cumin Vinaigrette and Shredded Greens (page 95). It's not quite the same recipe here as it was before—it's maybe even better than it once was—but I might not have thought about it if someone hadn't said that dressing was her favorite.

While I am quite comfortable with a mostly meatless diet, and actually prefer it, if you, dear reader, want to pair these recipes with lamb or beef or chicken or fish—or bison or yak or whatever—please do. Both approaches are fine—my recipes can be the vegetable side or in the center of the plate.

And finally, the "we" in this book refers to my husband, Patrick McFarlin, and me. We live in the country in northern New Mexico, which is far from the lush land of California where I grew up, so I'm often in the same position as a shopper as most people are. I am a big believer in the farmers' market and in the food and relationships one finds there. Though I have my own garden, I regard farmers as the experts, and I go to them for a great many foods, especially those I am still shy of growing myself. We are truly home cooks and eaters, and without a doubt, I deeply appreciate being able to cook something from scratch and do so daily. I hope you find these—some of my favorite recipes and approaches—delicious and that they enhance your life as they do mine.

A FEW THINGS I'VE LEARNED ABOUT VEGETARIAN COOKING

The elements of good vegetarian cooking are mostly the same as for any other kind of cooking: use good ingredients and understand how they work, cook the dishes that you feel comfortable making, make a few things well, and, above all, don't apologize. If you need a good vegetarian entrée for a special meal, be prepared to spend some time on it. Otherwise, consider keeping things simple; a sweet potato with some tangy goat cheese and a salad is a fine, little supper.

Good vegetarian cooking is so much more than "food minus the meat." That said, there are a few skills, attitudes, and practices that will help you enjoy cooking with vegetables. I hope they will bring pleasure and success to all your cooking.

Choose Your Ingredients Thoughtfully

Don't just toss produce in your shopping basket willy-nilly because it's on your list. Look at it to make sure it's as fresh as you want or need it to be. As you shop, keep in mind how long foods will last which should be cooked and eaten first and which will keep.

Learn to use your nose to tell you that a melon or peach will taste good (reject it if there is no perfume) or that a cheese will be a good one or that the milk at home is fresh. Train your fingers to find the right degree of give in an avocado. Develop an eye for the sturdiness of fresh leafy greens. Practice and attention will make you discerning; even with dried beans, there's a difference between ancient cracked ones and those no more than a year old. And when you encounter good food, be prepared to pay the price that it is worth.

Do Research If Possible

What is the quality of your eggs, your dairy, your vegetables? Where and how and by whom were they produced? Learning what's happening in farming and in food politics can prepare you to make informed and ethical choices. You can find good, current information about our food system on the Internet (the Cornucopia Institute is a good source; Civil Eats is another), in documentaries, and in books. If you have a farmers' market, use it. If you're so inclined and time allows, you might attend farming conferences; you can learn a lot there that you might not even hear of otherwise. If you want to cook with and eat the best-quality food, you have to know

what you're consuming, and to know what you're consuming, you have to work a bit. Sadly, there are good reasons to be concerned, so inform yourself however you can.

Grow Something!

Since I started to garden, my excitement about cooking has reignited. I have access to all kinds of edibles I can't find at the store. When sprouts of deep purple orach (also known as mountain spinach) appear each spring, for a few weeks they find their way into my salads. My herbs are so flavorful and so readily available, and they don't come in plastic containers that can't be recycled. I can enjoy vegetables at all stages, from tiny seedlings and sprouts all the way through to seeds again. The taste of truly fresh food that you've grown and picked yourself, whether it's the makings of an entire dish or a single tomato or a few zucchini, is nothing like anything the supermarket labels "farm-fresh." Real freshness has its own flavor and appearance— its own magic. Even if it's just a few chives and their blossoms or a summer squash, you'll see, taste, and relish the pleasures of utterly fresh food—and you'll know the difference from that moment on.

Learn to Use a Knife

Vegetables need cutting, slicing, trimming, paring—and you can't leave it all to the food processor. (I don't even have a food processor anymore.) Being proficient with a knife will pay you back many times over in terms of ease of preparation and time saved in the kitchen.

By "knife," I mean a *sharp* one, not some dull old thing you're going to hurt yourself with. And I mean the *right kind* for the job. Don't use a boning knife to cut vegetables— it doesn't provide enough points of contact to be effective. A knife with a long, flat blade is a better choice—more surface area means more opportunity for contact.

Here are the knives you need:

- An inexpensive paring knife or two because they're easily lost
- A heavy knife or cleaver for cutting big winter squashes and the like
- A knife with a flat, wide blade intended for chopping vegetables (a Japanese vegetable knife is ideal)
- A serrated knife for slicing bread and tomatoes

That makes four. That's not a lot of knives. Keep them clean and dry; store them in a block or on a magnetic strip; hone them regularly (except the serrated one); and have them sharpened professionally every year or so.

There are plenty of videos online that demonstrate knife skills; once you learn the basics, using a knife well just requires time and practice. Train on piles of leaves that are heading to the compost—just whale on them and get your arm working. Or take vegetables intended for a rustic or puréed soup, curl your fingers so that your knuckles guide your knife blade instead of your eyes (keep your head upright), and go for it—remember, for the blade to cut you while you are doing this, it would have to be turned at a really ineffective and highly unlikely angle. Don't worry about being machine-gun fast; you might be, or you might not be. You're a home cook, not a chef or line cook working twelve hours a day, so be kind to yourself and keep your expectations reasonable. If you work at it, you will gain the proficiency you need—which is, simply, to be comfortable and competent with a knife.

And give yourself plenty of room to work. Whether you use a plastic or wood cutting board, work on a large surface and don't cramp yourself. There's nothing worse than corralling an unruly pile of leaves on a little tiny board meant for cheese (and with a dull knife, to boot). My heart goes out to people trying to cook this way; it's so much harder. Keep your work area and your work surfaces spacious, clear, and open.

Coax Flavor from Sweet Vegetables

One excellent way of getting the best out of sweet vegetables (like peppers, onions, carrots, winter squash, sweet potatoes, or beets) is to embrace caramelizing. The sugars that abide so abundantly in these vegetables are drawn out with heat and in a hot pan with little or no liquid, they'll start to brown, or caramelize, as they come out. This caramelizing can be a great source of flavor and depth in a dish, because as the sugars caramelize, they take on a slight bitterness that helps temper and add complexity to the sweetness of these vegetables.

You can't rush browning, so here's where a glass of wine or another drink of your choice really helps. It's one of your cooking tools. You sip, talk, fiddle with corks and bottles, and once in a while give the pot a stir. Then all of a sudden you'll catch a scent that tells you that, yes, your vegetables have browned. Or your ear will tell you through a change in the sounds coming from the pan that it's time to give your dish active attention. Once you've got that nice brown surface, you can use a technique that's used with meat, namely, deglazing with wine or water or stock to lift those concentrated bits of flavor from the pan and spread them throughout the dish.

Use Good Fats and Use Them Effectively

Another tip for achieving good flavors in vegetable cooking is to use good fats. Oils and butter should be fresh tasting, never rancid, and always of the highest quality. You can tell if oil is rancid by its fishy, off smell when you heat it. Rancid oil not only tastes bad, it introduces free radicals into your body, which are not good for it. Good oil costs money; it has been expensive throughout human history. Only relatively recently, with the use of chemical solvents in the refining process, has oil become cheap—and the result is poor quality. As for butter, choose organic if you can. Pesticides tend to reside in fat, so this is one place you can try to avoid them.

Understanding the power of fats is of vital importance, especially in vegetarian cooking—we're always looking for ways to build flavor, and fats contribute to that. Not that vegetarian food has to be high in fat; it doesn't, nor should it. But fat does play an essential role in contributing good flavors to foods, and it's to the cook's advantage to know how fat works.

Fat both carries other flavors and is a source of flavor. Heating oil with garlic and rosemary creates a fragrant atmosphere that extends to the whole of the dish. But oils with distinct flavors of their own, such as roasted peanut oil, dark sesame oil, a really good olive or walnut oil, contribute *their* flavors to a dish. A vegetarian stir-fry that lacks that tasty bit of chicken or pork is ever so much better when finished with a fragrant roasted peanut oil—along with some roasted peanuts. A few drops of dark sesame oil or chile oil added to a bowl of miso soup make it spring to life; a spoonful—even a teaspoon—of cream can unite diverse flavors in a soup.

Nuts and seeds, such as hazelnut, walnut, sunflower seed, and avocado, are the source of many good oils. Before they become oils, nuts and seeds offer good flavors and interesting textures, and because of the satisfying sensation their richness provides, they can be a boon to the cook. Nuts provide a pleasant mouthfeel, making food satisfying. Whether you use nuts as butters or in a crunchier way, a vegetarian cook can do a lot with them. Not only is the quality of their fats good, nuts and seeds are also good protein sources. Like oils, however, you want them to be fresh, not rancid.

Nuts in their shells will keep for a very long time without spoiling. The shells also serve as a governor, keeping you eating them slowly and one at a time as you crack them, rather than pressing handfuls into your face. I keep a bowl of nuts (with nutcrackers) out in fall and winter, when they're fresh. People seem to enjoy dipping in and cracking a few nuts every so often. Often we put them on the table at the end of a meal to accompany pieces of dark chocolate or a dried fruit confection for dessert.

Grains and Beans

These two foods are always thought of as what vegetarians really live on, but of course, vegetarians eat all kinds of foods. Without going into a long discussion about how to cook them, which I've done in my other books, let me just say that it's essential that beans be thoroughly cooked if they're to be easily digestible. Beans can be simmered or gently cooked in the oven, a technique that's especially good for special and expensive heirloom beans. Beans cook quickly and thoroughly in a pressure cooker, plus you have the advantage of the broth, which is another ingredient, too. Or you can slow down their cooking in a slow cooker. Some grains, especially whole groats, take as long as beans to cook, so you might as well make extras and freeze them in 1-cup packets. It's much easier to incorporate them into the foods you eat if they're already prepared.

Try some heirloom beans or different grains if you want a change and a surprise. The differences may be subtle, but not all are alike. At a tasting of heirloom beans in Santa Fe, a farmer wanted to know which varieties the local chefs preferred so she could focus her efforts in growing only those. She had a few seeds at a time to begin with, so it was a meaningful question. The differences were surprising. Some beans actually tasted like dirt. Others were sweet and delicate. The most gorgeous purple ones were the most disappointing on the tongue, but we all pined for their color. What we usually regard as a bland, interchangeable food proved to be anything but.

As a country, we seem to go with one bean or one grain at a time in our cooking. But it's much more interesting to mix them up with each other and with other ingredients, such as pasta or potatoes. In Italy, for example, there are traditional rustic soups that include mixtures of legumes and grains, such as *jota*, a mixture of corn, barley, and white beans; or *imbrecciata*, a soup made with chickpeas, lentils, and beans; or *farro*, a soup based on white beans or chickpeas and farro. These mixtures are much more interesting than eating dishes based on only one bean or grain. They're pretty too—and, of course, we eat with our eyes.

You can combine beans and grains in all kinds of dishes, like a bean and pasta gratin. Or, instead of a salad based just on cracked wheat and parsley, you can make a more interesting one that consists of cracked wheat plus green lentils plus chickpeas, all seasoned with tarragon, walnuts, and walnut oil (page 67). However you mix them up, just make sure they're well seasoned with sea salt and freshly ground pepper and that they have enough butter or olive oil and plenty of fresh herbs and maybe some crisped bread crumbs for texture. You can't go wrong with a spoonful of these on a plate.

Learn How Foods and Flavors Work

Since vegetarians don't have all those dynamic meat flavors to work with, it becomes especially important for us to know how to preserve, deepen, and extend the flavors of the foods we cook. This is, of course, important for whatever food you're cooking, but I don't think that we're exposed to enough useful information about vegetables. The beet, for example, is a perfectly good vegetable that leaves many people confused. When people say they don't like them—and they usually say that adamantly—I'm convinced that it's because beets contain both earthy and sweet components, and that makes them confusing to the tongue. What bridges the spectrum are acids—lemon, vinegar, lime, orange—or pungent ingredients—olives, mustards, salty cheeses, arugula, watercress. Once you introduce these elements, you will see, and taste, beets very differently. You might even like them. And if not, then you probably really don't care for the vegetable, and that's fine, too.

Knowing how foods work—and work together—gives you the tools to cook well and intuitively. I could go on in this vein for every vegetable.

Vinegars

Vinegar, like oil, is a marvelous ingredient. And, like oils, vinegars vary. Highly acidic vinegars, such as sherry vinegar, go well with heavy, viscous oils like walnut or hazelnut. The lower the acidity (which is expressed in terms of the percentage of acetic acid, or grains), the more vinegar you can use in proportion to oil in a dressing. The standard 3:1 oil to vinegar ratio really depends on the acidity of your vinegar (or lemon). A dressing made with (highly acidic) sherry vinegar might be 6:1; with rice wine vinegar, 2:1. Fresh lemon juice might be closer to 3:1, but only if you're using Eureka or other tart lemons. Meyer lemons are less acidic, so you'll have to taste to get the proportion right. And true balsamic vinegar (not vinegar made sweet with caramelized sugar) is more acidic than other vinegars, but the natural sugars balance the acidity so well it seems less so.

Often, when you taste a finished soup or stew and think it needs salt, what it really needs is just a few drops of vinegar or lemon juice to bring up the flavors and get them into alignment. Or an onion frittata may already be delicious, but it's spectacular if you melt a teaspoon of butter and add a splash of sherry vinegar, then let it reduce to a sharp, deep-flavored sauce (page 178). The vinegar-butter amalgamation flatters the sweetness of the onion and makes the dish more interesting to eat.

Vegetable Stocks

One way of building and extending flavor is through the use of stocks. But let me say right away that, on a daily basis, I'd rather make a dish that doesn't need a stock; because, like you, I'm busy. Still, stocks don't have to be especially time-consuming. My most frequent approach is the quick stock—a thin stock based on the trimmings of the vegetables used in a soup or whatever dish I'm making, plus maybe a bay leaf or other appropriate herb. It's a stock that cooks in twenty-five minutes at most. It doesn't have the quality of a broth, but it does underscore the flavors already being featured in a dish.

Here are a few general tips for making stocks.

- A stock is not a catchall for old or spoiled vegetables. A mushroom that's dried or opened is fine; one that's slimy is not. A limp carrot is okay; a moldy one is not. My policy: If I'm in doubt, I throw it out.
- Chop your stock vegetables, because the more surface area that's exposed to the water, the more quickly the vegetables will yield their flavors.
- The more vegetables you use in proportion to water, the more flavor your stock will have.

- Allow a cooked stock to settle a few minutes before straining so that miscellaneous matter can fall to the bottom. On the other hand, don't let it steep too long; certain herbs can turn bitter, especially fine-textured dried ones.

- If you're not sure about how an ingredient works, boil some separately for fifteen minutes or so to see if you like the results. Some foods can turn grassy or bitter or just not be very good. Others might be surprisingly fine—like eggplant.

- Think imaginatively about what you can use. Corncobs stripped of their kernels; chard stems; the skins, seeds, and strings from winter squash; a handful of lentils or almonds; celery root peelings; and the roots and leaves of leeks are all great sources of flavor.

There are only a few things to avoid:

- Brassicas (the cabbage family members) with flavors that are very dominating and sulfurous
- Parsnips and beets, unless you want their particular flavors and colors
- Tiny celery seeds, powdered herbs, or ground pepper—they can turn bitter
- Artichoke trimmings
- Anything you definitely wouldn't want to eat

Composing a Vegetarian Menu

One place where vegetarian cooking does depart from meat-based cooking is in the expectations for how a menu should be composed. What's on the plate? What is the main attraction, and what are the supporting players? This, for most people, is the most difficult aspect of vegetarian cooking to deal with. Even after all these years, I can be stumped trying to plan the menu for a serious vegetarian dinner with guests who aren't vegetarian. It's never easy, especially if you think about it too much. Over the years I've tried many menu approaches. Here are the ones that work for me and why they do.

PICK A CENTRAL DISH Follow the classic meal pattern and have something impressive in the center of the plate—not a fake piece of meat, but something very specific and focused; essentially, a centerpiece that other dishes flatter and complement, just as the vegetables complement meat in a standard Western menu. This approach can help nonvegetarians relax because the form of the meal is at least familiar. The kinds of foods that best fill this center role are foods that have had something done to them; foods that have been layered, stacked, folded, or stuffed, for example.

Of course these refinements can be time consuming. But it's precisely this effort that produces a dish that has focus, clarity, and enough interest that the diner's eye isn't restlessly seeking for something to be "it." Recently I ordered a vegetarian meal that consisted of a pile of white rice with four vegetables. It came across as side dishes without the meat. However, if the cook had made the rice into a rice cake, placed the vegetables on it, and served my fellow diner's delicious Thai peanut sauce around it, it would have been ever so much better. It's a small shift in focus, but it makes a big difference.

Today, expectations about what's at the center of the plate are much more relaxed than they used to be. A lot of us have become happier with less, especially at dinner—and we certainly feel less stressed cooking more simply. A soup or salad, seared winter squash, a vegetable sauté, a quesadilla, supper sandwiches, an omelet—all these simple foods make perfectly fine, eminently doable weekday entrées. Taking extra care with presentation or table settings (see following) balances the simplicity of the menu so that a soup, salad, cheese plate, and dessert (or not) can work just as well for company as a more elaborate menu. And when I'm cooking for myself and my immediate family? My notion of what can be the main course has, many times, rested firmly on a single baked sweet potato.

PRESENTATION It turns out that some of the easier dishes to make are rather formless—stir-fries, sautés, pastas, and ragouts, for example. They just sit there loose on the plate. But you can still give them focus by serving your stew over firm polenta cut into triangles (see page 163) and your sauté over garlic-rubbed toast with some thin shavings of Parmigiano-Reggiano, or maybe tucked inside a popover. The simple act of nestling spaghetti in a wide-rimmed pasta plate gives it a visual tidiness while keeping it warm. When it comes to pasta, try to avoid it for a formal meal unless it's baked—it doesn't hold its heat well and it's meant to be eaten quickly. If you want your meal to go on for a while, make spaghetti a second course. For a main course, consider lasagna or another kind of baked pasta dish that has more "done" to it and will hold its heat.

AVOID REPETITION Is everything you're serving white, or based on onions? Does it all involve last-minute timing? Or is everything cooked on top of the stove? It's amazingly easy to repeat both ingredients and techniques without even noticing until it's nearly on the table. When you're sketching out your menu, look at the entire meal before starting to cook, especially if it's a big-deal dinner rather than just supper for the family. Notice if you've chosen a caramelized onion pasta, a garlic soup, and a leek gratin and plan to make a few changes if you have. (If it's too late, you can always cast such a meal as an allium festival.)

Making It All Possible

I love to find out from people what makes them want to cook and what makes it hard for them. Some people really enjoy the tactile quality of handling ingredients. Others love that they can come home from work and do something that they or their families can actually enjoy right then, not years later. Others dread the thought of dinner and shopping and would rather skip it, eat cereal, or order in. Recently I've met a number of retired couples who don't think twice about having their small dinner parties catered. There's a reason why there are personal chefs: there are just

a lot of people who don't cook, don't want to cook, or feel they don't have time. If you don't have the luxury of farming out your dinner prep, or you want to cook but need help getting started, here are some tips to help make cooking more possible.

LEARN TO WORK IN A NONLINEAR FASHION This will save you time and sanity. Only TV chefs, who have everything prepped ahead of time, *don't* do this. Cooking doesn't progress in a straight line but meanders from here to there. For example, you put the pasta water on to boil first, even though cooking the pasta is the last step. Or if the onions for a soup are going to cook for 15 minutes, you can use that time to prepare the rest of the ingredients. This is one reason why it's important to read your recipe through before starting. If you can see the whole picture, you have an enormous advantage, because several things are always going on simultaneously when you cook. Like tying a shoe, cooking in a nonlinear fashion is one of those things that is hopelessly complicated to describe. But it's crucial to cooking without going crazy. (I confess that I have the hardest time following a recipe, even my own—maybe *especially* my own—and this is one rule I should take more to heart than I do. It really does make a difference.)

LEARN TO MAKE A FEW THINGS WELL Trying too many new dishes at once makes cooking a chore unless you're hugely enthusiastic and energetic. It's better to build your cooking vocabulary dish by dish. Decide what you like to eat then practice cooking that type of dish until you feel confident. Once you understand the basics, you'll be able to cook creatively and easily, for most dishes of a particular type follow the same pattern. Then go on to something new—or do as a friend of mine does: cook the same three meals as long as your friends and family will let you.

SIMPLIFY THE MENU Consider making one- or two-dish meals standard. They're less taxing and there are fewer dishes to wash. Eggs make a great fast supper. Fruit for dessert isn't just healthy; it's easy. In winter try confections of dried fruits and nuts or walnut cookies (pages 102 and 265).

DEVELOP A ROUTINE In today's world of too much choice, having something of a routine can save time spent thinking about what to make for dinner. Besides, as eaters, we enjoy repetition, both in restaurants and at home. It's reassuring, and it's involving ("Oh, it was better last week" or "We're having my favorite dish!"). Our mothers and grandmothers were big on routines: a roast on Sunday, the leftovers on Tuesday, and so forth. They were busy women working and running households and farms. Having a menu plan made life simpler for them. It can for us, too.

HAVE DO-AHEADS Always working days in advance of a meal can be confusing, but having a few easy things done ahead of time does pay off later. For example, having prewashed salad greens often makes the difference between having a salad and not, so take the time to wash and thoroughly dry greens when you can. Or having some steamed beets or cooked beans and a few chopped onions on hand make getting a meal started much easier.

Certain foods can return to the table in another form, and often it takes only a little extra time to double a recipe. Leftover polenta can be served in all kinds of ways; beans, lentils, and chickpeas can go into salads, soups, stews, or purées; whole grains can be frozen and later added to soups. Leftover rice, quinoa, and couscous can be shaped into croquettes or made into salads. Soups usually taste better on the second or third day.

USE A FEW MACHINES Machines can helpfully speed things up or usefully slow things down. A pressure cooker makes short work of long-cooking foods, finishing them in about one-third the time. Slow cookers mean food can cook while you're at work or asleep. Some people swear by their rice cookers and food processors. My kitchen space is minimal so I have a blender, a pressure cooker, and a mixer. That's about it, and it's fine for me. You might want a few more kitchen gadgets—use whatever works best for you.

HAVE A FEW GOOD-QUALITY CONVENIENCE FOODS ON HAND Probably, your region has a specialty food, like tamales or pierogies, that can be bought frozen and set aside for those nights when you just can't cook. Canned organic chickpeas and black beans are a good resource, as are some frozen vegetables, such as lima beans, black-eyed peas, okra, and peas. Condiments like capers, olives, curry pastes, coconut milk, and roasted peppers can accomplish a lot. A spoonful of good olive oil adds a splendid finish to plain food of good quality, such as a plate of asparagus. Tofu couldn't be easier to cook.

ENLIST HELP About the time you think your children are able, get them started on some simple kitchen tasks. Eventually a child can be put in charge of the whole dinner once a week, from planning the menu to cooking it. Having kids work in the kitchen is undoubtedly a struggle at first, but later it can be a great gift for the parent who will get some relief from daily cooking while the child can take pride in making a meaningful contribution. The most interesting chapters to research and write about in my book *What We Eat When We Eat Alone* were about young people learning to cook, why they did so, and what it meant for their parents. Imagine being a parent walking into the house after a long day's work and smelling dinner cooking! Imagine your child competently cooking a meal for his or her friends. Actually, one of the most moving meals I've eaten was cooked by a seventeen-year-old girl for the friends of her parents who had known her since she was born. From appetizers to dessert, she pulled it off flawlessly. Such children, when they grow up, will leave home with a truly practical skill.

Holidays and Special Occasions

Most holidays have traditional foods that don't involve meat, as well as those that do, so vegetarians are not entirely excluded from what everyone else is eating. In fact, one way to approach the traditional holiday meal is just to make all those side dishes—they're usually more than ample and wonderfully varied—and ignore the traditional turkey, ham, lamb, or brisket. Generally, it's the candied yams, cranberries, and dressings that people love best at Thanksgiving. There's no need for tofurky—though if you like it, go ahead.

Another approach to holidays and special occasions is to simply make those foods that are special to you or your guests. These might include complicated dishes, like ravioli or lasagna made from scratch; foods that are richer than those we usually eat, such as a sizzling risotto gratin; or foods that are costly, such as truffles or a galette made with lots of wild mushrooms. Or you might wish to celebrate the day by using only foods from your farmers' market or garden—a truly local feast.

Of course, the other things that make holidays special are the joy of the occasion, the people we're with, and what's in our hearts. In my experience, the food ends up being important, but often not quite as important as we imagined it would be. In the end, it's about sitting down with friends—and quite often strangers or those in your community who you may not know well but who need a place to be for that holiday meal.

Above All, Don't Apologize

Your food may not taste as good to you as it does to those to whom you're serving it. If so, it's most likely because you've been inhaling it for a while so its flavors are no longer vivid and new. But that doesn't mean that others are faking their praise. Even if they are, don't worry about it. And if you feel you haven't met your own expectations, don't apologize because you feel your food is lacking. If you do that, you just take away the pleasure of others. In my experience, this can be a hard lesson to learn, yet I feel it's the most important one, and one I'm still learning.

ABOUT THE INGREDIENTS

Every cook has her or his own approach to ingredients, and these are a few of mine. For the most part I don't cook with foods that require label reading, but I do make sure that ingredients I use are organic or certified by the Non-GMO Project. I use plenty of vegetables, mostly olive oil, and always sea salt and freshly ground pepper. The rest is in the details, such as using nuts and nut oils that are as fresh as possible and not rancid. In this section, I'll talk about a few ingredients that I have changed my thinking about over time.

Balsamic Vinegar

I'm ruined. After tasting *real* balsamic vinegar, aged for sixteen years in its casks of seven different woods, I cannot go back to anything else. True, aged balsamic vinegar is costly, precious, and truly amazing. It's issued by the drop and is delicious on worthy fruit and caramel as well as some savory dishes. It is not poured into vinaigrettes and certainly not boiled with sugar to make a "gastrique." It is perfect as it is, and it is like nothing we usually encounter. A twelve-year-old vinegar can be used in place of the sixteen-year—or older—balsamic vinegar to, say, finish a soup. It should be dense, somewhat syrupy, and well balanced.

Eggs and Vegetables

I buy my eggs from a local farmer who gives his birds organic feed and allows them to live like chickens should, picking at bugs and greens and this and that. They are big, beautiful, brown-shelled eggs with bright yellow yolks. I trust this farmer and I love his product. There are farmers who sell their eggs at farmers' markets everywhere. They are bound to be better and fresher than those from a store.

I don't raise my own chickens, but I do grow some of my own vegetables and herbs. I also rely upon the purveyors at my farmers' markets who grow and sell super-fresh, organic produce. It's been a big learning experience about how hard it is feed oneself year-round when one doesn't live in California.

Flour

I look for flours that are USDA certified organic or certified by the Non-GMO Project because wheat is largely grown from genetically modified seed. I suspect that when people say they feel better when they don't eat wheat and are therefore gluten-free, they might be feeling better because they are eating fewer carbohydrates *and* they're avoiding these altered grains.

There are many small, independent sources of good-quality wheat. Sonoran wheat milled at Hayden Flour Mills in Arizona is soft enough that it can be used in place of cake flour in the Olive Oil Cake on page 173 or whenever cake flour is called for. Shepherd's Grain has a great website and online store, as does Bluebird Grain Farms, which has both organic wheat and ancient grains. Also consider Sunrise Flour Mill, in Minnesota, Bob's Red Mill, Anson Mills, and many others. Good grains of all kinds, as well as millers, are popping up in many places. Even in supermarkets, you can now find pasta made from organic einkorn wheat, such as that made by Jovial.

Garlic

The only garlic that used to be available was the soft-neck variety, which consists of small cloves surrounding some very tiny ones that are difficult to use. Today we have many more choices of garlic types, including many hard-neck, heirloom varieties, which produce very plump cloves that are often the equivalent of two, three, or more soft-neck cloves. When I call for "a plump garlic clove" it refers to these hard-neck varieties. When the cloves are really enormous, I sometimes use part of one and wrap the rest in plastic and refrigerate it to use the next day.

Nutritional Yeast

I used to use nutritional yeast in the '70s because I felt obligated to do so; then I stopped. I never cared for it that much. But recently I've encountered a product I really like called From the Fields Nutritional Yeast. I think it adds a lot of substance to a dish. If your market doesn't carry it, you can find it on the Internet. It's made in California and is GMO free.

Olive Oil

When I first began cooking, olives were pressed between mats and there was a difference between first and subsequent pressings, which yielded light, virgin, or extra-virgin olive oil, and so forth. Today most olives are pressed once in a machine. There is still extra-virgin oil, because that designation has to do with the acidity of the oil, but with just one pressing, a lot of the monikers we used to use no longer mean the same thing. What does make a difference to the quality and taste of olive oils is the variety of olive used, where it is grown, and how soon after being picked the olives are pressed, among other things.

I've called for "olive oil" and "best olive oil" throughout the book. By "olive oil" I mean one you don't mind using for cooking. By "best" I mean the one that is your best, that is special to you, that you probably use to dress a salad or finish a dish. I generally use a spicy, organic Arbequina for everyday use, and for my best oil,

one made by my brother's Yolo Press or another estate-bottled oil. When I lived in California, I had many choices as some fine oils are being made there. In New Mexico, my choices are more limited, but having just two seems to work well for me.

Organic and GMO-Free Foods

If I labeled every ingredient in the book, "organic" would apply to eggs, milk, flour, and oils as well as vegetables and fruits—everything, really. And even then I'm sure I'd miss some pesticides and GMOs—it's constant work to figure out what's what.

There are some foods that are more harmful than others, and the Environmental Working Group (EWG) publishes a useful list of foods to avoid and nonorganic foods that are probably okay to eat. It's worth looking at, if you haven't yet—did you know that nonorganic strawberries are at the top of the list of the most harmful foods? My own feeling about organic production is that it's not only about us. I choose organic even if the alternative is known to be fairly safe, because conventional agriculture harms or even destroys the environment, the health of farm workers who handle pesticides, and the lives of birds, fish, insects, bees, and a great many other creatures. Organic agriculture does not have the same negative impacts on ecosystems and people.

The more we learn about both genetically modified foods and foods grown with pesticides, the worse the news is. The best strategy, I feel, is not to buy them, and also to support campaigns that ask businesses to include GMO-based ingredients on the label. Look for foods that are part of the Non-GMO Project, or are certified organic by the USDA (which at this time does not allow for genetically modified organisms).

Salt and Pepper

I always use sea salt, which is stronger—and more complex—than iodized refined salt. In my cooking, pepper is always freshly cracked, ground, or pounded in a mortar. While I've given amounts of salt, in the end it's always best to season *to taste*—which means you taste it and add as much as you think it needs. Some cooks will want less, others more—it's always up to your judgment.

Soy Sauce

I try to find soy sauce that is unpasteurized (and therefore must be refrigerated) and has a pure, good, rich, full-bodied flavor. Ohsawa Organic Nama Shoyu, which I buy in my co-op, is one that's widely available. Carefully made soy sauces like this are delicious, and they go so far in a dish that they're worth looking for. I have found versions for sale in Japanese restaurants, but I can't provide the names because they are entirely written in Japanese.

Tofu

Modern tofu is, for the most part, with few exceptions, a travesty. It's tough, coarse, too firm, and oddly flavored. It is *not* exquisite, which is what I think tofu should be. That's probably because I grew up when tofu was a hand-made product—and because of the summer I ate tofu in Japan, where it was made daily. If you're not going to make tofu yourself (and it's a big project to take on), look for it in Asian markets. Brands like House are mass-produced, but they taste more like tofu should. The soft version is delicate and quivery and lovely to braise; the firm tofu keeps its shape but is not tough or chalky. You want tofu made with organically grown soy, as most soy is now genetically modified.

Tofu does have fat in it naturally, and it will turn golden when put in a skillet without the addition of oil. You can add oil, though, if you want it for flavor. Tofu also benefits by being salted while cooking, even if you're going to use soy sauce later in the dish.

The weights of tofu packs vary, but the ones I use are mostly 19-ounce packages. Except for those packed in small boxes, tofu packed in water will weigh about 1 pound.

THE RECIPES

ARTICHOKE AND SCALLION SAUTÉ OVER GARLIC-RUBBED TOAST

Serves 4; V

When I was spokesperson for the California Artichoke Board, boxes upon boxes of artichokes would arrive on my porch. I'd hear them land with a thud, heaved there by the UPS driver. Of course it was a thrill to be the recipient of so many of these glorious, large flower-vegetables, but where to put them? They went into big coolers with plenty of ice. Then I got busy developing recipes, many of which have ended up in my various books. This little sauté, which I cooked frequently on TV, is one, and it has stood up as a favorite. Happily, it can also incorporate asparagus if you wish to add some (briefly parboiled), making for a more complex seasonal spring stew. Use large artichokes if you like, or the babies I've used here. Because they grow low down on the large branches where they get little light, the so-called babies never develop a choke, or much size. They're very easy to work with, which I appreciate a lot.

Spoon these artichokes over garlic-rubbed toast and you have a good vegan supper sandwich. Sometimes I add a smear of chèvre flavored with pepper and a bit of orange zest. You can also serve this sauté over pasta, polenta, or another grain, either alongside another dish or by itself. CONTINUED

20 to 24 baby artichokes

Juice of 2 lemons

Sea salt

1 tablespoon mild vinegar

2 cloves garlic

2 heaping tablespoons of parsley

Zest from 1 large lemon

1 heaping tablespoon tarragon leaves

2 tablespoons olive oil, for cooking

1 bunch scallions, including an inch of the greens, thickly sliced

½ cup dry white wine

4 slices of strong country bread for toasting

Best olive oil, for the toast

Freshly ground pepper

Chives and chive blossoms, if available

Trim the top third off the artichoke leaves and discard them. As you work, put the trimmed artichokes in a bowl with the lemon juice and enough water to cover. When all are trimmed, drain them, and then simmer them in salted water to which you've added the vinegar (or use more lemon juice) until tender-firm, about 10 minutes. Drain the artichokes and slice them lengthwise into halves or quarters.

Finely chop one of the garlic cloves with the parsley, lemon zest, and tarragon, and set aside.

Heat the oil in a large skillet over high heat. Add the artichokes and sauté until they begin to color in places, after several minutes. Add the scallions and wine. When the wine boils off, add 1 cup of water and half the herb mixture. Lower the heat and simmer until the artichokes are fully tender, between 5 to 10 minutes.

Meanwhile, toast the bread. Cut the other garlic clove in half and rub it over the toast. When the artichokes are done, add the remainder of the herb mixture and season with salt and pepper. Tip them, with their juices, over the toast or onto a serving plate and garnish with snipped chives and chive blossoms if you have them.

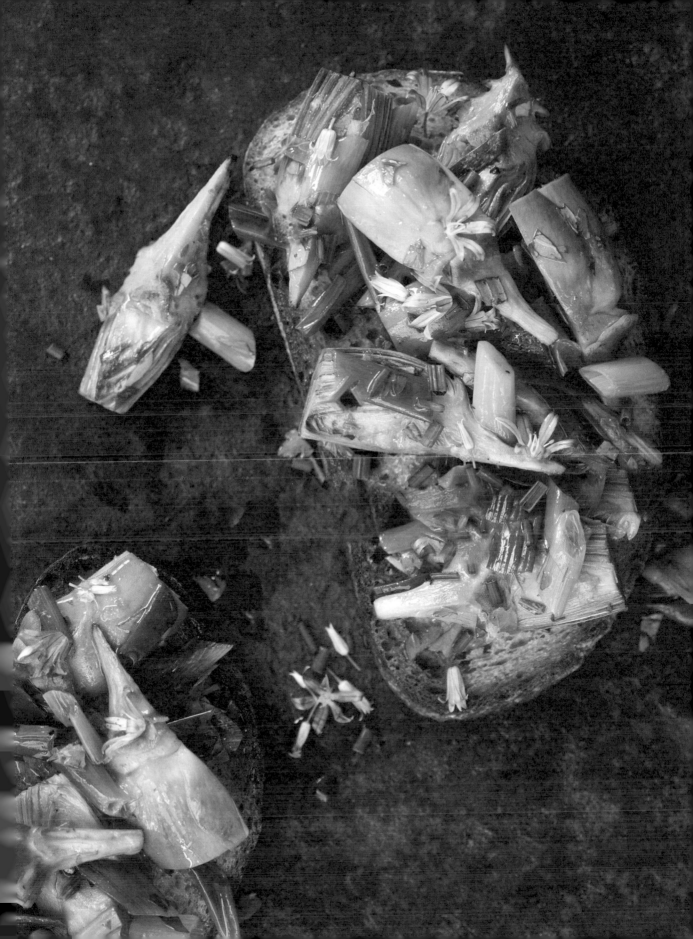

ROASTED ASPARAGUS AND ARUGULA WITH HARD-COOKED EGGS AND WALNUTS

Serves 4; GF

I finally got around to planting an eighteen by four-foot bed of asparagus. The crowns are the most hopeless looking things. They appear to be utterly dead, while the roots look like a handful of lifeless worms. I have to trust that they will flourish, as the package promises. And if they do, I know I will have to wait three years before harvesting. No wonder the young woman at the nursery quipped that it's better not to wait to plant asparagus.

In the meantime, asparagus comes into season—that is, it appears in our farmers' market—when the arugula is doing just fine in the garden, and I love the contrast these two plants offer.

Asparagus is grassy, the arugula is a bit hot and nutty, and the rather sober walnut vinaigrette brings it all together. I also think cooked egg is good here if you want to expand this salad into something heartier, as it flatters both arugula and asparagus. Have a few eggs either quartered and tucked among the leaves, or use just one as a polonaise, the whites finely chopped and the yolks pushed through a sieve to make a golden rain. This salad can be dinner or, made smaller, a first course.

Our farmers don't sell perfect bunches of asparagus trimmed at the base so that the stalks are all the same length. In fact, they don't sell bunches at all. They just have coolers full of spears, some thin, some wide, some long, some short, and your hands reach in with all these other hands and you pick the spears you want. People do have their preferences. Personally, I like them plump so there's something to bite into.

This recipe is written for thick spears of roasted asparagus, but if you prefer the ease of the stovetop, just simmer your spears in water to cover with a splash of olive oil and some salt until they are tender. Pour off the liquid at the end and let them fry a bit in the pan, but serve them hot, right on the greens. CONTINUED

1 pound or more thick asparagus	1½ tablespoons interesting vinegar
Olive oil	3½ tablespoons toasted walnut oil or good olive oil
Sea salt and freshly ground pepper	
3 handfuls of small arugula leaves, with blossoms, if possible	2 hard-cooked eggs, peeled and quartered
1 large shallot, finely diced	4 walnuts, freshly cracked and lightly toasted or left fresh

Heat the oven to 425°F. Trim and rinse the asparagus, then toss it with olive oil—not too much—and a few pinches of salt and some pepper. Put the asparagus in a large, shallow baking dish and bake for 20 minutes or as long as is needed (a little less for skinny asparagus), until tender, slightly shriveled, and aromatic. Wash the arugula leaves and spin them dry. If they're large leaves from the garden, break them down so that the stems are short. If they're very hot and spicy, use just two handfuls, or even a little less. If there are blossoms, set them aside and use them to garnish the salad.

Put the shallot in a small bowl with the vinegar and ¼ teaspoon of salt. Let stand for a few minutes, and then whisk in the walnut oil. Taste the dressing on an arugula leaf and add more vinegar or oil, if needed. Dress the arugula with about half of the dressing. Taste for salt.

Set the asparagus on a platter or individual plates. Heap the arugula over it. Tuck in the eggs and walnuts here and there. Spoon the remaining dressing over the asparagus, garnish with the flowers if there are any, and serve.

ANISE SEED SHORTBREAD
WITH STAR ANISE IMPRESSIONS

Makes 8 to 12 pieces or one 9-inch pan

I teach a hands-on cooking class at the spa Rancho la Puerta every year, and recently two yoga students were handed the recipe for my anise shortbread. When I went to see how they were doing, I saw these bright, shiny, and hard-looking pellets in the dough. What were they? They turned out to be the seeds of star anise instead of the smaller anise seed, which comes from a different plant altogether.

The star anise were too hard to use without fearing someone might break a tooth, so we decided to use both smaller anise seed and whole star anise to make impressions in the dough, which happily stayed through the baking. I love the way the impressions look, as well as the occasional whole star anise that I leave in.

You might want to serve this shortbread with a fruit compote.

½ cup butter, at room temperature

⅓ cup powdered sugar

¼ teaspoon sea salt,
unless salted butter was used

1 teaspoon orange flower water

2 teaspoons anise seed

1 cup white whole-wheat flour
or all-purpose flour

A few whole star anise

Heat the oven to 325°F.

Beat the butter with the sugar and salt in an electric mixer using the paddle until smooth, creamy, and pale. If the butter was soft, this won't take very long at all. (If it is pretty much cold from the refrigerator and you can't wait for it to soften, allow about 10 minutes of mixing for it to become creamy.) Add the orange flower water and anise seed, then reduce the speed to low and add the flour. When well mixed, remove the dough and press it into a 9-inch pie tin. Even the edges, then gently press the star anise into the dough and remove them so that they make an impression. You can leave a few in the dough during the baking or not, keeping in mind that you'll have to cut around them once the shortbreads are out of the oven.

Bake in the center of the oven until lightly browned, about 30 minutes. While the shortbread is still hot, slice it into twelve wedges with a sharp knife, then let it cool in the pan.

GREEN, YELLOW, OR PURPLE BEANS WITH SUN GOLD TOMATOES AND OPAL BASIL

1 pound serves about 4; V, GF

These are my basic beans, because whether they're green, purple, or yellow, slender or broad, truly fresh beans are just so good that I seldom venture into new culinary realms with them. Certainly there are all kinds of ways you can finish fresh beans, but I can't help myself—I cook them the same way every time and I'll probably continue to do so until someone says "Enough!" So far they haven't. Of course I might vary the tomatoes or the herbs, or include diced shallots or walking onions, but the basic method and dish remain pretty much the same. What's important? The freshness of the vegetables and the quality of the olive oil. If both are high, you needn't do anything fancy, really. Even with no more than oil and salt, these beans will be excellent.

I always grow some beans, mostly pole beans but also the skinny French green ones, and the broad, flat Romanos. Tomatoes are usually in when the beans are, and their simultaneity is what yields this combination. The beans are so succulent, the tomatoes have some acidity, and the colors are so fresh and pretty together: think of orange Sun Gold tomatoes covering yellow beans or green ones (the purples lose their color). At the same time, the garden (and market) is filled with basils of all colors and flavors; there's dill; tarragon is still going strong; and so forth. There are countless possibilities, yet it's still the same dish.

So here's what I do after picking about a pound of beans: I cut off the ends near the stems but leave the tails on (unless they're very large), then give them a rinse. If I'm using different varieties, I keep them separate because I'll cook them separately.

I drop each kind into plenty of boiling, well-salted water and cook them, without a lid, until they're almost as tender as I want, but not quite. You'll have to decide the doneness for yourself. I'm not fond of mushy beans, but I don't want them raw or super crunchy, either.

When they're nearly done, I scoop them out and dump them on a clean towel to absorb the cooking water. I never put them in ice water. This popular cheffy method is called "shocking," and I don't really want to shock my beans. I want to coddle them. They'll finish cooking as they dry, which takes about 35 seconds. CONTINUED

While the beans are cooking, I halve some tomatoes, often small Sun Golds or a mixture of various small tomatoes, and toss them with a little olive oil and a few pinches of salt. I also slice or dice a shallot and toss it, separately, with a few teaspoons of vinegar to pickle it.

Next I turn the beans into a bowl and toss them with good olive oil. The smell of the oil and the warm beans is intoxicating. I taste the beans for salt, and add some if need be, along with pepper from the grinder, and turn them onto a platter. I cover them with the sliced tomatoes and shallots, then cover the whole platter with torn or shredded leaves of opal basil, and serve. The beans will be warm. Invariably people eat them with their fingers until none are left.

Here are some other ingredients you can add if you get tired of the ones I've just described:

- Olives, especially black ones, pitted
- Tapenade (minced olives with chile flakes and more)
- Yogurt, Cumin, and Green Herb Sauce (page 273)
- Homemade garlic mayonnaise
- Plenty of dill instead of basil
- Pan-toasted pine nuts
- Salsa verde—one that emphasizes the herbs that are in season
- Capers

RIO ZAPE BEANS WITH SMOKED CHILE

Makes 2 quarts; GF

Black bean chili was on the menu at Greens from the day we opened. Why did we use black beans? They were the most exotic bean available at that time, and they not only looked dramatic, they were delicious. The chili quickly became a favorite dish, and it was thrilling to see other chefs pick up the recipe and make it at their restaurants. I was so naïve, I didn't even know that chili usually had meat—and sometimes only meat. Beans seemed like chili material to me.

It was Mark Miller, whom I had stood next to for months during the dinner shift at Chez Panisse, who told me about the smoky chipotle chiles that no one else seemed to know about. Then, chipotle chiles came in a can, imported from Mexico, and we puréed them so that their heat spread evenly. This was years before Californian farmers started smoking their jalapeños and selling dried, smoked chipotles, and there was no *molido* (ground chile) unless you dried and ground chiles yourself, or visited New Mexico and brought some back.

Today we have many beans and forms of chile to choose from. I am partial to the big, reddish Rio Zape beans from Rancho Gordo, and I call for them here. They both look and taste great. You'll need to soak them; if you think of it ahead of time, you can soak them overnight. If not, cover them with boiling water for an hour before cooking. In my experience (and at my altitude), they take a few hours to cook.

What else is different today? I use avocado leaves instead of bay leaf—same botanical family, but different flavor. At Greens, we served the chili over grated cheese, which made a kind of cheesy lump in the bottom of the bowl. Now I leave the cheese out but add a spoonful of sour cream and sprig of cilantro. I'm not especially fond of intense heat, but I add smoked paprika at the end for smokiness and mild heat. You might prefer to do otherwise.

This is a dish that will change form and appearance as it cooks. After adding the canned tomatoes and cooking the beans until they were nearly tender, I realized I didn't really like the looks of the dish. I crumbled up some dried tomatoes and added them for a brighter color (see picture on page 20) and kept on cooking the beans for another hour or more. When I finally went to serve them, all the tomato pieces had somehow disappeared, as had the excess broth, and my guests put the rich-looking reddish-brown beans on a plate instead of a bowl. They were amazingly good—mellow and complex. But normally I don't let all the liquid cook away—I like having some broth!

2 heaping cups Rio Zape or other large beans	2 plump garlic cloves, finely chopped or pounded in a mortar with a pinch of salt
5 or 6 dried avocado leaves, ground to a powder	1 (15-ounce) can peeled, seeded, and chopped tomatoes
Sea salt	2 teaspoons puréed chipotle chile, plus more to taste
4 teaspoons cumin seeds	
2 teaspoons coriander seeds	⅓ cup finely chopped cilantro stems and leaves
4 teaspoons dried oregano leaves	1 to 2 teaspoons sherry vinegar, to taste
4 teaspoons sweet or hot paprika	
1 tablespoon ground New Mexican chile	Smoked paprika (optional)
2 to 3 tablespoons olive or vegetable oil	Sour cream
3 white onions, cut into ¼-inch dice	Cilantro sprigs

Sort through the beans and discard any odd matter you find and then rinse them well. Either cover them with cold water and set aside to soak overnight or cover them with boiling water and set aside to soak for an hour. Drain the beans and, in a large pot, cover them with 11 cups of fresh water. Bring to a boil with the crushed avocado leaves. Lower the heat, add 2½ teaspoons of salt, and simmer the beans, partially covered, while you prepare the rest of the ingredients.

Heat a small skillet over medium heat. Add the cumin and coriander seeds. When they begin to color, add the oregano leaves. Shake the pan so the spices don't scorch. As soon as the fragrance is strong and robust, remove the pan from the heat and add the paprika and ground chile. Give everything a quick stir, turn out on a plate to cool, and then grind in a mortar or a spice mill.

Warm a deep wide pan and heat the oil. Add the onions and cook over medium heat, stirring occasionally, until they soften, about 10 minutes. Add the garlic, 1 teaspoon of salt, and the toasted ground spices, and cook another 5 minutes. Next, add the tomatoes along with their juice, and 2 teaspoons of the chipotle chile. Simmer this mixture for 15 minutes, and then add it to the beans along with the chopped cilantro. Continue cooking until the beans are soft, about 1½ to 2 hours or even longer. The exact time depends on the beans—what kind and how old they are—your altitude, and the hardness of your water. (At this point, if you're making the chili a day or two before serving, refrigerate it, and when ready to finish the chili, move it to the stove simmer until everything is amalgamated and dense, the tomatoes nearly disappeared, but some broth still remains. Add more water if you need to.)

Once the beans are done, taste them and add more chipotle chile if desired. Season with a little vinegar to soften any harshness, and taste for salt. If you wish, shower with smoked paprika, and then serve with a spoonful of sour cream and fresh cilantro sprigs.

GOLDEN BEETS WITH MÂCHE, PICKLED SHALLOTS, AND PURPLE ORACH

Serves 4 to 6; GF

Many find, as I do, that golden beets are a bit milder than the red ones. They're also drier, which is why a farmer recently told me he preferred red beets: he liked their juiciness! I find both quite acceptable, but I love to use golden beets for their color and for their delicious greens. In truth, any color of beet is good used in a salad and so is a mixture of beet varieties. And salads are one of the best ways to feature a mix of beets because the acid seems to unite their sweet and earthy flavors.

Beets and mâche are a perfect match, to my taste, but young arugula leaves are also very good, being nutty and spicy in contrast to the mild sweetness of the beets. For weeks in the early spring, my yard is covered with purple orach (mountain spinach) sprouts, which taste like spinach and look wonderful, plus there are hundreds of arugula plants as well. Sometimes I use both along with the mâche.

Shallots are cut into larger pieces than usual, then quickly pickled in apple cider vinegar or champagne vinegar. It turns them pinkish and sweetens them—perfect with the beets. The seasoned yogurt, which is infused with cilantro, basil, and dill, is entirely optional. I spoon it on or next to a cluster of beets.

There are many good companions for beets: walnuts, horseradish, grated carrots, paper-thin slivered fennel, pickled red onions, feta cheese, avocados and more. I have a hard time restraining myself, actually, and you should feel free to include any other garnishes and vegetables that appeal. CONTINUED

3 large golden beets

2 large shallots

3 tablespoons apple cider
or champagne vinegar

Sea salt and freshly ground pepper

4 tablespoons best olive oil

4 good handfuls or more of mâche
or arugula greens, washed and dried

Purple orach thinnings, if possible,
washed and dried

Yogurt, Cumin, and Green Herb Sauce
(page 273; optional)

Cut the stems off about an inch from the tops of the beets, then steam them over simmering water until tender but not too soft when pierced with a knife. Remove them, rinse under cool water, and slip off the skins with your hands. Cut the beets into ten to twelve wedges each and set aside in a bowl in the refrigerator.

Peel the shallots and then slice them crosswise a scant ¼ inch thick. Separate the rings and put them in a bowl with the vinegar and ¼ teaspoon of salt. Let stand for 5 minutes or so to color and soften, then whisk in the olive oil. Spoon a tablespoon or two of the dressing over the beets and toss. Taste for acid and salt, adding more vinegar or salt if needed. Season with pepper.

Dress the greens with the remaining dressing and heap them on individual plates.

Tuck the beets in and around the greens. If using the yogurt sauce, spoon some close to the clusters of beets.

BERRIES SCENTED WITH ROSE GERANIUM LEAVES AND FLOWERS

Serves 4; V, GF

I used to make desserts at Greens that brought together blackberries and rose-scented geranium leaves, and a version of this dish originally appeared in *The Greens Cookbook*. It was many years before I learned that rose and blackberries (and their many delicious relations) are members of the same botanical family—which makes it even more right that they should be paired. Rose and blackberries. Or tayberries. Or marionberries, or loganberries, or boysenberries. Or pure raspberries. All of these kinds of berries, alone or mixed with blackberries, are good with rose geranium.

Rose geranium, of course, is not a member of the rose family, but it does carry the scent of rose blossoms. There were some rose geranium plants at Green Gulch farm, and I could never resist running my hands over their leaves and then inhaling their scent on my skin. After walking around and breathing in "rose" for a while, blackberries would almost magically come to my mind. Today I keep a few rose geranium plants in my office for the sheer delight of their fragrant leaves. The berries don't appear until many weeks after the roses have bloomed, but the trusty geranium plants are there and ready to bring their fragrance to this dish. This is the simplest of desserts—blackberries (or their cousins) mingled with the leaves; the pink blossoms used as a garnish; cream to pour over, or not. I love the photograph of berries and rose geranium leaves and flowers on page 51, but when you make this, the proportions will be different and you'll macerate the berries before serving them.

I only rinse berries if they're dusty, and only just before making or serving a dish. Water can bring on spoilage, and it's hard to get the tender fruit really dry. And berries usually grow where it rains a lot, so pesticides are made to stick—it's a good reason to choose organic. **CONTINUED**

1 pint or more blackberries mixed with marionberries or another related berry (see page 49)

6 rose geranium leaves, rinsed

Light brown sugar, maple sugar, or honey if the berries are very tart

Rose geranium blossoms

½ cup heavy cream or cream stirred together with sour cream or crème fraîche (optional)

Remove any stems and leaves from the berries. Rinse them only briefly, if at all, and turn them onto a clean towel; blot dry. Crush the rose geranium leaves gently in your hands to release their perfume. Layer berries and leaves in a serving bowl, sprinkling the berries lightly with sugar if they are tart (maple sugar is especially nice). Cover the bowl tightly and let the berries sit for several hours in the refrigerator to macerate.

Before serving, bring the fruit to room temperature. Remove the rose geranium leaves, which will have a rather bruised appearance, and garnish the berries with pink blossoms or with fresh leaves, or both. Serve with the cream on the side, or not, as you prefer.

BLACK-EYED PEAS WITH YOGURT-TAHINI SAUCE AND THREE GREEN HERBS

Serves 4 to 6; GF

I adore black-eyed peas—but I can't seem to cook them without allspice, thyme, and bay leaves: before I know it, in go those seasonings. Since black-eyed peas thrive in the Mediterranean, I figured they'd be good with a yogurt-tahini sauce as well. I serve the peas and the sauce over white, brown, or black rice. If I'm reheating the peas, I stir in some of the sauce, which melts into the dish and enriches it nicely.

Black-eyed peas are odd-looking and beautiful plants. Each summer I grow enough to make this dish once or twice. Otherwise, I use frozen peas. Since they're not a Southwestern food, the "fresh" ones aren't really fresh, the way they are in the South. Fresh or frozen, they all seem to take about the same amount of time to cook—somewhere between 15 and 30 minutes.

The Yogurt-Tahini Sauce
1 clove garlic

Sea salt

½ cup yogurt

3 tablespoons tahini

The Black-Eyed Peas
1 tablespoon olive oil

1 onion, finely diced

1 small green bell pepper, finely diced

1 celery stalk, finely diced, the pale green leaves chopped

2 bay leaves

¼ teaspoon dried thyme

½ teaspoon ground allspice

2 pinches of red pepper flakes

3 cups frozen black-eyed peas or other cowpeas

Sea salt

4 cups water or vegetable stock

Smoked paprika

Cooked rice, to serve

3 tablespoons chopped green herbs, a mixture of dill, cilantro, and parsley

TO MAKE THE YOGURT-TAHINI SAUCE Pound the garlic in a mortar with a few pinches of salt until creamy and smooth. Stir it into the yogurt and tahini.

TO MAKE THE PEAS Warm a soup pot over medium-low heat and add the oil, onion, pepper, celery, bay leaves, and thyme. Cook for 15 minutes, stirring occasionally, then add the allspice, pepper flakes, black-eyed peas, a teaspoon of salt, and the water. Raise the heat, bring to a boil, then lower the heat and simmer until the peas are tender, from 15 to 30 minutes. Taste and season with salt and with smoked paprika.

Serve the peas over the rice, with the chopped fresh herbs and the yogurt-tahini sauce.

BLACK RICE WITH MIXED BEETS, THEIR GREENS, AVOCADO, FETA, AND POMEGRANATE SEEDS

Serves 6; GF

I first made this salad—or another version of it, I should say—because I was inspired by a bunch of quinoa leaves and I couldn't resist pairing them with the quinoa itself. Quinoa greens are, sadly, seldom seen, but beet greens are common. Quinoa and beets are in the same botanical family, and their greens have similar flavors. Before long, I was making the salad with different colored beets and their leaves, along with feta and avocado, plus pomegranate seeds and a sparky lemon vinaigrette. Of course beets of all hues look striking against black quinoa, but if you find the texture of black quinoa a little gritty for your taste, consider making this salad using black rice (as I do here) or black lentils, or even the two mixed together. I have also made it with a very dark, chewy, smoky freekeh, and that's good too.

Steaming the beets and cooking the greens involve extra (though pretty easy) steps. If you don't happen to have the beets already cooked, you'll want to start them first so they'll have a chance to cool. Although I've called for larger beets here, it's quite possible you'll come across a bunch or two of small ones, which cook more quickly—and are delectable.

3 medium to large beets, golden, red, Chioggia, or a combination, with their greens

1 cup black rice

Sea salt

Zest of 1 large Meyer lemon

3 tablespoons lemon juice, or more to taste

5 tablespoons best olive oil

1 teaspoon ground toasted cumin seed

12 mint leaves, slivered

3 tablespoons finely sliced chives, or a bunch of scallions, including the firm greens, finely sliced

1 large or 2 medium, firm but ripe avocados, diced

½ cup crumbled feta

Seeds from 1 small pomegranate

If you haven't already cooked the beets, do that first. Cut off the greens, leaving an inch of the stems and all of the tails, and set them aside. Steam the beets until tender when pierced with a knife, but not soft, 25 to 40 minutes depending on their size. When they're done, rinse them under cold water to stop the cooking, then slip or slice off the skins. Dice the beets into small cubes (½ inch or less), or if you prefer larger, irregular pieces, you can cut them that way instead.

Cover the rice with 2 cups of water in a small saucepan. Bring to a boil, add ½ teaspoon of salt, and then lower the heat and simmer, covered, until the rice is fully cooked. Black rice can take a good 30 minutes or so. When it's done, take the saucepan off the heat but leave the lid on so the rice can steam further, then turn it into a bowl and fluff it with a fork. (If the rice is done but there's water in the pan, simply drain it.) Leave it to cool.

Sort through the beet greens and discard any that are ragged or otherwise unappealing. Remove and discard the stems of the ones you're keeping. Wash the leaves well and then, with the water clinging to the leaves, cook them in a wide pan over medium-high heat, turning them frequently until wilted, after a few minutes. Drain well, pressing out the excess liquid, and chop fairly fine.

When you're ready to assemble the salad, use your fingers to toss the cooked rice with the chopped cooked greens, and all but ⅓ cup or so of the diced beets.

In a small bowl, combine the lemon zest, lemon juice, oil, ¼ teaspoon of salt, and the cumin. Pour it over the rice and beet mixture, add the mint and chives, and toss. Taste for salt and acidity. Meyer lemons can be very low acid, so you might want to add a little more lemon juice.

Mound the rice in a shallow bowl and then scatter the avocado, feta, pomegranate seeds, and the rest of the diced beets on the rice. Present the salad like this, but toss it before serving so that all those goodies are well distributed.

BREAKFAST BREAD WITH ROSEMARY AND LEMON

Serves 6 to 8

Rosemary and lemon aren't only for savory dishes, although they certainly are good there. They are oddly good in sweeter recipes, too, like this breakfast bread. To me, the rosemary comes off like pine, especially with the currants, honey, and pine nuts scattered over the surface. While I usually make this with butter, olive oil is also very good in its place here. If you're adventurous, give it a try.

In the past, this was my yeasted holiday bread (the original recipe is in *Vegetarian Cooking for Everyone*). But because I like to be able to get up and make it on a Sunday morning, I've turned that recipe into this quick bread. As such, it does come together, more quickly than if you were relying on yeast. The crumb is as fine as in the yeasted version, even if you use half or more whole-wheat flour, but it is crumbly. I leave the flour mix up to you. I use a combination of white and white whole wheat, and it's Sunday-morning light, but not just white. Big raisins sink to the bottom, so I use smaller currants instead.

I've had several runs at this bread. The first time it was a little blah: it just needed more of everything—especially honey and fruit. Eventually I switched from sweet milk to buttermilk, which I always believe makes the most tender cakes and breads. You can't really warm it without its curdling, so there is an extra step, which is melting the butter (or warming the olive oil) with the rosemary, lemon, and honey. Other than that, it's pretty straightforward. And like all breads, this one is best still warm from the oven, but leftovers make great toast! CONTINUED

6 to 8 tablespoons butter, cut into pieces, plus more to serve, or use olive oil

2 heaping teaspoons minced rosemary

Finely grated zest of 1 large lemon

½ cup honey

1 cup diced currants

1 cup buttermilk

2 large eggs

2 cups flour (whole wheat, white whole wheat, all-purpose, or a mixture)

1 teaspoon baking powder

½ teaspoon baking soda

¾ teaspoon sea salt

⅓ cup pine nuts

Butter and flour a 9-inch springform pan. Heat the oven to 350°F.

Melt the butter with the rosemary, lemon, and honey in a small skillet. If the currants are hard, cover them with hot water, let them stand until they soften, then drain and squeeze out the excess water. Beat the buttermilk and eggs together. Combine the flour with the baking powder, baking soda, and salt in a spacious bowl.

Make a well in the flour, add the milk and egg mixture, and quickly bring the ingredients partially together with a fork. Pour in the melted butter mixture, add the currants, and continue mixing with a light hand until all have come together. Turn the batter into the prepared pan and toss the pine nuts over the surface.

Bake until risen and browned, 35 to 40 minutes. Remove from the oven and let stand for at least 10 minutes, then carefully loosen the rim of the springform pan. Slide the bread onto a serving plate and serve warm, with soft butter.

BROCCOLI WITH ROASTED PEPPERS, FETA, OLIVES, AND HERBS

Serves 4 or more; GF

This is one of those salads I end up making the same way every time—more or less. Sometimes my peppers are from a jar, other times I'll roast a fresh one. Sometimes they're red, other times yellow. If I have big Greek capers in the freezer I use those; if not, I use smaller ones or even leave them out. The cheese is often feta but it might also be ricotta salata, as pictured on page 60, manouri, or a tangy goat cheese. Even the broccoli might be something else, like romanesco! And while I always dress the broccoli while it's warm, by the time it's served, it's cool enough that you might want to scatter some salad greens over everything. Arugula would be an especially good choice.

I first made this salad at Greens, so it's an older approach to what is, for many, a challenging vegetable. But it's also a timeless one. I've learned broccoli is often best liked when it's paired with flavors that are bright and sharp, as in this recipe. So despite other changes that might take place, I find that fresh oregano or marjoram and parsley are good bright herbs to use with broccoli. As for amounts, it's hard to gauge without becoming obsessive about everything, so these amounts are all suggestions. Have the rest of your ingredients ready when you start the broccoli so you can dress it while warm; that makes the salad its most aromatic. CONTINUED

1 broccoli crown per person (about 1½ pounds in all)

Sea salt

Red pepper flakes

1 heaping tablespoon chopped fresh oregano or marjoram

1 heaping tablespoon chopped parsley

1 or 2 tablespoons capers

3 to 4 tablespoons good strong olive oil

1 large red or yellow pepper, roasted, peeled, seeded, and cut into strips

12 kalamata olives, pits removed

A few ounces feta, ricotta salata, or manouri

Red wine vinegar or lemon juice

Slice the broccoli crowns into florets. If you wish to use the stems, peel them with a paring knife, getting under the epidermis, then slice them into rounds or julienne strips. Steam the crowns and stems over boiling water until they're bright green and tender-firm. Turn them into a shallow bowl and, while they're still warm, season with several pinches of salt, a few pinches of red pepper flakes, and the herbs, then toss with 3 tablespoons of the olive oil. Add the capers, parsley, roasted pepper, olives, and cheese and toss again. Taste and add more olive oil or salt if needed. Finally, add a few teaspoons of vinegar or a good squeeze of lemon juice to sharpen everything and make it sing.

YEASTED BUCKWHEAT WAFFLES

Serves 4

I don't think there is anything better than these light, crisp buckwheat waffles with warm maple syrup, unless it's these waffles with sautéed apples or applesauce or any of a host of other syrups and fruits. Warmed molasses, for example, is very good with buckwheat.

Marion Cunningham, of Fannie Farmer (and other) fame, put yeasted waffles on the breakfast menu of a Berkeley restaurant where she was the menu consultant in the '80s. You got two, the second one served after you'd finished your first, so that the crispness and warmth would hold. They were divine and very popular. I owe quite a debt to Marion Cunningham; in fact, her wonderfully appealing *Breakfast Book* is the source of many of my favorite baked goods—like her luscious Sunday morning cornbread covered with cream and then baked, her Dutch Babies, her cream biscuits, and a host of other classics.

I've been making these yeasted waffles ever since I first had them, playing with amounts (mostly of butter) and with types of flour—white whole wheat, whole wheat pastry, quinoa, spelt, stone-ground corn meal from the farmers' market, semolina, and so forth. All these different flours and grains are delicious, but buckwheat is my favorite, so it is featured here. But play around with the flours that appeal to you. Because of the yeast in this recipe, with its power to raise and hold things together, you can use a lower-gluten flour; but I do think it works best if you use some wheat flour.

Although the recipe does ask you to start these the night before, you can manage to pull the whole thing together in the morning if you have an hour or two for the yeast to rise. But it's nice to wake up and know that your work, minimal as it is, is pretty much done. You can spend your time with a second cup of coffee and a book, or use it to make a fruit salad (or the aforementioned applesauce and sautéed apples) to go with the waffles.

1 package (2¼ teaspoons) active dry yeast

½ teaspoon sugar or honey

2 cups milk

1 teaspoon vanilla

¾ cup buckwheat flour

1¼ cups all-purpose flour

¾ teaspoon sea salt

5 to 8 tablespoons melted butter or sunflower oil

2 large eggs, beaten

½ teaspoon baking soda

Maple syrup or molasses (optional)

Pour ½ cup of warm water into a small bowl and sprinkle the yeast over it. Stir in the sugar or honey and let stand until foamy over the surface, about 10 minutes.

Meanwhile, warm the milk so it's lukewarm and not super hot and then pour it into a deep bowl (since the batter will rise). Add the bloomed yeast and vanilla. Whisk in the flours and salt. Cover and refrigerate overnight. (A shower cap, the kind you find in your hotel room, works perfectly for covering the bowl.)

The next morning, remove the bowl from the refrigerator and stir down the batter. Add the remaining ingredients—the melted butter, eggs, and baking soda. (If you're making this the morning of, leave the bowl at room temperature. It should be ready to stir down after an hour, or longer if your kitchen is cold.) Yeasted batter will resist mixing a bit, but stay with it. Eventually it will yield. You'll end up with four cups of batter, enough for eight Belgian waffles. (This batter also makes good pancakes if you don't have a waffle iron.)

If you're using maple syrup or molasses, warm it while the waffle iron heats. Make the waffles according to your iron's directions and serve as soon as they come off the iron!

SMOKY-SPICY BUTTER FOR THREE ORANGE VEGETABLES

Makes about ½ cup; GF

I've found that if you're a person who likes winter squash, you probably also like sweet potatoes and carrots—three orange vegetables that are from different botanical families, but all of which are on the sweet side. Not surprisingly, all of them are enhanced by this reddish-orange smoky-spicy butter. The butter does wonders for a squash soup or purée, roasted chunks of squash, or rounds of butternut squash seared in the skillet. It makes a great finish to a carrot soup or a dish of braised carrots, to a sweet potato purée or soup, or to a previously cooked sweet potato that's sliced then seared on a grill. These vegetables all have plenty of sugars that are well aligned with smoke and spice. And outside of the vegetable realm, consider using this butter with brown rice or brush it, when soft, over a roasting chicken.

I often call for the seedless, dense neck end of the butternut squash because not only is that a very good squash, that part of it is especially easy to peel and slice. But what to do with the round seed end or, for that matter, other (delicious) squash varieties that are all round and don't have a straight neck to work with? Whether you roast them or steam them and make a purée or a soup, this compound butter will finish them nicely.

This will probably be more butter than you need at a single sitting. If so, freeze the remainder; ideally, shape it into a log and freeze it until hard, then cut it into thin disks to flavor a soup or a vegetable. Make it hotter by using the hot paprika and perhaps a few pinches of cayenne.

2 tablespoons finely sliced green onion, including some of the greens

2 plump garlic cloves, coarsely chopped

2 teaspoons hot or sweet paprika (not smoked)

2 teaspoons hot or sweet paprika (smoked)

2 teaspoons ground toasted cumin

½ teaspoon ground coriander

2 tablespoons chopped parsley and/or cilantro

Sea salt

Grated zest and juice of 1 lime

½ cup butter, at room temperature or somewhat softened

Pound the green onion and garlic, paprikas, cumin, coriander, parsley, ¼ teaspoon of salt, lime zest, and lime juice in a mortar to form a rough paste. Stir the paste into the soft butter with the lime juice. You might want to use your hands to bring everything together and make sure it's well blended. If you plan to keep this butter for later, roll it in waxed paper or plastic wrap to make a cylinder and freeze it. Slice off rounds to float in a soup or add to a dish.

BULGUR AND GREEN LENTIL SALAD WITH CHICKPEAS AND PRESERVED LEMON

Serves 6 or more; V, GF (if quinoa is used in place of bulgur)

When I went to make this recipe recently, I had plenty of Hearty Lentil Minestrone with Kale (page 144) in the refrigerator. I didn't want to cook even more lentils since I was the only one eating from a considerable volume of the leftover soup, so I used the lentils from the soup (yes, we do that). It was studded with carrots and celery, and the vegetables looked so great in this dish, I decided to include them in this version.

This is a good salad for winter, when there's a dearth of fresh vegetables, but you can take it into other seasons as well. In summer, for example, you might want to omit the preserved lemon and add tomatoes, cucumbers, and peppers, all finely diced in a relish. Purslane is also a possible summer addition. In early spring or winter, try roasted Jerusalem artichokes or walnuts instead of or in addition to preserved lemon. Some other changes you might make include using smoky freekeh mixed with or in place of bulgur, or farro, or another ancient grain, or the pseudograin quinoa. Smoked paprika and smoked salt might be brought into play as well. But before you get too deep into the other possibilities, consider the combination of the cracked wheat, lentils, and chickpeas. Their subtle earthy flavors and colors always make me think of beach stones when I put this salad together.

If time allows, soak the lentils for at least a half hour, or longer. They cook more quickly, closer to the time you might expect, and I feel they emerge with more flavor and a better texture. CONTINUED

½ cup green French or black Beluga lentils

1 bay leaf

1 deep orange carrot, diced into small pieces

Sea salt and freshly ground pepper

½ cup fine or medium bulgur

1 plump garlic clove, finely minced or pounded in a mortar with a pinch of salt

3 tablespoons lemon juice

⅓ cup best olive oil

8 scallions, thinly sliced, including some of the greens

1½ cups home-cooked or canned chickpeas, well rinsed and drained

1 preserved lemon, skin only, finely diced

½ cup finely chopped parsley

1 rounded tablespoon chopped tarragon

2 celery stalks, diced, plus their pale leaves, finely chopped

If you have time, soak the lentils in water to cover for 30 to 60 minutes. Drain the lentils, then put them in a small saucepan and cover with water by at least 2 inches. Add the bay leaf, carrot, and ½ teaspoon of salt, and bring to a boil. Reduce the heat to medium-low and simmer until tender-firm, 25 minutes or longer. Check to make sure there is ample water and add more as the lentils cook, if needed.

Meanwhile, put the bulgur in a small bowl, add 2 cups of water, and let stand until the liquid is absorbed and the grains are tender, about 30 minutes. When a grain tastes done, drain the bulgur and press out any excess water.

Whisk the garlic, lemon juice, oil, scallions, and ½ teaspoon of salt in a large bowl. When the lentils are done, drain them and add them to the bowl along with the bulgur and chickpeas, preserved lemon, parsley, tarragon, and celery stalks and leaves. Turn gently and thoroughly. Taste for salt and season with pepper. Mound the finished salad into a handsome serving dish. Serve immediately or cover and set aside to serve later.

SAVOY CABBAGE, LEEK, AND MUSHROOM BRAISE ON TOAST WITH HORSERADISH CREAM

Serves 4 to 6

The scent of tarragon, mushrooms, and wine drifting toward me from the pan make this irresistible as a vegetable dish. It's light, complex, and aromatic, and excellent over a sturdy, whole-wheat pasta or garlic-rubbed and olive oil– or butter-washed toast. Leftovers, I've been told, are also good spread on rye crisp crackers, bachelor style. The horseradish sauce is a must though, however you serve these vegetables.

Originally this was a filling for a savory galette. A pastry filling needs to be fairly dry so that the crust doesn't become soggy. But over toast (or pasta), you needn't worry about that; in fact, you'll want some moisture, and that can come from the cooking liquid or a splash of wine added to the pan.

Aside from dropping the crust in favor of another farinaceous food, I use the tarragon a bit differently than I did originally. It's the first herb to appear in my garden, and it comes at a time when crinkly savoy cabbage still appeals. I like to use a lot—a heaping tablespoon is not too much—and I add it twice—at the beginning, while the leeks and mushrooms cook, and at the last, sprinkled over the cabbage and toast to give it fresh flavor.

The photo on the next page is of the wonderfully bizarre looking broccoli Romanesco, not savoy cabbage. But it's there to suggest that you might use this vegetable in place of the cabbage, or alongside it. Being in the same botanical family, they do share flavor characteristics and give you more options to consider. To use, cut it into small florets and add it to the pan when you'd add the cabbage. **CONTINUED**

Horseradish Cream

1 cup yogurt or sour cream or a combination

1 tablespoon snipped chives
or thinly sliced scallions

2 to 3 heaping teaspoons prepared
horseradish or more, to taste

½ teaspoon tarragon vinegar

Pinch of sea salt, or to taste

2 tablespoons butter or butter
and olive oil mixed

2 leeks, sliced into thin rounds and rinsed
well (between 1 and 2 cups)

8 ounces mushrooms, thinly sliced, stems
discarded unless they're very firm

1 rounded teaspoon chopped thyme,
or ½ teaspoon dried

1 heaping tablespoon chopped tarragon

¼ cup white wine

About 1 pound of savoy cabbage,
thinly sliced (4 to 6 cups)

Sea salt and freshly ground pepper

¼ cup chopped parsley

1 teaspoon tarragon vinegar, or to taste

4 pieces ciabatta or other favorite bread

A clove of garlic, halved

Olive oil

TO MAKE THE HORSERADISH CREAM Combine all the ingredients in a small bowl and set aside until time to serve.

Melt the butter in a wide skillet set over medium heat. Add the leeks, mushrooms, thyme, and two-thirds of the tarragon. Cook until the leeks have softened, about 5 minutes, and then add the wine and allow it to bubble away.

Add the cabbage, season it with 1 teaspoon of salt, and add ½ cup of water to the pan. Cover and cook gently, lowering the heat if need be, until the cabbage is tender, about 12 to 15 minutes, turning it occasionally. Add more liquid if needed, but if it's covered, it will probably be fine. Stir in the parsley, season with vinegar, taste for salt, and add pepper.

Toast the bread, rub it with garlic, and brush it with olive oil. Cover the toast with the cabbage mélange and spoon some horseradish cream over all. Garnish with the remaining tarragon.

WARM RED CABBAGE SALAD
WITH TOGARASHI TOFU CRISPS

Serves 4 to 6; V, GF

When I decided to revisit the peppered tofu crisps from my book *This Can't Be Tofu!*
I was surprised at how unnecessarily complicated they seemed. I decided do them
far more simply, only using the Japanese spice mixture, togarashi, instead of pepper.
People standing around the kitchen kept eating them, proving to me that, as promised,
they can do service as a snack or an appetizer.

At the same time my little crisps were disappearing, I was thinking they'd make a
good "crouton" for a warm red cabbage salad, only to find I had put just such a recipe
in the same book. (We do forget these things!) But the salad, too, seemed unnecessarily
complicated. I didn't have the golden bell pepper or snow peas, so I just left them
out and it was fine, although I know they make a bright and sweet addition. (They're
shown in the photo, and listed here in case you have them.) Instead, I added other
ingredients that seemed essential and that I had on hand—lots of fresh ginger, more
scallions and cilantro, and a mild red jalapeño-sized pepper. I simplified the dressing
ingredients, too, taking away those that weren't needed.

One reason for the changes, other than that it was winter and there were no snow peas
and yellow peppers in season, is that the pantry ingredients we have now are better
and different. Then I didn't have the rich, good, unpasteurized soy sauce that I buy
at my co-op, hence the miso to make up for the thinness of what we did have. Mirin—
the real thing, that is—wasn't a staple, hence the use of sugar and cheap balsamic
vinegar. In addition, we didn't have organic or GMO-free cornstarch as we do now.
The changes I made resulted in a recipe that's far easier to make and just as good,
if not better.

Red cabbage makes a good winter salad, but I do think it tastes better if it's cooked
just enough to warm and wilt it, no more. The wilting brings up both the flavor and
the color and tenderizes the cabbage a bit, too. Although I would always serve this
with just that hint of warmth, I am also happy eating leftovers for lunch the next day,
cold from the refrigerator.

On a cold January night, I served this salad for dinner, preceded by a winter squash
soup (page 269) and followed by sliced blood oranges for dessert. There was so much
color and flavor. Who says winter vegetables are drab? CONTINUED

The Togorashi Tofu Crisps

1 pound (more or less) firm tofu

1 scant teaspoon togorashi or 1 heaping teaspoon freshly ground black pepper

½ teaspoon red pepper flakes, if using pepper

1 rounded teaspoon sea salt

Organic cornstarch

½ cup peanut or oil, for frying

The Dressing

4 tablespoons rice wine vinegar

2 tablespoons good Japanese soy sauce or tamari

2 tablespoons dark sesame oil

1 tablespoon light sesame or peanut oil

⅛ teaspoon salt

The Cabbage Salad

1 small red cabbage (a scant 2 pounds)

1 small red onion, thinly sliced

1 large yellow bell pepper, sliced about ¼ inch thick (optional)

1 red jalapeño-sized pepper, thinly sliced

A chunk of ginger, peeled and sliced into very thin strips to make 1 heaping tablespoon

1 cup (or so) snow peas, if available, tips and strings removed, sliced diagonally

2 good handfuls of chopped cilantro leaves

6 scallions, including some of the greens, sliced diagonally

1 tablespoon toasted black sesame seeds or ¼ cup toasted peanuts or cashews

TO MAKE THE CRISPS Drain the tofu, then wrap it in a clean cotton towel, place a heavy object on top, and set it aside while you prepare the rest of the ingredients for the tofu and the salad. You want the tofu to be dry so that there won't be any bits of water sputtering in the hot oil. When it has drained, cut the block of tofu into ½- to 1-inch cubes.

Put the togarashi or pepper, pepper flakes, and salt in a large bowl. Heat the oil in a 9-inch skillet. While it's heating, take a third of the tofu pieces and toss them in a few tablespoons of cornstarch. When the oil is hot enough to sizzle a bit of tofu, add the batch and cook over medium-high heat, turning them every so often until they are golden and crisp, about 4 to 5 minutes. Remove the tofu and turn it onto paper toweling to drain. Repeat with the last two batches. (There should be plenty of oil.) When done, toss the still-warm tofu with the togarashi mixture.

TO MAKE THE DRESSING Whisk the dressing ingredients together and set the dressing aside.

TO MAKE THE SALAD Prepare all the vegetables before you begin cooking. Quarter the cabbage, cut out the cores, and using a sharp knife or running a chunk of cabbage over a sharp blade (a mandoline), slice it as thinly as you can. You'll need 4 to 5 cups.

Heat a third of the dressing in a wide skillet set over high heat. Add the onion, yellow pepper, red pepper, and ginger and cook briskly, stirring often until softened, about 2 minutes. Remove to a platter or shallow salad bowl.

Return the skillet to the heat and add the rest of the dressing. When it's hot, add the cabbage and cook, turning frequently, until it has softened but still retains its bright color, about 2 minutes if very thinly sliced, longer if thicker. Add the snow peas during the last minute. Slide the cabbage into the bowl with the onion and toss with most of the tofu crisps, scallions, cilantro, and seeds or nuts. Taste for salt and add more if needed. Garnish with the remaining ingredients and serve while still warm.

CARROT SOUP WITH ZESTY RELISH
OR SMOKY-SPICY BUTTER

Serves 4 to 6; GF

Carrots are great fun to grow, harvest, and cook. I am especially happy when those carrots I overlooked the previous fall bloom in their second year, making big, lacey umbels that go to seed, resulting in a new crop of carrots that pop up all over the garden. Ladybugs are powerfully attracted to the flowers at the end of summer, when aphids are also heading to the fading blooms for a last meal. After the ladybugs have had *their* aphid feast, they go to their ladybug house to spend a cozy winter huddled in a pile of dead leaves.

Carrots are just good vegetables in general: sturdy, versatile, good cooked or raw, colorful. They're especially good for soups. Because they tend toward sweetness, carrots take well to spicy garnishes—like harissa, tomatillo salsa, the smoky-spicy butter on page 64, and pickled onions to name but a few—as well as the more delicate but robust-flavored tops of the carrots, finely chopped and scattered over the surface. Another approach is to take a few teaspoons of berbere (page 151), stir in some olive oil to make a sauce, and then drizzle that over the surface. Some creamy yogurt stirred into the soup would be good with the berbere, too. In the version here, you have a choice between the spicy compound butter to use if you're serving the soup hot, or a quick relish of pickled onion, fresh chile, cilantro, and lime, which works whether you are serving the soup hot or cold.

Carrots offer endless possibilities, and a good basic soup seems like a fundamental recipe to have in your repertoire. If you prefer, you can stay away from the spices here and turn instead to dill, parsley, lovage, caraway, and other familial herbs—all are umbellifers, like the carrots themselves—and do best with butter as a fat rather than ghee or coconut oil. Rice is the thickener—the carrots need a little starch.

2 tablespoons ghee or coconut oil

1 onion, thinly sliced

1 pound (or more) carrots, scrubbed well and sliced (you'll want at least 3 cups sliced)

Sea salt and freshly ground pepper

3 tablespoons white rice

1½ teaspoons toasted ground cumin seeds

1 teaspoon ground coriander

1 teaspoon paprika (smoked or not)

¼ teaspoon turmeric

2 tablespoons finely minced cilantro stems

Smoky-Spicy Butter (page 64), if serving the soup hot

The Relish (optional)

¼ cup finely diced pickled red onions (see page 175) or finely diced scallions or chives

¼ serrano or jalapeño chile, seeded and finely diced

2 tablespoons chopped cilantro

Juice and grated zest of 2 limes

Melt the ghee or coconut oil in a soup pot set over medium heat. Add the onion, carrots, and rice. Cook, stirring frequently, until the onions have softened, about 5 minutes, then add the cumin, coriander, paprika, and turmeric, along with about 1 rounded teaspoon of salt and some freshly ground pepper. Continue cooking for another 5 minutes. Add 5½ cups of water and bring it to a boil, then lower the heat and simmer, partially covered, for 25 minutes. Let the soup cool somewhat, then purée at least 2 cups of it until smooth; return this to the pot to give it a more dense background. Or purée all the soup if a smooth texture is to your liking.

While the soup is cooking, make the compound butter if you haven't any in the freezer. Or, assemble the relish, stirring together the onions, diced chile, cilantro, and lime zest and juice in a bowl.

Serve the soup hot, with a slice of the butter in each bowl, or cold or hot with a spoonful of relish in each.

CAULIFLOWER AND SWEET PEPPERS, SAFFRON, PARSLEY, AND OLIVES

Serves 4 or more; GF

Cauliflower is a bit on the bland side—that is, until you add saffron, garlic, red pepper, and plenty of parsley. In *Vegetable Literacy,* I made this with pasta shells but also suggested using einkorn or whole-wheat spaghetti; the seasoned cauliflower is robust enough to stand up to these heartier pastas. Cutting the cauliflower into small pieces that can nestle right inside the openings of the shells makes this a visually and texturally fetching dish. Today I tend to make just the cauliflower (still in small florets), leaving out the pasta altogether unless there are heartier eaters at the table than I—then I offer the pasta, or black rice, to round out the dish. The black adds to the visual excitement along with its flavor; the peppers add succulence. And as for peppers, bells are great, but you might be tempted to try pimentos (Lipstick has thick, red flesh) or Corno di Toro peppers from the farmers' market. They are sweet and excellent with the cauliflower.

Be sure to use the core of the cauliflower. There's no reason to throw it out. It's dense but not pithy or stringy, and it tastes pretty much the same as the florets. The pale leaves that wrap around the head are also quite edible.

1 cauliflower (about 1½ pounds)	½ teaspoon red pepper flakes, or less
2 tablespoons olive oil	Sea salt and freshly ground black pepper
1 onion, finely diced	4 tablespoons finely chopped parsley,
1 red pepper, diced into ½-inch squares	or a mixture of fresh oregano and parsley
1 yellow pepper, diced into ½-inch squares	8 oil-cured olives, halved or chopped
2 pinches of saffron threads	Crumbled feta or manouri cheese
1 plump garlic clove, minced	Pasta, rice, or quinoa, to serve

Cut the cauliflower into small florets and dice the core. Steam both over boiling water for 2 to 4 minutes, or until the cauliflower is on the verge of being utterly tender, but is not quite there. Set it aside but don't discard the steaming water.

Heat the oil in a wide skillet. Add the onion, peppers, and saffron. Cook over medium heat, stirring frequently, until the onion is cooked, 6 minutes or so. The steam that the vegetables release will activate the saffron so that it stains and flavors the onion. Next add the garlic, red pepper flakes, 1 teaspoon of salt, a few big pinches of the parsley, and finally the steamed cauliflower. Toss all together, add ½ cup of the water left from steaming the cauliflower, and cook over medium heat until the cauliflower is fully tender. Taste for salt, season with pepper, and toss with the remaining parsley and the olives. Add the cheese. Serve as is, or over pasta, rice, or quinoa.

ROASTED CAULIFLOWER WITH ROMESCO SAUCE AND A SHOWER OF PARSLEY

Serves 2 to 4; V, GF

The way this dish looks depends on how large the cauliflower is and how determined you are to present large golden planks of the vegetable over smaller pieces. This choice will itself depend on whether you're putting this out as a first course, an appetizer, or a main dish. Regardless, roasted cauliflower is excellent paired with rusty red romesco sauce and a flurry of bracing green parsley—romesco sauce simply makes everything taste infinitely better. Don't despair if your cauliflower doesn't want so stay connected to the core and prefers to fall into florets—just roast them anyway. You're only likely to get two or three—possibly four—intact pieces out of one large cauliflower.

Depending on where you're going to use roasted cauliflower, you can toss the florets with different kinds of fats. I use coconut oil or ghee when roasting them for a curry but olive oil for this recipe.

1 large cauliflower (the larger it is, the more slabs you'll get)

Olive oil

Sea salt and freshly ground pepper

Romesco Sauce (page 218)

Italian parsley leaves

Heat the oven to 375°F and line a sheet pan with parchment. Halve the cauliflower, keeping the core intact, and make as many slices as you can, each ½ to ¾ inch thick, cutting from the center out, ideally achieving three or four slabs that are joined at the core. If your cauliflower isn't cooperative or simply isn't very large, just cut large florets so that each has a flat side.

Brush the cauliflower with olive oil and season well with salt and pepper.

Warm a cast-iron skillet over medium-high heat, add the cauliflower, and cook until golden brown on the bottom, then carefully turn and cook the second side. In all, this should take about 12 minutes. Transfer the finished slabs and any remaining florets to the prepared sheet pan. Slide the pan into the oven and bake until the cauliflower is tender when pierced with a knife in the core, about 10 minutes.

Arrange the pieces on plates and add a generous spoonful of the sauce either on top of or next to the cauliflower. Shower all with the parsley leaves and serve.

CELERY ROOT AND POTATO MASH
WITH TRUFFLE SALT

Serves 4 to 6; GF

Celery root and potatoes make a most delicious vegetable purée, or mash. There are all kinds of things you can do with it. You can use it to blanket a vegetable shepherd's pie, or you could flavor the purée with ghee and black garlic, or you could include other vegetables in the mix—turnips, parsnips, and fennel are all delicious. If the purée is thick enough and you have some left over, mix it with some Gruyère cheese, form it into cakes, and brown them in clarified butter. This is very luxurious, rich and good: a perfect small first course.

You have to improvise with what you have. If you're rich with celery root, you might use much more in proportion to potatoes. If you have only a small celery root, know that it will still lend its flavor to the mash; it just won't be as strong.

To me, celery root always cries out for truffle and, since I seldom find (or can afford) a whole truffle, it's here in the form of truffle salt, added at the end. But this is a fine dish on its own, even without the truffle salt.

1 to 2 pounds Yellow Finn or other boiling potatoes, peeled

1 large celery root, rinsed and peeled

Sea salt and freshly ground pepper

Approximately ½ cup warmed milk, cream, or cooking water

4 tablespoons butter or nut oil, more or less, to taste

¼ cup, more or less, finely chopped celery leaves (optional)

Truffle salt

Cut the potato and celery root into large pieces. Put each vegetable in a saucepan with cold water to cover and a teaspoon of salt. Bring to a boil, then lower the heat and simmer until the vegetables are tender, about 15 minutes for the potatoes and 10 minutes for the celery root, depending on their size. Drain, reserving the cooking water: you can use this instead of milk or cream for thinning the mash, or save it to use as a soup stock.

Pass the cooked vegetables together through a food mill or mash by hand, adding warm liquid (cream, milk, or cooking water) to thin them as you go. Taste for salt, season with pepper, and stir in butter to taste. Finally, stir in the celery leaves. You can keep this warm in a double boiler. When you're ready to serve, scoop the purée into a serving dish and sprinkle generously with truffle salt.

SILKY BRAISED CHARD AND CILANTRO

Serves 4; V, GF

It's because of this recipe that I learned to adore the combination of chard and cilantro in any form, but especially when it's cooked slowly until soft and intense, as it is here. As I use chard from my garden, the stems are often thin and tender and need only be sliced crosswise. If you have chard with big fat stems, consider running a peeler over them, then slicing them into ¼-inch strips and then crosswise into small pieces to use in this dish. You'll just need a cup, more or less.

I turn to this dish regardless of how much or how little chard I have. If you're shopping at the farmers' market or cooking from the garden, you no doubt realize that chard doesn't grow in bunches. You pick what needs picking and take it from there. You can also mix beet greens and spinach with the chard—they're all close relatives—or use other greens as well: collards, lambsquarters, what have you. By the time the greens are really cooked down, there won't be a lot, but it will be an intense few spoonfuls to accompany something else. If I'm not serving rice elsewhere in the meal, I add white rice to the pot, which will absorb the moisture from the greens and be fully cooked by the time they are. The chard goes great with the Yogurt-Tahini Sauce on page 53.

It has become customary for recipe writers to say things like "set aside the stems for another use" when speaking of chard. But do they get used? Most likely not, I suspect. But the following recipe (Chard Stems with Lemon) makes use of them, and why not serve those extras alongside the leaves? In part, I like to cook chard stems because, well, why waste them? But I also like them because they taste good, both earthy and mild.

About 2 pounds chard, or chard
mixed with other greens

⅓ cup white rice (optional)

1 small onion, finely diced

½ cup chopped cilantro

¼ cup olive oil

1 teaspoon paprika

Sea salt

Stem the chard leaves and cut into 1-inch ribbons—you'll have about 12 cups. Trim the tough parts off a few of the stems and dice them into small pieces (you'll want a cup, more or less). Place the sliced ribbons and stems in a large pot with a tight-fitting cover, along with the rice, if using, and the onion, cilantro, oil, and paprika. Season with ½ teaspoon of salt. Cover and cook over low heat, covered, for 40 to 50 minutes. During this time, check once or twice to make sure there's enough moisture and that nothing is sticking. Add a few tablespoons of water if it is or the pot seems dry. In the end, the chard will be silky and very fragrant.

CHARD STEMS WITH LEMON

V, GF

This is a great way to use the stems from the chard and cilantro from the previous recipe—or from any other chard dish that only calls for the leaves. Chard stems can be cut into 3-inch lengths and served chilled with a wedge of lemon on a summer's night, or, once cooked, they can be diced and served as a relish, maybe with a bit of preserved lemon, over the *trouchia* on page 122, or alongside Silky Braised Chard and Cilantro (opposite). Any color chard stem can be used in this simple braise, which can be augmented with saffron, diced tomatoes, and the like, if desired. Some color will be lost in the cooking, but not all. And the exact cooking time will depend on the tenderness of the stalks. They can be done in as little as seven minutes or as long as twenty. You'll just have to test their tenderness, as they cook, with the point of a knife. I haven't included measurements because you don't really need them. Just be sure you have enough water to cover.

Chard stems	Grated zest of 1 lemon
Several thyme sprigs	Best olive oil
Lemon juice	Chopped parsley
Sea salt and freshly ground pepper	A garden tomato, peeled, seeded and neatly diced (optional)

Trim the stems so that they're even on the top and the bottom and then cut them into 3-inch lengths. Put 1 to 2 quarts of water in a sauté pan—as much as you think you need to cover the stems. Add the thyme and lemon juice and about 1 teaspoon of salt for each quart of water. Bring to a simmer, stir to dissolve the salt, add the stems, and cook until tender, testing them for doneness with the tip of a knife or taking a bite. Drain and then put the cooked stems on a platter and turn them with lemon zest, olive oil, and parsley. Taste for salt and season with pepper. Spoon the tomato over and serve.

CHARD AND SAFFRON FLAN IN AN ALMOND CRUST WITH SPRING GREENS

Serves 4 to 6; GF

If anyone asked me how my cooking has changed over the years, I would say that the flavors I'm drawn to are much the same but that I construct dishes differently. For example, a tart shell holding a filling of chard and saffron scented cream (a dish I started making long ago at Greens) is something I love, and others do, too. But in *Vegetable Literacy*, I found myself keeping the flavors but forming the ingredients to make little skillet cakes, which are so satisfying as little pass-arounds garnished with a spoonful of crème fraîche and some microgreens—a different texture and presentation altogether. Today, and in this recipe, I've mingled two favorites: the aforementioned Chard and Saffron Tart and a reconfigured Green Herb Torta, omitting the crust in the former and featuring the latter's spring greens in a salad to serve under or along side of the flan. A somewhat different dish, but one whose flavors I would recognize blindfolded.

What it comes down to is this: if I want to include cream, cheese, and nuts in the tart, then something has to go, and that is the crust. That isn't to say I don't love its crispness and buttery succulence—I do. It's just that its richness is problematic. (However, I would include it if pieces were to be sliced into thin wedges for a first course.) In lieu of the crust, I butter a gratin dish and grind almonds and dust the dish liberally with them. It's not really a crust, but it offers a bit of crunch as do the nuts scattered over the top surface.

As for the spring greens salad, what I search for are such goodies as the first lovage leaves, those humorous walking onions, the sorrel plant's first leaves, and arugula greens, which grow weedlike everywhere, as does purple-flowered musk mustard. I'd also include some early lettuce leaves or a head of Belgian endive, the leaves left uncut. Herbs can go in the mix as well—tarragon, hyssop, parsley, and maybe some sheltered chervil. The more of these oddballs you can put in your salad, the more interesting it will be. CONTINUED

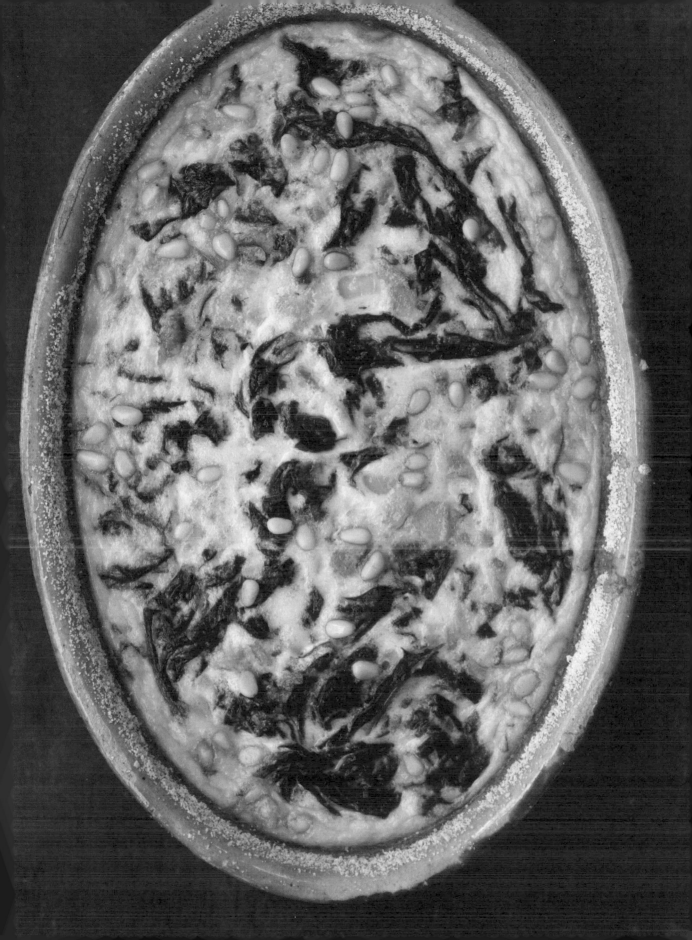

1 pound chard (enough leaves to make 8 cups, minus the stems)

2 tablespoons olive oil

1 hefty spring onion, quartered lengthwise and diced into small pieces (enough to make about a cup), or 1 medium onion, finely diced

Sea salt and freshly ground pepper

2 large eggs

A big pinch of saffron threads soaked in 1 tablespoon near-boiling water

1½ cups cream or ¾ cup half-and-half mixed with ¾ cup ricotta

Grated zest of 1 lemon

¼ cup freshly grated Parmigiano-Reggiano

Butter

About ½ cup almonds, ground or finely chopped

3 tablespoons pine nuts or slivered almonds

The Spring Greens

Several handfuls of greens and herbs (see page 88)

Sea salt

Olive oil

Lemon juice or vinegar

Heat the oven to 375°F. Tear or chop the chard into pieces, then wash and drain the pieces, but do not dry them. Heat the oil over medium-high heat in a wide skillet and add the onion. Move it around the pan to cook for about a minute, then add the chard with the water clinging to its leaves. Sprinkle over ½ teaspoon of salt and cook, turning the leaves occasionally, until they're soft, about 8 to 10 minutes for later-season chard, which can be tough, less for more tender leaves. Turn off the heat. Taste for salt and season with pepper.

Beat the eggs in a bowl, then stir in the saffron water (plus threads), cream, lemon zest, and grated Parmigiano-Reggiano. Stir in the chard and season with pepper.

To finish, butter a 4-cup gratin dish, then dust the bottom and sides of the dish with the finely chopped almonds. Pour in the filling and scatter the pine nuts or almonds over the surface. Bake until the flan is golden and set, about 30 minutes.

TO MAKE THE GREENS Tear the herbs into large pieces and keep the more salady greens larger. Toss them with salt, just enough olive oil to coat lightly, and a few drops of lemon juice or vinegar to sharpen the flavors.

Put the dressed spring greens on individual plates and spoon the flan carefully over or next to them. The heat of the flan will wilt them a bit and bring out their aromas.

A CHEESE SOUFFLÉ—MY GO-TO RECIPE

Serves 4

A cheese soufflé is something you can easily (yes, *easily*) whip up. Most people think it's very difficult to make a soufflé, but it's not, and you don't have to tell anyone how really straightforward it is. Let them be impressed and in awe of you when you carry your creation to the table. Smile and say thank you when they rave. This is my go-to recipe when people drop in for dinner or my husband and I want to enjoy a dish that's both light and nourishing.

Here are a few tips. First, you can use a number of cheeses. I happen to love a goat cheese soufflé, but I also like a soufflé that's based on an aged Cheddar, or on Gruyère. I've also been known to throw one together using bits and pieces of odds and ends of cheese, but not blue cheese, which has a way of turning a soufflé an unappealing blue-gray color. Second, while a soufflé dish with its high sides produces a lofty and impressive item, you can also use a shallow earthenware dish—even a glass pie plate. The soufflé will still rise; it will cook more quickly and there will be lots of crust for the taking, which is every person's favorite part. I have long since relegated my soufflé dish to the storage shed in favor of an earthenware dish with low sides, but both work very well. Third, you can if you wish, incorporate cooked vegetables into a soufflé. To a cheese soufflé base, add a cup of cooked vegetables such as puréed winter squash, asparagus, spinach, chard, or beet greens. And don't forget herbs. I often lace my soufflés with aromatic flecks of green from thyme leaves, marjoram, parsley, fresh (not dried) oregano, and so forth. They are not in the oven long enough so that they become gray and dingy or lose their flavor, and they do add complexity to the dish.

2 tablespoons grated Parmigiano-Reggiano or dry bread crumbs

1¼ cups milk

1 bay leaf

Several sprigs of thyme

A branch of parsley

2 or 3 thin slices of onion

4 large eggs, separated

Sea salt and freshly ground pepper

3 tablespoons butter

4 tablespoons flour

Pinch of cayenne

1 cup grated aged, Cheddar or crumbled goat cheese

2 tablespoons finely minced herbs, such as marjoram or oregano (if available)

Heat the oven to 375°F. Butter a 6-cup soufflé dish or shallow earthenware dish and coat it with either the Parmigiano-Reggiano or the bread crumbs.

Slowly warm the milk with the bay leaf, thyme, parsley, and onion slices. When the milk just comes to a boil, turn off the heat, cover, and let it sit for the flavors to steep while you go on to the next step.

Whisk the egg whites with a pinch of salt until they form firm, but not stiff, peaks. (If the peaks are too stiff, they'll be hard to fold into the base.)

Melt 3 tablespoons of butter in a 2-quart saucepan over low heat. When it bubbles, add the flour and cook for several minutes, stirring it about with a flat-bottomed wooden spoon. Pour the still warm milk through a sieve into the pan while whisking. Stir vigorously for a minute or so as it thickens, then add ¾ teaspoon of salt, a few twists of pepper, and the cayenne. Turn off the heat and beat in the egg yolks one at a time until well blended; then stir in the cheese.

Stir in a quarter of the beaten egg whites to loosen the base and then fold in the remainder. Add the minced herbs. Scrape the batter into the prepared dish and then slide it into the center of the oven. Bake for 30 minutes or until golden and just a bit wobbly in the center. Remove and serve immediately. Soufflés wait for no one!

CITRUS AND AVOCADO WITH LIME-CUMIN VINAIGRETTE AND SHREDDED GREENS

Serves 4; V, GF

I started making this dressing at Greens to use on a salad that was based on hearty romaine leaves tossed with jicama, radishes, cucumbers, and such. It was a perfect salad to serve with the black bean enchiladas—crisp, sweet, and spicy in contrast to the dense beans. I've since learned that it works equally well as a dressing on a winter salad of citrus fruits and avocado. If this salad is what you're having for dinner, by all means include the avocado; when I serve it with something substantial, I leave the avocado out—it's just too rich.

You might think of winter as root dominated, but citrus fruits arrive starting in November with the first satsumas and going on with mandarins of all kinds, small citrus such as kumquats and limequats, giant ones like grapefruits and pomelos, then Meyer lemons, various kinds of limes, and so forth. Seedless oranges—navels, Cara Caras, and bloods—are bright and cheerful, and their taste is clean and, in the case of blood oranges, perfumed. Sliced oranges in an orange caramel sauce is one of my favorite desserts, while oranges with this dressing is one of my favorite winter salads. The avocado has the perfect creamy and contrasting texture (and color) to complement the fruit. And although it's not necessary, I like to scatter a few handfuls of thinly sliced romaine, napa cabbage, or radicchio over the salad for a contrast in texture and, once again, color.

I'm not a big fan of bowls, but if you are, you might start with some quinoa, then add the oranges along with avocados, then sprigs of cilantro and leafy greens, ending with the dressing and the pickled red onions on page 175. This would be very pretty and would make a complete meal for a light eater.

Jalapeños used to be smaller and more consistent in their heat levels. Now they're much larger and they vary greatly: some are searing while others are bland, and marketers don't always tell you which is which. They probably don't know. I used a fairly hot pepper here, and measured a tablespoon, which was about a quarter of a pepper. You're just going to have to taste your chile, if you're using one. And if you're using all blood oranges, you might want to use more, as they are smaller than navels or Cara Caras.

CONTINUED

6 oranges, different varieties, preferably
seedless, plus a few kumquats, if desired

1 large ripe but firm avocado

2 handfuls finely shredded radicchio,
napa cabbage, or romaine lettuce

¼ cup pistachio nuts

The Dressing
1 small clove garlic

Sea salt

Grated zest of 2 limes

3 tablespoons lime juice

2 scallions, including an inch or so
of the greens, finely sliced

1 tablespoon finely diced jalapeño chile
(optional)

½ teaspoon cumin seeds

½ teaspoon coriander seeds

¼ teaspoon dry mustard

¼ teaspoons sweet paprika

4 tablespoons olive oil

2 tablespoons finely chopped cilantro

Take a slice off the stem end and flower end of each orange so that the fruit stands on a cutting board without wobbling. Using a sharp knife, slice down the sides, cutting just beneath the white pith. (Sometimes it takes a few strokes to get under it.) When you've removed most of the pith, hold the orange in your hand and slice off any patches that remain, then slice the fruit into rounds about ¼ inch thick. Do this with all the oranges and put the slices in a shallow bowl. (If you wish to include thin slices of kumquats with their skins, do so.) Cover and refrigerate until you're ready to serve.

TO MAKE THE DRESSING Begin by pounding the garlic in a mortar with ½ teaspoon of salt until it's smooth, after half a minute or so. Add the lime zest, juice, scallions, and chile if using. Set aside.

Toast the cumin and coriander seeds in a dry skillet until aromatic, then turn them out on a plate to cool briefly. Grind them to a powder in a spice grinder. Add them, along with the rest of the spices, to the mortar and then whisk in the oil and add the cilantro. Taste a little dressing on a piece of orange to make sure the balance is right. Halve the avocado, scoop out the flesh, cut it lengthwise into slices, and lay them on the oranges.

Pour the dressing over all, then scatter the shredded greens and the pistachios over the top. Present the salad like this, but toss it a bit as you serve it so that everything is well mixed.

COLLARDS SIMMERED IN COCONUT MILK WITH SHALLOTS

Serves 4; V, GF

When coconut oil first became popular, I used it often with narrow ribbons of collard greens, which I then used to garnish a carrot soup. The collards were hard to find, and the leaves were huge, expensive, and not really all that great. But then I started growing them and could pick them to my heart's content. I started cooking masses of the smaller, more tender leaves and found that they are especially delicious when cooked in coconut milk. The coconut milk makes a sauce that you can spoon over coconut rice (page 213) with triangles of tofu simply seared and splashed with soy sauce. These three dishes make a dynamic and complete meal, quite possible to make even on a weeknight.

2 bunches of collard leaves, about 8 cups sliced, minus the stems

2 teaspoons coconut oil

2 hefty shallots, peeled and sliced crosswise

½ cup coconut milk

Sea salt and freshly ground pepper

Juice of 1 large lime

Slice the leaves off the tough stems of the collards and discard the stems. Wash the leaves well, agitating them vigorously in cold water. Drain the leaves, then stack a few together, roll them (or leave them flat if they're small), and slice them crosswise into strips about ½ inch wide. If you have small, tender leaves you can just chop them.

Heat the coconut oil in a pan with sides high enough to hold the greens. When hot, add the shallots and cook over medium heat for about a minute. Pour in the coconut milk followed by the greens and several pinches of salt. Cook until the leaves are tender; taste them to be sure. Young greens may take just a few minutes; larger, older greens will take more like 12 to 15 minutes. Squeeze the lime over the collards, taste for salt, and season with pepper.

CORN, SHIITAKE MUSHROOMS, AND SAGE WITH MILLET

Serves 4 to 6; GF

Golden millet is an old, old grain, one we should become acquainted with if we're not already. It has more copper, manganese, phosphorus, and magnesium than most foods, plus it's gluten free, it's fluffy, and very mild, which allows other flavors to come forward. I sometimes make it ahead of time and then crisp slabs of it in ghee, even though the pieces tend to break up and not stay together that well. The other alternative is to serve it soft, as it comes from the pot. And of course, polenta, either soft from the pot, or cooled then fried, is yet another accompaniment for this dish.

The corn takes but moments to cook, but it does take a few minutes longer to slice the kernels off the cobs. Fresh is so much better than frozen that I make this dish, or some variation of it, at least once a year. Frozen corn is convenient, but the kernels are cut a little too deeply and can get caught in your teeth. Plus, they retain a kind of toughness that isn't so pleasant.

3 tablespoons ghee or butter, plus more for frying

1 cup millet

3 cups water or stock

Sea salt and freshly ground pepper

1 ounce dried shiitake mushrooms covered with 1 cup boiling water

8 plump ears of corn, shucked and rinsed

1 cup or 1 large bunch finely minced green onions, including their firm greens

8 sage leaves, finely slivered

Paprika (smoked or not), for sprinkling

1 small tomato, diced (optional)

1 tablespoon chopped parsley, marjoram, or sage

Melt half the ghee in a 2- to 3-quart saucepan. Add the millet, stir it about and cook for about 5 minutes, or until it starts to darken and even pop. Pour in the water, add ¾ teaspoon of salt, and bring to a boil. Lower the heat, cover the pan, and simmer until the water is absorbed, about 35 minutes. If you're not going to serve the millet immediately, pour it into an 8 by 10-inch or smaller dish, smooth it out, and set aside to firm up.

Pour the mushroom soaking water through a fine-mesh sieve set over a bowl. Cut the stems off the mushrooms, then slice them into ½-inch pieces.

Using a good, sharp knife, slice the kernels off the corn cobs, going slightly less than halfway through them. Put the kernels in a bowl. You should have about 3 cups. Next, take one cob at a time and drag the flat edge of the knife down each cob, forcing out the milky liquid, also known as corn milk. Add this to the bowl of corn kernels.

Melt the remaining ghee in a 10-inch skillet. Add the green onions, mushrooms, and sage. Give a stir to combine, then add the corn kernels and corn milk. Cook at a lively temperature to heat everything through, then add the mushroom-soaking liquid and cook for another few minutes. Season with salt and pepper to taste. If you wish, add some paprika, a diced tomato, or nothing at all.

Divide the millet pieces, whether soft or fried, among plates and spoon the corn and mushroom ragout over them. Serve, garnished with fresh, chopped parsley or other herb.

CURRY MAYONNAISE FOR ROASTED CAULIFLOWER OR STEAMED BROCCOLI

Makes about 1 cup; GF

Say you need an appetizer, and all you have is a cauliflower. When that happened to me, I roasted the florets as described for the curry on page 252, adding a little extra curry powder, then made this curry mayonnaise from the vegan mayonnaise I always have on hand and some other ingredients. It's a rather retro mayonnaise, and it used to embarrass me, but it's really good with vegetables of all kinds. And it happily goes lots of other places as well.

The cauliflower is better hot than cold. It becomes kind of limp when cool; still tasty, but not so appealing. You can make it ahead of time. Just reheat it on top of the stove in a skillet and put it out, hot, with the mayonnaise. Broccoli, cut into florets and lightly steamed, is better chilled.

¾ cup prepared mayonnaise

¼ cup yogurt or sour cream

1½ teaspoons curry powder

1 teaspoon Patak's curry paste, or more, to taste

¼ cup Major Grey's mango chutney

Juice of 1 lime, or more, to taste

Snipped chives or green scallion leaves, for garnish

Mix together the mayonnaise, yogurt, curry powder, curry paste, and chutney. Taste and then add the lime juice. Taste again to see if needs more.

Scrape the mayonnaise into a bowl and garnish with the snipped chives just before serving.

QUICK CUCUMBER PICKLES

Makes about 2 cups; V, GF

These take a little longer than the Easy Pink Onion Pickles on page 175—they are better if they can rest a few hours in the vinegar. They'll keep for about five days.

⅔ cup white wine or apple cider vinegar

⅓ cup sugar

Pinch of sea salt

1 small red or white onion, thinly sliced in rounds

1½ cups thinly sliced cucumbers (peel the cucumbers only if the skins are tough)

1 teaspoon mixed whole peppercorns

A few lovage leaves, fennel greens, or dill sprigs

Mix the vinegar, sugar, and salt, stirring occasionally, until the sugar is dissolved.

Toss the onions with the cucumbers, peppercorns, and herbs in a noncorrosive bowl. Pour the vinegar mixture over the vegetables and herbs. Toss well, cover, and refrigerate well before using.

THREE WINTER CONFECTIONS
USING DRIED FRUIT

V, GF

Little bites of goodness, that's what these are. I've made these little jewel-like fruits during the holidays for years. I still like to make them and they're a perfect response to today's desire for less sugary desserts. One or two will suffice after a meal.

Dried Fruits with Fennel, Sesame Seeds, and Orange Flower Water

Enough for twenty-four 1-inch sweetmeats

The original description of this ancient recipe included cumin seeds, and although I'm very fond of cumin, it is perhaps better in savory dishes, so I've left it out. Anise seed can take the place of fennel seeds if you're out of the latter.

1 pound mixed dried fruits: dates, figs, large raisins, prunes

¾ cup white sesame seeds, toasted until golden in a dry skillet

½ cup walnuts

The grated zest and juice of 1 orange

½ teaspoon ground cinnamon or cardamom

1 teaspoon fennel seeds (or anise seed)

2 to 3 teaspoons orange flower water, to taste

Small pieces of dark chocolate (optional)

Green pistachio nuts (optional)

If the fruit is rock hard, soften it over steaming water. Remove any stems and pits, then add ¼ cup sesame seeds along with the remaining ingredients, except for the orange flower water, to a food processor. The goal is produce a rough paste. Add 2 teaspoons of the orange flower water. Taste it and add more of anything that's needed—orange, fennel, or cinnamon. If you wish, add a few tablespoons of dark chocolate chunks or green pistachio nuts. Break off pieces of the paste, roll them into balls, then roll the balls in the remaining sesame seeds to coat them.

Figs with Toasted Almonds and Anise Seed

This is a fine use of the dried figs available in the winter, either dark or light varieties. While figs and almonds alone make a fine little confection, anise seed makes an excellent addition. You might also consider adding toasted fennel seeds, star anise, 5-spice powder, lightly toasted cardamom seeds, and orange zest. Marcona almonds would also be interesting, and almonds seasoned with rosemary or truffle salt would make a compelling savory dessert or appetizer.

An equal number of dried figs and almonds

Toasted fennel seeds, anise seed, 5-spice powder, cardamom seeds, orange zest (all optional)

Count out as many dried figs as you want to serve, and the same number of almonds with their skin on. **CONTINUED**

If the figs are hard like little stones, soften them by steaming them over simmering water until they're pliable. Drop the almonds into boiling water, let stand for a minute, then take one out and see if the skin will come off easily. If so, drain all of them. If not, let them stand in the water a bit longer, until the skins do come off. Pop off the skins, then toast the almonds at a low heat, until golden and crisp. Insert a toasted almond into each fig with a pinch of any combination of fennel, anise, 5-spice, cardamom, or orange zest. Close up the figs and serve.

Dates with Almond Paste or Marzipan

Enough for 8 to 12 sweetmeats

For this confection, use big plump Medjools or the more slender Black Sphinx dates. Both are dramatic and delicious. You can make your own almond paste—the recipe is in *The Savory Way*—or buy a 7-ounce tube, which is enough to fill 8 to 12 dates. I use either almond paste or marzipan, and prefer the one made by Odense. It has a good almond flavor. Others don't, so you might need to knead them with a drop of almond extract. I add a few drops of rose flower water to the almond paste if I'm using dried rose petals for a garnish, or I knead the paste with chopped pistachio nuts, rolling the finished dates in the finest bits.

8 to 12 Medjool or Black Sphinx dates	Rose flower water (optional)
7 ounces almond paste or Marzipan	Finely chopped pistachio nuts (optional)

Slice each date lengthwise and remove the pit inside. Roll a piece of almond paste between you palms. You can make a piece that's slender enough that you can slip it inside the date and close the flesh completely around it. Or you can make it thicker and leave some of the almond paste exposed. Serve the dates whole, or slice those that cover the almond paste completely into rounds, and put them on a dessert plate with pieces of chocolate and some cracked nuts.

EGG SALAD FOR SPRING WITH TARRAGON, LOVAGE, AND CHIVES

Makes about 1 cup; GF

With spring's longer and warmer days come more eggs from the chickens along with the first herbs in the garden. Together, they are a perfect match.

I wanted to make deviled eggs with the same herbs, but you really do need older eggs to do that. We buy our eggs from a neighbor farmer, and they are always so fresh that you can't peel them. I had to ask myself, are deviled eggs so important that I have to wait until my eggs are a few weeks old? I decided they weren't. But if you do have older eggs, seasoning the yolks and scooping them back into the halved whites is a great way to go. Everyone loves a deviled egg. If that's not an option for you, remember you can pile egg salad on crackers or a dark rye bread, garnish it with chive blossoms, and be very happy.

For a long time I had forgotten about egg salad, but now that it's back on my culinary horizon, I love it. I should mention, because this is my husband's preference, a bit of curry powder is good, too. If you go in that direction, I'd leave out the tarragon and lovage.

4 fresh eggs	1 tablespoon minced parsley
1 shallot, finely diced	2 teaspoons slivered lovage
Tarragon or white wine vinegar	3 tablespoons mayonnaise, or as needed
1 heaping tablespoon minced tarragon leaves	Sea salt and freshly ground pepper
1 tablespoon finely snipped chives	Chive blossoms or little herb thinnings, if available, for garnish

Cover the eggs with cold water in a saucepan, bring them to a lively boil, and boil for 1 minute. Turn off the heat, cover the pan, and let stand for 7 minutes. Pour off the hot water, rinse with cool, then peel and chop the eggs. If they're very hard to peel, cut them in half crosswise and scoop out the eggs with a spoon.

While the eggs are cooking, cover the shallots with a little vinegar and chop the herbs. Put the chopped eggs in a bowl with the herbs and mayonnaise. Taste before you add salt—commercial mayonnaise can be salty, so if that's what you're using, you may not need any more salt. Season with pepper, then add the shallot, holding back the vinegar. Garnish with the chive blossoms or tiny herb thinnings.

SCRAMBLED EGGS SMOTHERED WITH CRISPY BREAD CRUMBS

Serves 2

This is a simple sort of inversion that surprises: spooning toasted bread crumbs over your scrambled eggs instead of putting your eggs on top of toast. It's the same bread—though it can easily be about half the amount you might eat at breakfast—and, while I didn't have this in mind when I first starting preparing eggs this way, the buttery, crisp crumbs do fill the desire for something crunchy. One slice of bread will suffice for two servings, but you might also make two slices into crumbs if the pieces are small. Use whatever bread you like—a sturdy whole wheat, a white sandwich bread, a gluten-free bread, ciabatta, and so forth. I especially like Ezekiel sprouted whole-grain bread for these crumbs. I also like a thin sliver of goat's milk Gouda set over the eggs, but that's entirely optional.

Three large eggs are more than ample for two of us at breakfast. If your eggs are smaller, use four, or whatever you consider right for breakfast—you know best.

2 slices bread	Sea salt and a grind of pepper
Butter	Cream or water, if you wish
3 or 4 large eggs	Thin slices of a favorite cheese (optional)

Cut the crusts off the bread if they're very thick and tough, then make the remaining bread into crumbs in a food processor. Melt a teaspoon or more of butter in a skillet, add the bread crumbs, and cook them over medium heat, stirring frequently, until they're toasty and crisp, about 5 minutes—longer if the bread is very fresh and dense.

Crack the eggs into a bowl and whisk them with a few pinches of salt and some pepper. If you wish, add a few spoonfuls of cream or water. Melt about a tablespoon of butter in an 8-inch skillet over medium-low heat. When it bubbles, pour in the eggs. Using a wooden spoon or rubber scraper, move the eggs around the pan until they're as moist or dry as you like them. Divide between two warm plates, add a slice of cheese if you wish, and then spoon the bread crumbs over all.

EGGPLANT GRATIN WITH A GOLDEN DOME OF SAFFRON-RICOTTA CUSTARD

Serves 4 to 6; GF

This has long been one of my favorite main dishes. I love that little dome of golden ricotta and I love that it's just as good cold, sliced into handsome wedges, as it is warm from the oven. It holds together well, and with a splash of good balsamic vinegar it is a perfect dish for hot weather.

In rereading the recipe for this gratin from *The Greens Cookbook*, I was reminded that we had added a layer of Gruyère to the eggplant "to make it more substantial as a main dish." Such were our concerns then, long before vegetables were valued for themselves. Even before revisiting that last line, I had taken the Gruyère out, thinking it unnecessary.

What matters most is making this when the eggplants and tomatoes are plentiful, in season, and full of flavor: late summer would be the time. It takes extra time to make your own tomato sauce, so you want it to be as good as possible. If you don't have lots of great tomatoes, a good commercial crushed tomato sauce works beautifully here. Smallish, delicate Rosa Bianca eggplants are a good choice here, and they're now available in many farmers' markets.

There are three parts to this gratin: the eggplant, the fresh tomato sauce, and the custard. I used to brown the eggplant in oil on the stove, probably because the ovens at the restaurant were otherwise full. Today I choose the oven, which means I can use a little less oil and it's a bit easier, too. You can get all three elements done at once if you take them in the right order: eggplant, then the tomato sauce, and finally the custard.

CONTINUED

2 pounds (or a bit more) small globe or larger oblong eggplants

Olive oil

1 small red onion, finely diced

1 plump clove garlic, minced

½ teaspoon herbes de Provence or a tablespoon marjoram leaves, chopped

2½ pounds ripe full-sized tomatoes peeled, seeded, and chopped or 2 cups crushed canned tomatoes

Sea salt and freshly ground pepper

2 eggs

1 cup ricotta

¼ cup milk

1 good pinch saffron threads, crumbled and soaked in 1 tablespoon hot water

½ cup freshly grated Parmigiano-Reggiano

10 large basil leaves, torn into pieces

Heat the oven to 400°F.

Cut the eggplants in half, lengthwise. If you've got one large eggplant, cut it in quarters. Slice each piece crosswise about ½ inch thick. Brush the slices lightly with the oil, set them on a sheet pan, then bake until the bottom sides have browned, about 15 minutes. Turn them over and brown the second side; this often takes less time, so check after about 8 minutes. When the eggplant is done, remove it from the oven and reduce the heat to 350°F.

To make the tomato sauce, warm 2 tablespoons of olive oil in a wide skillet. When hot, add the onion, garlic, and herbes de Provence (crushed first between the fingers), or the fresh marjoram. Stir to coat the onion with the oil, then reduce the heat to medium-low, and cook slowly until it is soft, 12 to 15 minutes. Add the chopped fresh or canned tomatoes, raise the heat, and cook, stirring occasionally, until the liquid has cooked off and the sauce is fairly thick. Season to taste with salt and pepper.

To make the custard, whisk the eggs and stir in the ricotta, milk, saffron, and Parmigiano-Reggiano. Season with a few pinches of salt and some freshly ground pepper.

Choose an earthenware casserole with 2-inch sides and an 8-cup capacity. A larger pan, say an oval dish 8 inches wide at the center and about 12 inches long, allows the ingredients to spread to a thin layer along with the custard topping.

Spread a cup of the sauce in the dish and then set down an overlapping layer of eggplant. Season it with salt and pepper. Scatter half the torn basil over the surface. Dab about ¼ cup of the sauce over the eggplant and then make another layer of eggplant, season with salt and pepper and the torn basil, and cover with the rest of the tomato sauce. Pour the custard over all and bake until it has gently swelled and is browned in places, about 40 minutes. Remove from the oven and let the gratin rest for about 10 minutes before serving.

ROASTED EGGPLANT, TWO WAYS

Eggplant needn't be fried or otherwise saturated with oil. One of my favorite treatments is to cook smallish ones right in the flame or roast larger ones in a hot (425°F) oven until they've softened to the point of collapse. The now-limp vegetables go into a bowl to cool, where they'll give up their juices all by themselves. At this point, you slice them open and carefully spoon out the flesh, which will be pale and soft. Then you can leave it with texture or pound it to a purée and proceed with as few or as many additions as you wish.

One possibility is to serve it as a vegetable with olive oil or butter, salt and pepper, parsley, and a squeeze of lemon. Is this an appetizer? A filling in a pita sandwich? A small side dish? It can be all of these and no doubt more.

You really can use any size or variety of eggplant, but smaller varieties are truly best— and sweetest—in season. I suggest roasting really large ones in the oven rather than on the stove. Make a few slits and fill them with pieces of garlic or simply poke the eggplants in a few places so they won't explode (they really will do that!) and then bake them until they've collapsed.

In general, I prefer to use the oblong varieties of eggplants, from tiny Fairy Tales, which can be enormously prolific, to larger purple ones such as Orient Express or Orient Charm and the smaller Ichiban. Among the Italian eggplants, there are some that are definitely more oblong than round but plumper and heavier than the Asian ones, such as Dancer, Nubia, or Traviata. There are so many varieties. Just a look in one catalogue showed seventeen, and these are just new ones for the most part. Purple, white, green, striped, magenta—the color doesn't matter in this easy recipe.

The tool that makes this recipe easiest to make is an *asador*, essentially a heavy wire-mesh disk on legs, with handles, that you can set right over your burner. But if you don't have one, or an equivalent, you can cook the eggplants right in the flame.
CONTINUED

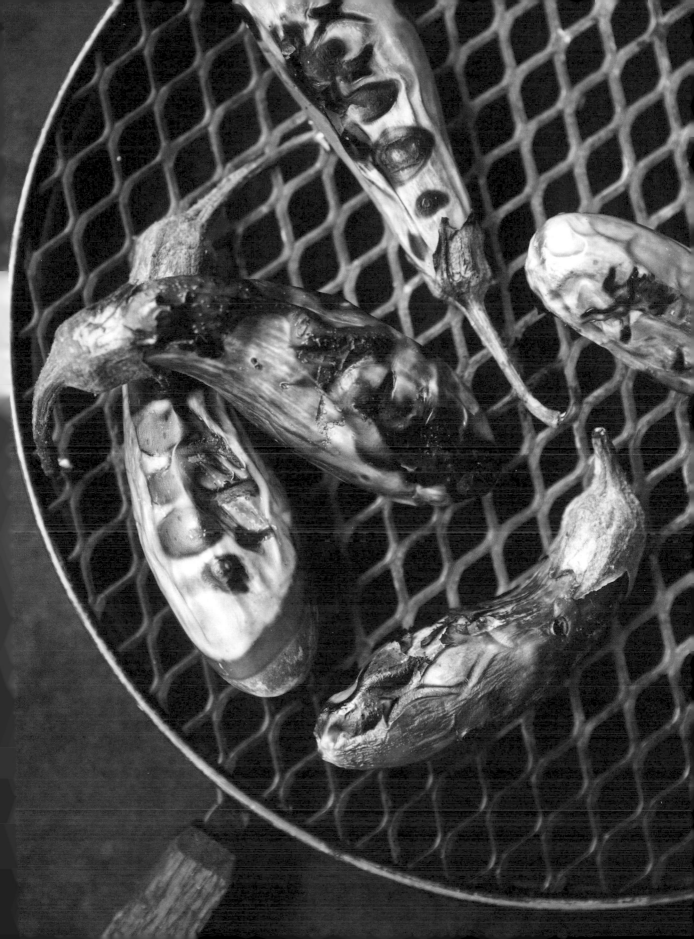

Roasted Eggplant on the Stovetop

Makes 1 cup or more; V, GF

This simple version of roasted eggplant can be served with any number of things. Here are some options: thick, creamy yogurt; ground roasted cumin; toasted black sesame seeds; cilantro; salsa verde of any kind; tahini (this gets it moving toward baba ghanouj); smoked paprika; or simply additional garlic and lemon.

2 pounds, more or less, smallish eggplants

Sea salt and freshly ground pepper

Best olive oil

Gremolata: a tablespoon of parsley minced with a clove of garlic and the grated zest of ½ a lemon

Set an asador or equivalent, if you have one, over a flame. Put the eggplants on top and cook over high heat, turning them and moving them about so that all surfaces are exposed to the flame. Eventually the eggplants will become wrinkled, charred, and very soft to the touch. When this happens, move them to a bowl to cool.

Cut the eggplants in half lengthwise. Scoop out the flesh and put it in a bowl. Mash the flesh with a fork to break up large chunks, making it as rough or smooth as you like. Season it with salt, pepper, and a little olive oil. Scoop into a serving dish and sprinkle the gremolata over all.

Roasted Eggplant with Dill, Yogurt, and Walnuts

Makes about 1½ cups; GF

Dill, yogurt, and walnuts take this roasted eggplant in a very different direction. Serve it with flatbreads or crackers before dinner or with dinner.

2 medium eggplants, about 1½ pounds in all

2 plump garlic cloves or 3 smaller ones

⅓ cup walnuts, halved and pieces

Sea salt and freshly ground pepper

½ cup chopped dill

2 to 3 tablespoons best olive oil

⅓ to ½ cup thick, creamy yogurt

Heat the oven to 425°F. Make four or five short incisions in the eggplants. Thinly slice one of the garlic cloves and insert a slice in each incision. Roast the eggplants in the oven until they've collapsed, 30 to 40 minutes, depending on the size of the vegetable.

Meanwhile, toast the walnuts on a small sheet pan. Watch them carefully in that hot oven. They'll burn easily. Once toasted, chop them lightly.

Pound the remaining garlic with ½ teaspoon of salt in a large mortar until smooth. Add the dill and olive oil and work it into a rough purée. Peel the eggplant and add the flesh to the mortar; pound just enough to make a coarse purée. Stir in the yogurt, fold in the nuts, and season with salt and pepper to taste.

MISSION FIGS ROASTED WITH OLIVE OIL, HONEY, AND THYME

Serves 4 to 6; GF

As a California girl, I know figs, both the June crop and the fall crop. In New Mexico, good fresh figs are a rarity, though people do grow them at lower elevations where it is warm enough for them. But somehow, when I do get figs in Santa Fe, they aren't quite as rich and plummy as I remember. One way to enhance their flavor is to roast them and serve them warm with crème fraîche or mascarpone and a drizzle of honey. You could also serve them with a good grass-milk yogurt or ice cream.

Veronica Vallejo, who was preparing foods to be photographed for the book, decided to dress these figs with olive oil and thyme as well as the honey. We had figs that weren't that flavorful at the Berkeley photo shoot, just like I do at home in New Mexico, and this method helped build up flavor. Dead ripe they're even better, and the combination of olive oil, honey, and thyme is just as beguiling.

This is an easy recipe to make for any number of people, in this case allowing three or four figs per person. If you're just a few eaters and you're loath to turn on the oven in summer, use your toaster oven to bake the figs. It may not get as hot, but eventually it will do the job. The stovetop will also work for a quicker sauté. This is a good dish to serve with the Walnut Nugget Cookies on page 265.

12 to 16 plump figs	3 cloves
2 tablespoons, rich olive oil (or butter)	A few cloves of star anise
2 tablespoons honey	5 sprigs of thyme (lemon thyme would be especially good)
A few pinches sugar	Crème fraîche, yogurt, or mascarpone for serving
A tiny pinch of salt	

Heat the oven to 425°F. Rinse the figs and pat them dry, then cut off the stems and slice some in half while leaving others whole. Set the figs in a dish that will leave a little room between the fruits. Pour over the olive oil, drizzle over the honey, and scatter a little sugar over the figs along with the salt. Tuck in the cloves, star anise, and thyme.

Bake until the sauce is bubbling and the fruit is heated through, about 15 minutes. Serve warm with a drizzle of crème fraîche, a spoonful of good yogurt, or mascarpone.

WARM FETA WITH TOASTED SESAME SEEDS

Makes 14 to 16 pieces; GF

Something magical happens when feta cheese is warmed: its strong salty character falls into a softer, more complex bundle of flavors, and the texture goes from chalky and dry to melting and moist. As a small bite to have with a glass of wine, it completely works, belying how really easy it is to prepare. As with the tofu crisps that go in the red cabbage salad on page 73, all you need do is sift a little cornstarch over the cheese, then cook it in a little butter or olive oil. It's browned and ready to eat in just a bit more than a minute.

In my original recipe, I covered the finished bits with toasted sesame seeds and I still do. They can be white or black, and I sometimes use inky black nigella seeds. I suspect poppy seeds could be very nice too. The seeds offer a bit of contrasting texture to the velvety cheese. But then, so does the cracker or flat bread you might be serving it on. I also finish these with plenty of coarse black pepper and sometimes red pepper flakes. Another thing I used to do is to simmer the cheese in some fresh lemon juice at the end, but the cheese is so delicate it can be tricky. I think it works better to have some lemon wedges on the side to squeeze over the finished, plated cheese, if desired. Or just omit them altogether.

Although I give amounts, in truth, when I make this, it's more a matter of taking out whatever feta is there and preparing it. Serve this as a stand-alone appetizer, or put it out perched on crackers, a selection of your favorite olives, some roasted red peppers, toasted almonds, and other small nibbles.

1 (8-ounce) piece of feta cheese	1 bay leaf
1 teaspoon sesame or nigella seeds	Freshly ground black pepper and/or red pepper flakes
Organic cornstarch	
1 tablespoon butter or olive oil	4 lemon wedges (optional)

Cut the cheese in half and then cut each half crosswise into seven or eight pieces about ½ inch thick. Set the pieces on paper toweling to absorb any excess water. Blot the tops of the pieces as well.

While the cheese is drying, toast the seeds in a dry 8-inch skillet until aromatic and, in the case of white sesame seeds, golden. Set them aside and return the pan to the heat.

Remove the pieces of cheese to a plate covered with cornstarch and dust the tops with more cornstarch. Meanwhile, melt the butter with the bay leaf until the butter is foamy. Lay the cheese in the pan and cook until golden on the bottom, about 40 seconds. Carefully turn and cook the second side and cook for another half minute or until golden. Sometimes the crust separates from the cheese. If you can, scrape it up and set it on top of the piece. It will taste amazingly good. Carefully remove the cheese pieces to a plate or set each on a cracker. Grind pepper over all and sprinkle over the toasted seeds. Serve with lemon wedges, if you like.

SHAVED FENNEL SALAD WITH FENNEL BLOSSOMS, FRONDS, AND PISTACHIOS

Serves 4; V, GF

Slow-growing fennel is costly to buy, but shaving it into paper-thin slices not only makes it tasty as a raw vegetable, but also makes it go farther. If you are handy with your (sharp) knife or have a mandoline or other vegetable slicer, a shaved fennel salad is a snap to put together. Shaved fennel with a lemon vinaigrette and some shaved cheese is something that will always please my palate, although its charm may have run its course for some. There are many other ways you can use this vegetable—it plays well with other edibles. In the spring, I toss it with small arugula leaves and purple orach sprouts from the garden. In summer, I include the big fleshy leaves of purslane (preferably a cultivar, though you can also use the smaller-leafed weed). Walnuts, mushrooms, and thin shavings of Parmigiano-Reggiano are also good at any time of the year, with or without greens mixed in. Here it is simply finished with fennel blossoms, the chopped fronds, and pistachio nuts.

If fennel is really costly, you can use just one bulb and mix it with other leaves; or if you wish to use two bulbs without any other leaves, there's that option too.

1 large or 2 smaller fennel bulbs

A blooming umbel of fennel flowers, if possible

About 2 tablespoons finely chopped fennel fronds

2 tablespoons apple cider or white wine vinegar

1 large shallot, finely diced

Sea salt and freshly ground pepper

4 tablespoons best olive oil or walnut oil

A small handful of pistachio nuts

Trim the base of the fennel and remove the tough, scarred outer leaves. Slice the bulb paper thin on a mandoline and put it in a bowl. Toss it to separate the slices, then toss with the fennel blossoms and chopped fronds.

To make the dressing, combine the vinegar, shallot, and ¼ teaspoon of salt in a bowl or jar and let stand for several minutes, then whisk in the olive oil. Taste on a piece of fennel and adjust the vinegar and oil if necessary to your taste. You can do this much an hour or so beforehand.

When it's time to finish the salad, toss the fennel with the dressing, season with pepper, and toss again with the pistachios.

TROUCHIA: FAILED-TO-CATCH-A-TROUT FRITTATA

Serves 4 to 6; GF

I live not far from the mountain village of Truchas, New Mexico; *truchas* means "trout," as do the Provençale words *troucha* and *touchia*. For a long time, I thought that this frittata of onions and chard was perhaps what you made if you failed to catch a trout. But now I think that maybe it refers to what one might take along to eat while fishing, for *trouchia* is a sturdy food, one that can travel to a river bank or on a picnic. Nathalie Waag taught me this dish many years ago at her home in southern France, and it has been a favorite since then. I make this with chard, but you could also use spinach.

As I always grow lots of chard, I use plenty of the tender leaves in this frittata; you can use a lot or a little, depending on what's available to you. The important thing—what makes this frittata so exceptionally good—is to take your time with the onions, cooking them slowly until they melt, and then the same with the chard leaves, which follow in the pan. The eggs too, should be cooked over a low, gentle heat. All should be luscious and tender. The color will be golden, but also purple and red if you use red chard. It's as good cold as it is warm (or at room temperature) and sturdy enough to travel well in a backpack. It can also do service as a main dish or, cut into small pieces, as an appetizer.

I like to serve this with a spoonful of saffron mayonnaise on top and a few purple orach leaves from the spring garden. To me, this is one of the great reasons to have a garden—to glean such treasures as these gorgeous leaves.

1 large red onion, cut into sixths
and thinly sliced crosswise

2 tablespoons olive oil

1 clove garlic

Sea salt and freshly ground pepper

6 large eggs, lightly beaten

2 tablespoons finely chopped parsley

6 to 8 large basil leaves, slivered
(about 3 heaping tablespoons)

2 teaspoons chopped thyme
or lemon thyme leaves

6 cups (more or less) young chard leaves,
stems removed and leaves chopped

1 cup grated Gruyère or Gouda cheese

2 tablespoons freshly grated
Parmigiano-Reggiano

Begin with the onion, because it's going to cook very slowly, giving you time enough to do everything else that's needed. Heat half of the oil in a warm 10-inch skillet, add the onion, and cook over low heat, stirring occasionally, until completely soft but not browned, about 15 minutes. Don't rush this, take your time.

While the onions are cooking, smash the garlic in a mortar with ¼ teaspoon of salt, and then stir it into the eggs along with herbs. Let the eggs stand while you slice the chard.

When the onions are very soft, add the chard and continue cooking, stirring occasionally, until the moisture has cooked off and the chard is fully tender, about 15 minutes. Season well with salt and freshly ground pepper. When the mixture has cooled some, stir it into the eggs and add the Gruyère and half the Parmigiano-Reggiano.

Heat the broiler. Heat the remaining oil, plus a little butter if you like, in a 9-inch skillet. When it's hot, add the eggs. Give a stir and keep the heat at medium-high for about a minute, then turn it to low. Cook until the eggs are set but still moist on top. Scatter the remaining cheese over the surface and broil until golden. Serve warm, at room temperature, or even chilled, alone or with a saffron mayonnaise and small fresh greens, such as orach or mâche.

HERB (AND WILD GREEN) SALAD

Makes 4 to 6 small salads; V, GF

Although largely an extemporaneous affair, composing an herb salad does ask for a moment of thought before you start. This is not, after all, the best place for aggressive, chewy, wintry herbs such as rosemary, mature sage, savory, hyssop, and the perennial culinary thyme. More suitable are the volatile soft-leaf herbs—chervil, marjoram, the basils, tarragon, chives, dill, and lovage, to name a few. Lemon thyme is good in small quantities—use the leaves only, not the stems—as are the other lemon-scented herbs, like lemon verbena. I always include some lettuce, preferably a soft buttery leaf type, as background, along with a few handfuls of odd greens, such as purple orach, amaranth, miners' lettuce, young spinach leaves, and herb blossoms—although tiny and fragile looking, these tiny flowers convey more than you might expect of the personality of the herbs they come from. Besides, what could be prettier than violet chive flowers, purple sage blossoms, sky-blue borage, periwinkle rosemary, purple anise hyssop, delicate cilantro, or the bright and fragrant yellow-orange blossoms of Mexican tarragon (mint marigold)? If your garden has cilantro that's going to seed, by all means use the little green spheres of coriander, (that is, if you like them).

I'm just learning about wild plants and what they can add to a salad. For example, if it's early spring and you have drifts of purple flowering musk mustard, include those plants as well, leaves and flowers, in your salad. Purslane is another, more common but intruding wild plant. Add lambsquarters, as well. Even the green seedpods of the Siberian elm, samaras, can play a part in the spring salad.

Whether they contain only some torn lovage leaves or an entire garden's worth of herbs, salads that are laced with fresh herbs, blossoms, and wild plants offer a vivid parade of flavor that marches across your tongue with each bite, leaving it surprised and awake. Such salads don't need additions like croutons or cheese, but good bread makes an accompaniment that tempers the salad and prolongs its enjoyment.

An herb salad can be simple or complex. Here's a sample to guide you, along with some other ideas. CONTINUED

2 cups butter lettuce leaves

2 cups mixed greens, such as amaranth, orach, young spinach, watercress

½ cup purslane sprigs (preferably from an upright variety)

A handful or two of musk mustard, leaves and blossoms, if available, or arugula leaves

2 tablespoons basil leaves

½ cup celery leaves

Several small, tender lovage leaves

½ cup parsley leaves, plucked from their stems

Sea salt

Good olive oil or fresh walnut oil in the fall

Apple cider vinegar

Herb blossoms, such as rosemary, chive, or thyme

Tear the greens into bite-size pieces. Keep the marjoram leaves whole and tear the basil leaves, unless they're the tiny Piccolo Verde Fino variety. Tear the celery, lovage, and parsley leaves, keeping them in fairly large pieces. Snap the purslane into clumps and wash it well, especially if you're using garden purslane that creeps across the ground. It can be sandy.

Toss all the leaves in a bowl with a pinch of salt and then again with just enough oil to coat. Season with vinegar to taste, check the salt and then toss again with the blossoms.

Of course there's no one way when it comes to such salads, but there are combinations of flavors and textures that are especially pleasing. Here are some I enjoy:

- Parsley, dill, basil, cilantro (plus green coriander seeds), watercress, and mint
- Thai basil, perilla, lemon verbena, chives, cilantro leaves, and green coriander
- Chervil, chives, parsley, tarragon, and salad burnet or the mild musk mustard
- Arugula, mint, basil, lemon verbena, anise hyssop, and a little curly cress
- Dill, salad burnet, tarragon, red sorrel leaves for appearance, and green sorrel, torn into small pieces, for flavor.

HERB-LACED FRITTERS MADE WITH GOOD STALE BREAD AND RICOTTA

Serves 6

Somehow we end up with half-loaves of very good bread that are gradually becoming stale. These fritters are what keep those stale loaves from going into the compost, plus they make a delicious little dinner, served with tomato sauce. While they are very light, they also have a dense texture, due to the bread, and a deep flavor because of the herbs.

A lot depends on the bread, which should have good texture and strong crumb. It needs to be dry enough and strong enough not to disintegrate when soaked in milk. Bread that's bone dry will absorb more liquid than fresher bread or bread without much structure, so you will have to play with your ingredients to end up with a mixture that can be shaped into spheres that will hold together and keep their shape. What you're aiming for is moist bread, not wet, falling-apart bread. I've erred on the side of too wet a mixture and had to scramble to make it dry enough to hold its shape, adding bread crumbs, and the like. If the bread mix is too dry, it's easier to correct: you always have the option of adding an extra egg.

In the past I served these golden spheres with spaghetti squash, which is good, and also makes a silly reference to spaghetti and meatballs. But a simple tomato sauce is also good, and that's what I've used here. I have what seems to be an endless supply of tomato purée in my freezer, and it works perfectly as a base for a light tomato sauce. Or you can use canned tomatoes to make the sauce, or fresh, in summer (three recipes for tomato sauce are on pages 250 to 251).

The mixture freezes well. You can make it—not really a big deal—freeze it, and pull it out when you need it. In addition to fritters, you could also use this to fill a stuffed pepper or a cabbage leaf, but I must say the browning that comes from a brief fry in olive oil is too delicious to lose. CONTINUED

4 thick slices stale but not rock-hard country bread (about 8 ounces)	½ cup freshly grated Parmigiano-Reggiano
½ cup milk, or as needed	Sea salt and freshly ground pepper
2 tablespoons chopped marjoram or oregano or 1 heaping teaspoon dried marjoram	1 or 2 eggs
	Olive oil
½ cup parsley leaves	Almond meal or dried bread crumbs, if needed
1 clove garlic	Tomato sauce (see pages 250 to 251 for three options)
½ cup finely diced onion	
1 cup ricotta cheese	Additional chopped parsley or marjoram, for garnish

Cut the crusts off the bread. Put the pieces in a pie plate and pour over the milk. If the bread is on the soft side, use less milk; if it's hard, use more. I know this is vague, but it's hard to be more precise since we're all starting from different places. Better to have it a little too dry than too wet.

While the bread is soaking up the milk, chop the garlic with the herbs. Return to the bread now and then and move it around, squeezing the wet pieces over the drier ones. When all the bread is soft, squeeze out the excess milk. Use your hands or a quick turn in a food processor to just break it up into coarse, large, moist crumbs; then turn it into a bowl.

Add the herb-garlic mixture and the onion to the bread along with the ricotta and Parmigiano-Reggiano and 1 egg. Season with 1 teaspoon of salt and plenty of pepper. Mix everything together—your hands are the best tool—then fry a little in some olive oil and taste it for salt, adding more if it's needed. If the mixture is too dry to shape, add another egg. If it's too wet, add almond meal or dried bread crumbs to absorb some of the moisture. You want to be able to shape the batter into spheres or ovals that will both hold together and keep their shape when fried. When you've got your dough to a place you like, form it into spheres or ovals, 2 to 3 teaspoons each. As you work, set the pieces on a clean surface.

Fill a cast-iron or nonstick skillet with an inch of olive oil and set it over medium heat. When hot, add the morsels, taking care not to crowd them, and cook over medium heat, shuffling the pan frequently so that all the surfaces brown. To serve, spoon a little tomato sauce on each plate, add the herb-laced fritters, and garnish with the additional chopped herbs.

HUMMUS WORTH MAKING

Makes about 2⅓ cups; V, GF

Is this recipe really worth making, you ask? Well, yes.

Because what's happened to hummus is both good and not so good. It's good that so many people know and like hummus that it inhabits a significant niche in the grocery store. But that's the downside, too. How many parties have you been to where you're served it cold, right from the plastic container it was bought in? Do you notice the cheap oil listed among the ingredients rather than olive oil, which you'd use if you made it? Young cookbook writers seem to call any vegetable purée "hummus"—red pepper hummus, green chile hummus, beet hummus, and even hummus flavored with siracha or hummus made with white beans. Those ideas might be good, but perhaps it's better to call these dishes by another name. Green chile and chickpea purée? Does that still work for you?

While there are different approaches that traditional cooks take to hummus, I can promise you that if you take the time to make your own, then garnish it handsomely and set it out for people to eat with vegetables or crackers, they will be amazed. "That's hummus?" they'll ask. Yes, it really is.

We made hummus at Greens long before you could just buy it. We used it mostly on composed salad plates or to line a pita sandwich, so it never was finished the way it is here—scraped onto a platter, its surface swirled into small hills and depressions, then garnished with chickpeas, pine nuts, olive oil, and so forth. And of course, it's finishing the dish that's the pleasure of making—and serving—hummus. I always drizzle plenty of warmed olive oil over the surface, include some skinned chickpeas (they really do have a better color), some sumac, some pepper flakes, then something green, like minced parsley or mint leaves.

One cup of dried chickpeas swells to about three cups once cooked, and your own home-cooked chickpeas are important to use since you'll need their liquid to make the hummus. Water isn't as good, nor is the liquid that surrounds canned chickpeas.

I often turn to food writer and scholar Clifford Wright when I have a food question. In his book *A Mediterranean Feast*, he writes that the Arabic word for chickpea is, in fact, *hummus*, so white beans make a white bean purée, not hummus. He also says that it's absolutely necessary to remove the skins from the cooked chickpeas. I know that may not happen for you. Personally, I enjoy that fiddly kind of task. While I'm pinching the skins off the chickpeas and they're floating to the surface of the bowl of water, I'm thinking about the dish, the rest of the meal, the leaves that need raking in the garden and when that might happen, the botany class I need to study for. Such a mindless task offers a rare chance to line up the many things that have to happen that day or that week.

I suggest using a pressure cooker for the chickpeas. For me, with my hard water and high altitude, it's really necessary. Alternatively, you can simmer soaked chickpeas on the stovetop until they're tender. But a pressure cooker is an amazing tool that makes homemade hummus well within reach, even if you cook the chickpeas one day and make the hummus the next.

1 cup dried chickpeas	⅓ cup tahini
¼ cup olive oil	⅓ cup fresh lemon juice, or more, to taste
Sea salt	Warm olive oil, to finish
1 small clove garlic, pounded to a paste with a good pinch of salt	Sumac, pepper flakes, minced parsley, fresh mint leaves, to finish (optional)

Rinse the chickpeas and put them in a pressure cooker with 6 cups of water. Bring up to pressure, then reduce the heat and cook for 40 minutes. Turn off the heat and allow the pressure to fall by itself rather than doing a quick release. When the pressure has fallen, remove the lid and taste a chickpea. If it isn't yet soft, bring the pressure back up for 5 minutes, repeating if necessary. If done a day before you plan to make the hummus, refrigerate the cooked chickpeas in their liquid.

If you're up for it, transfer the chickpeas to a bowl of water and slip the skins off them. Tip the water and skins into the sink when done and set aside a few of the chickpeas for garnish. (Maybe just take the time to skin those few chickpeas rather than all of them.)

Put the chickpeas in a food processor or blender with ½ cup of the cooking liquid, the olive oil, and 1 teaspoon of salt. Process or blend until creamy. Add the pounded garlic, tahini, and lemon juice and work again until smooth. Now taste and adjust, adding more salt and lemon juice or chickpea water as needed to get the consistency and flavor you want. I've found I usually need to add more chickpea liquid to my blender jar to get it smooth. But I've also noticed that hummus thickens as it cools, so don't worry if it seems a tad on the thin side.

Scrape the hummus onto a platter rather than a bowl and use a spatula or rubber scraper to make furrows or waves as you would if you were icing a cake. Garnish the hummus as you wish, using the reserved chickpeas, for sure. Drizzle plenty of warmed olive oil over the surface, include some skinned chickpeas, some sumac and pepper flakes, and then some minced parsley or mint. But there's more you can do if you wish. Make your dish beautiful.

ROASTED JERUSALEM ARTICHOKE SOUP WITH SUNFLOWER SPROUTS AND SEEDS

Serves 6, GF

Years ago, when I first started to garden, I jumped to attention when more experienced gardeners said things like, "Do not plant those! You'll never get rid of them." They were often referring to Jerusalem artichokes, and I thought if you couldn't get rid of them you'd definitely *have* them, and that was hugely appealing to a nervous novice. So I planted them.

They were right, of course, those gardeners. I've had Jerusalem artichokes ever since; but finally, not as many as I used to have. They're well contained in a bed with strong sides and wire on the bottom from which they cannot drift too easily. Although the bed is only four by four feet, the number of tubers that emerge from it is truly impressive. There are far more than I can use or store over the winter, so I'm always shocked that they cost as much as they do, grocery stores are making a lot of money at $6 a pound for what is pretty much a weed in the garden!

They do however, make an excellent soup for chilly weather. I once made twelve gallons of this soup with Jerusalem artichokes bought at the New York City Greenmarket. I featured it there the next day, and the farmers who were trying to sell their crop were thrilled as their overlooked tubers flew off the tables. People loved the nutty flavor, although there were, of course, some who complained that the soup could have used more salt. I mean, it was 12 gallons of soup made in a tiny apartment kitchen!

These knobby tubers are in the sunflower family, so I like to keep them with their relatives, using sunflower seed oil for roasting and nutty flavored sunflower sprouts as a garnish along with toasted sunflower seeds. Walnut oil, however, would have a good flavor for finishing the soup, as would pumpkin oil. Smoked salt is also a great finisher, alone or with a little minced rosemary. For a dish based on such humble beginnings, this ends up as something quite elegant. CONTINUED

1 pound (or a bit more) Jerusalem artichokes, scrubbed and cut into ⅓-inch slices

2 small potatoes (about 8 ounces), peeled (unless organic) and sliced

3 plump cloves garlic, unpeeled

3 tablespoons sunflower seed oil

Sea salt and freshly ground pepper

1 small onion, thinly sliced

2 bay leaves

2 heaping teaspoons minced rosemary

6 cups water

¼ cup cream or half-and-half

A handful of big, fleshy sunflower seed sprouts

A tablespoon or so toasted sunflower seeds

Heat the oven to 425°F. Toss the Jerusalem artichokes, potatoes, and garlic cloves with two-thirds of the oil and several pinches of salt. Put them in a 9 by 12-inch or larger baking dish and roast for 45 minutes, or until they're browned in places, giving them an occasional turn. They will shrink and shrivel some.

Heat the remaining oil in a soup pot and add the onion, bay leaves, and rosemary. Cook over medium heat, stirring occasionally, until softened, about 5 minutes. Then add the roasted vegetables, 1 teaspoon of salt, and ½ cup of the water. Cook over medium heat, stirring occasionally, for another 4 to 5 minutes and then add the remaining water and scrape any browned juices from the pan. Bring to a boil, then reduce the heat to a simmer, cover the pan, and cook until the vegetables are soft, about 20 minutes.

Purée the soup, leaving a bit of texture and flecks of brown from the Jerusalem artichokes. Stir in the cream, taste for salt, and season with pepper. Serve garnished with a lofty pile of the sprouts in each bowl and a few pinches of the sunflower seeds.

KALE AND WALNUT PESTO WITH ROASTED OR SEARED WINTER SQUASH

Serves 4; GF

Before lacinato kale was the rage, there really was a time when it was a "new" vegetable for American cooks. I interviewed a grower of this then-exotic green who told me not that kale salads would be all the rage (who knew?), but that, as an Italian, he liked to make a pesto with the leaves. This struck me as a good thing to do with kale, and so it is. I especially like to make it when the season has cooled and the kale is sweet.

You can make this pesto in a small food processor, but the quantity of garlic is too small to really work it into a paste using the machine. I suggest you do that first in a mortar and pestle and then add it to the kale so that you don't end up with small chunks of garlic.

Pan-seared or roasted winter squashes are good vehicles for this green sauce, and so are cauliflower, crostini, and seared halloumi cheese, among other foods. I sometimes offer the kale with roasted rings of delicata squash or rounds of pan-seared butternut squash as a before-dinner nibble or first course.

A note about delicata squash: you can cook them with their skins on, which become soft and edible. They're in the same genus as zucchini and other summer squash, which we eat skin and all. We tend to treat them as a winter squash though, and they're offered throughout the winter and early spring, but they really are best when they're newer, in the fall.

2 delicata squash or the small neck of a butternut squash, sliced into ⅓-inch rounds	1 clove garlic
	¼ cup walnuts
Olive oil for roasting or searing	Best olive oil, for the pesto
Sea salt and freshly ground pepper	A few tablespoons of grated Parmigiano-Reggiano
1 hefty bunch of lacinato kale	

If you are using delicata squash, heat the oven to 375°F. Wash the squash well, as you will be leaving the skins on. Slice off the two ends of each squash, then reach inside with a narrow spoon and scoop out the seeds. Slice crosswise into rounds somewhat less than ½ inch thick. Toss them in a bowl with enough olive oil to coat lightly; season with several pinches of salt and some freshly ground pepper. Spread them out on a sheet pan and bake until browned and tender, about 10 minutes per side.

If you're using butternut squash, peel it or not as you prefer. Film a cast-iron skillet with olive oil, then add the squash rounds, and cook over medium heat until blistered. Turn and cook on the second side until the squash is tender when pierced with a knife. This should take about 20 minutes in all.

Meanwhile, make the pesto. Bring a few cups water to a boil in a 3-quart saucepan. While that heats, slice the leaves off the tough kale stems and discard the stems. Rinse the leaves well. When the water boils, add the leaves to the pot and cook until they're bright green and wilted, about a minute. Drain, rinse with cold water and then squeeze the excess water out of the kale. Chop finely or purée in a food processor.

Smash the garlic in a large mortar with a few pinches of salt to make a purée, then add the walnuts and work into a paste. Add the kale and continue working with the pestle (or transfer to a small food processor), adding your best olive oil as needed to loosen the mixture, using about 2 tablespoons in all. Taste for salt, season with pepper, and stir in the cheese.

To serve, put the squash on a plate and dab the pesto here and there, or serve it separately in a bowl.

About Roasted Squash

Roasting is one of the best treatments for winter squash, including those that have warty, bubbly surfaces that resist peeling because roasted squash needn't be peeled, but just cut into wedges, brushed with oil, and roasted at a moderate temperature until tender and golden-brown. You can use all kinds of interesting heirlooms. If the skins are hard, the eater will simply cut them away from the flesh. There are many ways you can serve roasted squash—with toasted bread crumbs, the kale pesto (above), Smoky-Spicy Butter (page 64), toasted sesame seeds, and chopped herbs, especially parsley and sage.

KALE AND QUINOA GRATIN

Serves 4

Even if you're a kale hater, believe me, you won't think "kale" when you eat this. When the kale is cooked and puréed, it is very mild, a lively green, and not at all stodgy.

I came up with this more than twenty years ago when farmers were producing tons of kale and shoppers were still trying to figure out how to use it. (Kale is a strong plant that doesn't crumble the minute it gets cold, so farmers liked growing it. Even I can manage a crop.) As this was well before kale salads were in vogue, I paired it with this and that, including pearled barley. Barley is on the heavy side, though, and many people don't eat it, so now I make this gratin with quinoa, which is lighter and cooks more quickly.

This pretty dish can easily be made vegan by changing the fat and leaving out the cheese. It does need a little something to serve with it, though. A tomato sauce (see pages 250 to 251) is good, as is a healthy dab of the curry mayonnaise on page 100, or a spoonful of the marjoram sauce on page 152 with, perhaps, a cluster of small sprouts for a final flourish. The kale can be any variety, a mixture of varieties, or you can use another green altogether, like collards. CONTINUED

Butter or olive oil	2 tablespoons all-purpose flour
1 cup white quinoa with a little black mixed in	1½ cups warm quinoa cooking water or milk
Sea salt and freshly ground pepper	½ teaspoon ground allspice
A very large bunch of kale, about 1¼ pounds (mixed varieties are fine)	⅛ teaspoon freshly ground nutmeg
2 tablespoons butter	½ to 1 cup grated Gruyère or goats' milk Gouda

Heat the oven to 375°F. Butter or oil a 2-quart gratin dish and set it aside.

Rinse the quinoa well. Put it in a saucepan with ½ teaspoon of salt and 4 cups of water. Bring to a boil, then lower the heat and simmer until tender, 15 minutes. When the quinoa is cooked, drain it but save the liquid; you'll be using it.

While the quinoa is cooking, slice the leaves off the kale stems and discard the stems. Wash the leaves and then cook them in 2 cups of water with ½ teaspoon of salt until tender, 5 minutes or so. Purée with ¼ cup of the cooking water until smooth.

Melt the 2 tablespoons of butter in a 1-quart saucepan. Whisk in the flour, then pour in the 1½ cups warm quinoa cooking water or milk, or a mixture. Cook over medium heat, stirring, until the sauce has thickened and then cook for several minutes more for the flour to cook. Season with the spices, a few pinches of salt, and some freshly ground pepper. Combine the sauce with the quinoa and kale and stir in the cheese. Transfer to the baking dish. Bake until firm, about 35 minutes. Cut into pieces and serve.

HEARTY LENTIL MINESTRONE WITH KALE

Serves 6; V if you omit the cheese, GF

This soup merges two recipes, and the result is a hearty soup, studded with interesting pasta shapes (or you could use an unusual grain), and finished with plenty of chopped celery leaf, robust olive oil, and a shaving of cheese (or not). It's a dish I'd serve for a winter Sunday supper with toast and a salad. It's a pleasure to craft this soup, especially at the end when you put it all together, layer by layer. That's when the flavor comes together in a big way.

I often reach for my jar of French green lentils, but I think the dusty-green German lentils would work well, too. In fact, some people call them "soup lentils." They're larger than the little Puy lentils (or Belugas, for that matter) and not as visually dramatic, but they're far less expensive and they taste just fine. In any case, I cover my lentils with water to soak while I prepare the vegetables. Soaking yields a fuller flavor and quicker cooking time.

I'm giving the amounts here in cups as well as more singular units, because I know if you're cooking from your garden, you may have carrots and such that don't conform to regulated "store" size. However, if you find you have a little extra of anything, do put it in the soup rather than throw it away. For the most part, soups are hugely accommodating dishes.

Two caveats: First, cook your pasta or grain separately and add it to each serving, otherwise it will swell as it drinks up all the liquid. If you find you have a very thick pot of leftover soup and pasta the following day, thin it with water or vegetable stock. Or pluck out the swollen pasta pieces and heat the lentils to serve with a drizzle of olive oil and a grating of Parmigiano-Reggiano.

The second caveat has to do with the greens. If you bypass the kale and use bagged "baby" spinach, be sure to wash it, even if a triple wash has been promised. Moist leaves blacken and stick to leaves that may be good, and the rotted leaves taste terrible. You'll want to discard the blackened ones and those that have yellowed. And if you don't mind a finicky task, snip off the stems with a scissors; otherwise you'll end up with a stemmy mass at the end. While all greens are naturals with lentils, I've called for kale because I appreciate its dark color and robust quality, but you can use any green that appeals.

1½ cups dark green lentils

2 tablespoons olive oil for the pot, plus your best olive oil to finish

1 large onion, finely diced (about 2 cups)

1 heaping tablespoon nutritional yeast

2 bay leaves

6 sprigs fresh thyme or ½ teaspoon dried

3 tablespoons (or more) chopped parsley

1 cup diced carrots (a mix of varieties is great)

1 cup finely diced celery, pale leaves reserved and finely chopped to make ¼ cup

2 tablespoons tomato paste

2 plump garlic cloves, finely minced or mashed in a mortar with 1 teaspoon of salt

½ cup white wine or water

Sea salt and freshly ground pepper

1 tablespoon smooth mustard

1 tablespoon sherry vinegar or red wine vinegar

3 to 4 cups stemmed, chopped kale leaves

1 cup interesting dried pasta shapes or 2 cups cooked whole grain, such as spelt

Parmigiano-Reggiano, for grating

Cover the lentils with warm water and set them aside to soak while you prepare the vegetables.

Warm the oil in a heated soup pot, then add the onion, nutritional yeast, bay leaves, thyme, carrots, celery, and parsley. Give a stir and cook over medium heat, occasionally giving the vegetables a turn, until the onions are well wilted, about 10 minutes. Add the tomato paste, smash it against the bottom of the pot, and cook until a glaze has formed on the bottom of the soup pot. Add the garlic and the wine, scrape up the glaze from the bottom, and cook until the wine is mostly reduced.

Pour the water off the soaking lentils and add them to the pot along with 2 teaspoons of salt and 7 cups of water. Bring to a boil, then lower the heat to a simmer and cook, covered, until the lentils are soft, about 30 minutes. When the soup is done, stir in the mustard and vinegar and then taste for salt and season with pepper. Add the greens and let them cook until tender, about 7 minutes.

Cook the pasta in salted water just before serving. Ladle the soup into each bowl, add a few spoonfuls of pasta, then drizzle with your favorite olive oil. Finally, grate some Parmigiano-Reggiano over each serving and garnish with the reserved celery leaves.

GREEN LENTILS WITH YOGURT, SORREL, AND PARSLEY SAUCE

Serves 6; GF

The tart sorrel in this yogurt sauce really perks up the lentils, and you can use it with other legumes as well. It's also very good with beets, broccoli, and a host of other vegetables (and grains too). I always have sorrel plants in the garden that leaf out come spring, and how much sorrel I use varies as the summer progresses. Early in the season, it might be just a few tender leaves; later it could be a few handfuls of larger, tougher ones. Your access to sorrel may also vary. For yogurt, use a good, creamy full-fat yogurt rather than a nonfat version.

1 clove garlic, pounded to a paste with a pinch of sea salt

1 handful sorrel leaves (or more if you wish or you have them)

1 handful parsley leaves

3 green onions, including an inch of the greens, thinly sliced

1 cup creamy full-fat Greek yogurt, or a mixture of yogurt and sour cream

1 tablespoon best olive oil

1 cup French green lentils, soaked for 1 hour or more if there's time

1 bay leaf

Sea salt and freshly ground pepper

To make the yogurt sauce, pound the garlic and chop the herbs fairly finely. Put them in a small food processor with the yogurt and purée until the yogurt is pale green and flecked with herbs. Scrape into a bowl and spoon the olive oil over the top. Serve right away, or refrigerate and serve chilled, if desired. A cold sauce, if served with warm food, should be allowed to sit on the counter for 30 minutes to come to room temperature.

To cook the lentils, drain them of their soaking water (if you soaked them) and put them in a pot. Cover generously with fresh water and add the bay leaf and a teaspoon of salt. Bring to a boil, then lower the heat and simmer until tender, about 25 minutes for soaked lentils, longer if they're unsoaked. When they're done, drain them.

Stir in the yogurt sauce and taste for salt again, adding more if needed, and season with pepper.

RED LENTIL SOUP WITH BERBERE

Serves 4 to 6; V, GF

Red lentil soup with turmeric and lime has long been a favorite in our house. It's light, aromatic, and the ultimate in versatility as there are many ways you can finish it—surrounded with rice, spinach, crisped triangles of pita bread, slivered scallions, and so forth. It also has plenty of turmeric, which I appreciate. The recipe itself came from a friend who lives half the year in India, and she used even more turmeric than what I call for—and that's already a lot—and a great deal more ghee as well. Still, this soup is plenty rich as is with ghee (or coconut oil).

Even though I taught this for years in classes, I believe that every single time I forgot the lime juice at the end—that is, until I tasted the soup and thought, "Something's missing." And it is if you don't include plenty of lime. Somehow the juice balances the acrid flavor of the turmeric, rendering it present but more gentle.

Today when I make this soup, I do it slightly differently. I cook the lentils until they're soft but still hold their shape, just short of falling into a rough purée. Then I add the cooked onions and garnishes. It gives it more complexity and texture than adding the onions to the puréed lentils, as I used to do. I also sometimes use coconut oil in place of ghee, a fat we didn't have access to when I first started making this recipe, and on occasion I've stirred in some coconut cream left over from another dish. But the most recent addition I've turned to is berbere, the incredibly aromatic and feisty Ethiopian spice mix, scattered over the surface. This is the best! You can buy berbere as a prepared mix or make it yourself. I use my riff on Marcus Samuelsson's recipe (in his book *Marcus Off Duty*) as a place to start.

Since I started adding berbere to this soup, a new Ethiopian restaurant has opened in Santa Fe that in fact serves red lentils with berbere as part of their vegetarian plate. So this isn't at all farfetched. The chef stirs olive oil into the spice mix to make a deep red burnishing sauce that's delicious on her sliced, roasted potatoes as well as just about anywhere else it goes. CONTINUED

2 cups split red lentils, picked over and rinsed several times

2 teaspoons turmeric

3 tablespoons ghee or coconut oil

Sea salt

1 large onion, finely diced

2 teaspoons ground cumin

1½ teaspoons black mustard seeds

2 teaspoons berbere (recipe follows)

1 small bunch cilantro, the stems finely sliced and the leaves chopped

Juice of 2 or 3 limes, to taste

4 teaspoons olive oil

Put the lentils in a soup pot with 2½ quarts of water, the turmeric, 2 tablespoons of the ghee, and 2½ teaspoons of salt. Bring to a boil, then lower the heat and simmer until the lentils are soft and just short of falling apart, 15 minutes. (If you prefer a smoother soup, purée the lentils.)

While the soup is cooking, heat a medium skillet over medium heat and add the last bit of ghee. When it's hot, add the onion with the cumin, mustard seeds, 1 teaspoon of the berbere, and cilantro stems, stirring occasionally. When the onions are soft, add them to the lentils with the chopped cilantro leaves and then add the juice from two limes. Taste and add more, if needed, to bring up the flavors. It should be a tad sour.

At this point, if the soup seems too thick, you can add extra water, stock, coconut cream, or coconut milk. Mix the remaining teaspoon of berbere with the olive oil. Drizzle it on the surface of each bowl.

Berbere

Makes about ½ cup; V, GF

I don't believe that traditional berbere calls for smoked paprika. Still, the smoky flavor is awfully good here. Frankly, I can't resist it.

2 teaspoons coriander seeds

1 teaspoon fenugreek seeds

½ teaspoon black peppercorns

4 allspice berries

6 cardamom pods, husks discarded

4 cloves

3 tablespoons or more ground New Mexican chile

3 tablespoons smoked paprika or regular paprika, sweet or hot

2 teaspoons salt

½ teaspoon powdered ginger

½ teaspoon grated nutmeg

½ teaspoon cinnamon

Put the coriander, fenugreek, peppercorns, allspice, cardamom, and cloves in a dry skillet over medium heat. Toast until fragrant, then turn the seeds and berries out onto a plate and let cool for several minutes. Grind to a powder in a spice grinder, then put in a bowl, add the remaining ingredients, and give everything a stir to mix. Store in a tightly covered jar.

THICK MARJORAM SAUCE
FOR BEETS (AND OTHER VEGETABLES)

Serves 4 to 6; V

The original inspiration for this salsa verde came from Ada Boni's book *Italian Regional Cooking*, which was published in the seventies. The color photographs were strange-looking, with off colors, but I mined it relentlessly for ideas. A Ligurian recipe for a Genoese fish salad had a sauce that was something like this one, and along with the featured fish there were a number of vegetables, which was what caught my eye in the first place. I don't really recall how I got from her recipe to this one, but I've made and taught this sauce for years, and it never fails to surprise and delight.

I adore marjoram in summer sauces like this one. Basil is good, of course, but marjoram is less expected and every bit as summery. In my classes, students commonly become enthusiastic converts to this herb. Even if you live where your marjoram succumbs to the first hard frost, you can buy a few plants in late spring, tuck them in a sunny spot, and use the herb all summer. When they finally freeze, you'll be ready to move on to rosemary, sage, and winter savory.

This sauce is so thick that it's almost a paste. You can loosen it by adding more oil, or water if you like, but know that you can spread it as a paste on hard-cooked eggs or grilled fish. It's phenomenally good with vegetables of all kinds—grilled leeks, sliced tomatoes, roasted cauliflower, steamed fennel, or these beets. You can also toss it with pasta and stir it into rice, put it on a hard-cooked egg, and add it to summery vegetable soups and ragouts. This sauce is not difficult to make in an ample mortar with a heavy pestle, but you can also use a food processor if you prefer. I have made this without the bread for a student with celiac disease; I added more nuts for bulk, and it was fine.

4 golden beets or a mixture of golden, Chioggia, and red beets (3 or 4 ounces each)

1 slice country bread, crusts trimmed

2 tablespoons aged red wine vinegar

1 clove garlic, coarsely chopped

Sea salt and freshly ground pepper

⅓ cup marjoram leaves, stripped from their stems

3 tablespoons capers, drained

½ cup pine nuts or walnuts

1 cup finely chopped parsley

10 green olives, pitted and chopped

½ cup best olive oil

To prepare the beets, cut off all but an inch of their stems and leave the tails on so that the juices stay mostly within the beet. Rinse off any sand or mud and then steam them until tender-firm when pierced with a knife, from 25 to 40 minutes, depending on their size. Rinse to cool and then slip off the skins. Refrigerate the beets until they're well chilled, if desired, or use them at room temperature. (Beets can be steamed days before you need them.)

To make the sauce, put the bread on a plate and sprinkle the vinegar over it.

Pound the garlic in a mortar with ½ teaspoon of salt until smooth, then work in the marjoram, capers, pine nuts, parsley, and olives. Pound them with the pestle until you have a coarse mash. (Alternatively, you can do this in a food processor.) Add the bread and olive oil and work until the sauce is well amalgamated. Season with pepper and taste for vinegar, adding a little more if you think it needs it. The sauce should be very thick and very green.

Slice the beets into rounds about ⅜-inch thick and arrange them on a plate. Add a spoonful of the sauce to each.

MASA CRÊPES WITH CHARD, BLACK BEANS, AVOCADO, AND PICKLED ONIONS

Serves 4 to 8

Maybe because I've made them for so many years, whipping up crêpe batter and turning it into breakfast or supper crêpes is easy to do and a treat for your eaters. Crepes don't have to be gooey and rich or complicated. And when they're filled with something, they naturally bring a focus to the plate where there is no meat.

Once again, the combination of chard, cilantro, and chiles is featured here—it's one of my unabashed favorites. It is, in fact, the constant in this recipe, which has gone through more than a few transformations. It started out as a Mexican casserole that was rich with tortillas, sour cream, and cheese—too much even for me. I then put the elements together, substituting masa crêpes for the dense corn tortillas, but still including some cheese and serving two plump crêpes per person. Finally I decided that one crêpe is probably sufficient for most eaters, especially when that crêpe is served with black beans and avocado. There is enough filling here for eight crêpes, so you can judge your eaters accordingly. I also feel that the cheese, while good, is in the end, quite optional. How our tastes change over time.

These crêpes are delicate since the masa harina doesn't have gluten and there's little flour. Handle them with care. There's enough batter that you can have a few accidents. Eight cups of coarsely chopped chard leaves will make two cups of filling, or half a cup per crepe. It looks like a lot, but it cooks down. You can also use more per crepe if you wish.

I serve these with a green tomatillo salsa, one that I buy when local tomatillos are not in season. I admit I succumb to some convenience. The salsa is tangy and enlivens the chard greatly. If you can find a good salsa where you live, use it. CONTINUED

The Crêpe Batter

3 large eggs

1½ cups milk

½ cup masa harina or fine cornmeal

½ cup plus 2 tablespoons all-purpose flour

½ teaspoon salt

3 tablespoons melted butter or oil, plus more for the pan

The Chard Filling

1 tablespoon olive oil

1 onion, finely diced

1 jalapeño, finely diced, seeds removed if you don't want their heat (you'll have about 1 heaping tablespoon)

1½ teaspoons oregano

2 cloves garlic, minced

1 heaping cup chopped cilantro

12 chard leaves, stems removed, leaves coarsely chopped, and washed (you'll have about 8 cups)

Sea salt

⅓ cup sour cream, plus extra for serving

To Finish

1 (15-ounce) can black beans

1 clove garlic, pounded or pressed into a paste

½ teaspoon toasted, ground cumin seeds

Sea salt

1 cup grated cheese, such as Oaxacan string cheese, queso blanco, Jack, or crumbled feta

Easy Pink Onion Pickles (page 175)

Slices of avocado

Cilantro sprigs or leaves

Tomatillo salsa

TO MAKE THE CRÊPE BATTER Combine the eggs, milk, masa harina, flour, salt, and butter in a blender and blend until smooth, scraping down the sides once or twice as needed. Pour into a liquid measuring cup and let rest while you gather the ingredients for the filling.

TO MAKE THE FILLING Heat the oil in a large skillet or Dutch oven. Add the onion, jalapeño, and oregano and cook over medium heat, stirring occasionally, until the onion has softened, about 5 minutes. Add the garlic and cilantro and cook a few minutes more, then add the chard with any water clinging to its leaves and ½ teaspoon of salt. Reduce the heat and cook, turning the leaves occasionally until they are wilted and fully tender. Over low heat, this will take at least 10 minutes. Take your time. Turn the chard often and taste it to make sure it's done and that it has enough salt. Stir in the sour cream.

To cook the crêpes, heat a 10-inch nonstick skillet or well-seasoned crêpe pan over medium heat with a little butter. When the butter has melted and the pan is hot, pour in ¼ cup of batter and swirl it around the pan. Set the pan down and watch for little pinprick-like holes to emerge over the surface. Slide a knife or offset spatula under the edge, lift the crêpe with your fingers and quickly turn it over. Cook on the second side until you can slide it easily in the pan, abut 20 seconds. Slide the crêpe onto a plate and continue with the rest of the batter. (Note—the first crêpe often fails, so don't worry if that happens.)

Simmer the beans in a small pan with the garlic and cumin seeds. Taste for salt; there should be enough if using canned beans. If not, add more to taste.

To fill the crêpes, set the prettier side of a crêpe facing down, spread half the crêpe with ½ cup of chard mixture and add some cheese. Fold the top part of the crêpe over the filling, then fold again once more. You'll have a plump, triangular crêpe. Lightly film a wide skillet set over medium heat with oil. Add the filled crêpes and cook on both sides, the pan covered if need be, until heated through, about 6 minutes.

To serve, spoon some of the beans onto a small plate and add some pickled onions and avocado slices and finally one or two crêpes. Sprinkle with some cilantro leaves and, if you like, slide a spoonful of sour cream under one section of each crêpe so that it spills out just a little. Serve with a spoonful of salsa on the plate as well, if you like.

MUSHROOM SOUP FOR COMPANY

Serves 4

This really is a favorite soup of mine, and it's still true, what I wrote in my soup book, that this soup is a joy to make and a pleasure to view. It's all pebbly with its swirls of cream and black pepper—you don't even need an herb or a garnish. It's good hot in winter or chilled in summer.

Even though I view it as a great soup for a company dinner, I make it often for just the two of us at home. And yes, you can use water, provided that you allow for some of the changes I've made to the original recipe. What are those? If I'm using just regular mushrooms, I sauté them with a few dried porcini for their flavor. I might finish the soup with a mushroom salt I bought at a Maine farmers' market or with a pinch of truffle salt. Or, if I'm luckily endowed with more exotic fresh mushrooms, I'll use those. But really, just a few dried porcini will enhance the flavor greatly, and if you wish to use a stock, you can make a mushroom stock or use a commercial one. If you have just a few wild or exotic mushrooms, you can slice and sauté these for the final garnish.

This soup is thickened with bread rather than flour, and when you add it, it looks truly shabby and hopeless. But by the time the soup has been puréed, it will be fine. And while I seldom make anything with cream anymore, this soup is one exception, because a good splash really brings all the flavors together. Maybe that's what makes it a company soup—the touch of cream. **CONTINUED**

2 tablespoons butter, plus a little to sauté the mushroom garnish

½ cup chopped shallot or onion

A few slices of dried porcini

2 tablespoons chopped parsley

1 bushy thyme sprig

1 pound mushrooms, a few whole mushrooms reserved for garnish if you don't have any wild ones (see below), the rest washed and chopped

1 clove garlic, chopped

Sea salt and freshly ground pepper

1 slice firm-textured bread (can be gluten free)

4 cups water or mushroom stock, either homemade or commercial

¼ to ½ cup cream

A few wild mushrooms, for garnish

Mushroom salt or truffle salt, if available

Melt the butter in a wide soup pot over medium-high heat. When it foams, add the shallot, cook for several minutes until translucent, then add the porcini slices, and cook a minute more. Add the chopped mushrooms and stir well to coat them with the butter. Season with 1 teaspoon of salt and cook over medium heat until their liquid is released. Add the garlic, bread, and water or stock. Bring to a boil and then lower the heat and simmer, covered, for 15 minutes.

Purée the soup in a blender, leaving it a bit textured with flecks of mushroom or making it utterly creamy, and then return the soup to its pot. Taste for salt. Swirl in the cream with a spoon and season with pepper.

Before serving, slice the mushrooms you held back (or the wild mushrooms) about ¼ inch thick. Sauté them briefly in a bit of butter. Spoon them into each bowl of soup. Finally, add a pinch of mushroom or truffle salt and serve.

DRIED PORCINI, FRESH MUSHROOM, AND WHOLE TOMATO RAGOUT WITH SEARED POLENTA

Serves 4; GF

I have a long history with mushrooms and tomatoes. It began with a soup that featured dried porcini and tomatoes. That quickly turned into a stew, or mushroom ragout. It turned out to be a good way to produce a center-of-the-plate vegetable dish that wasn't heavy or cheesy—although I did do variations with cream and sour cream. In summer, the tomatoes were fresh. In winter, they were canned. Tomato paste was usually included, too, for its intensity.

In this dish, instead of the usual diced canned tomatoes, which are fine (and certainly better than winter tomatoes), I use whole peeled San Marzanos, which give more stature to the dish. This happened originally because San Marzanos were what I had on hand. I was planning to dice them, but then I thought, why not leave them whole? After all, if I had good roma-type tomatoes in my garden, I'd do that, dipping them in boiling water first to make the skins easy to remove. I have often made this with red wine, but if white is what I have open, I'll use it. It gives the right bit of acidity this dish needs. So often a dish is shaped by what's on hand.

Where I live, porcini appear about the same time as tomatoes, so it's possible to make this with fresh porcini—which are spectacular, of course. But more often than not, I slice and then dry the fungi I manage to find, putting them aside to use in the winter, when this dish is especially appealing. Rosemary and sage are good winter herbs; marjoram, basil and oregano are good in the summer.

This dish doesn't take long to make, and it can easily be reheated, but make the polenta first so that it has time to firm up, unless you wish to serve the mushrooms over soft polenta or another farinaceous food—say, a different grain, a fresh pasta, or big slabs of toasted hearth bread that have been rubbed with garlic, brushed with olive oil, and broken into large shards. CONTINUED

1 cup polenta

Sea salt and freshly ground pepper

1 tablespoon butter, plus more to finish

1 cup, more or less, dried porcini mushrooms

3 tablespoons olive oil

1 small onion, finely diced

2 tablespoons chopped parsley

1 tablespoon finely chopped herbs
(see headnote)

1 plump garlic clove, chopped finely

2 teaspoons tomato paste

½ cup red or white wine

1 pound large fresh mushrooms,
gills still closed if possible, thickly sliced
at odd angles

8 to 12 peeled whole roma-type tomatoes

Parmigiano-Reggiano, for grating

Bring 4 cups of water to a boil, add 1½ teaspoons of salt, and then whisk in the polenta. Cook over medium-high heat until the polenta begins to thicken, then reduce the heat to low and cook, stirring frequently, until it is quite thick. (If you're doing other things, you can cook the polenta in a double boiler and pretty much ignore it for an hour.) Stir in 1 tablespoon of butter, taste for salt, and season with pepper. Scrape the polenta into an 8 by 10-inch dish and smooth the top. Set it aside to cool and set.

Cover the dried mushrooms with 1½ cups of very warm water and set aside while you assemble and chop the rest of the ingredients, at least 20 minutes. Drain, reserving the liquid. If there is soil grit in the liquid, pour it through a mesh fine strainer.

Heat a wide skillet over medium heat with a tablespoon of the oil. When it's warm, add the onion and the drained porcini. Cook, stirring frequently, until the onion is golden, 4 to 5 minutes, then add half the parsley, winter or summer herbs, garlic, and work in the tomato paste. Pour in the wine and cook until it's reduced to a syrupy consistency. Season with a few pinches of salt and plenty of pepper and remove to a bowl.

Return the pan to the heat, add the rest of the oil, and when it's hot, add the fresh mushrooms. Sauté over high heat until they start to color, add a few good pinches of salt, and then cook until they release and then absorb their juices, about 6 to 8 minutes. Add the onion mixture to the mushrooms and pour in the mushroom soaking liquid. Nestle the tomatoes here and there among the mushrooms. Reduce the heat and simmer until the mushrooms are cooked; at least 15 minutes. Add the remaining herbs and garlic, along with a spoonful of butter for added richness.

To serve, cut the polenta into four portions, making whatever shapes you wish. Warm a skillet over medium heat and film it with a little oil. Add the polenta pieces and cook on each side until golden, and a bit crisp. Arrange these on plates or in shallow bowls and spoon the mushrooms over. Grate a little Parmigiano-Reggiano over the top. If you have fresh sprigs or leaves of herbs, use them to garnish each dish.

STINGING NETTLE SOUP
WITH NIGELLA SEEDS

Serves 6; GF

They're called "stinging nettles" for a reason. Tiny barbs on the undersides of the leaves sting any flesh they encounter. The burn is uncomfortable for a few minutes, like a bee string and then it goes away, but you don't want to be picking nettles with your bare hands. Happily, once they're submerged in boiling water, the stingers stop stinging and you can handle them with impunity.

I've had my own private love affair with nettles for years. They love the foggy California coast and I used them a lot at Greens. Sadly, they don't flourish in the desert where I live now so they've become something of a rarity for me, but when some intrepid farmer who has enough water to grow them brings a bunch to the market, I jump on them.

An online search for nettles once led me to Nettles Farm on Lummi Island, in Washington. The owners laughed in disbelief when I told them that I was looking for nettles. When they saw my confusion, they explained that the first thing they had to do when they bought their farm was clear five acres of nettles. But they still used them when they grew back in places—in pasta dough, in a ravioli filling, with eggs, on crostini, and of course, in soup. A friend told me that eating this soup made her feel like an animal that had been out grazing in the wild, which is just how a bowl of nettle soup should make one feel.

I don't think people paid much attention to my nettle soup in *Local Flavors* until I made it and took a picture. Once it was posted on Facebook, it got some attention—it's that gorgeous a green. I broke it up with a garnish of black nigella seeds, added more for their striking looks than anything else. (You can use black sesame seeds as well.)

This version is tempered somewhat with chard and other greens, but the nettles will definitely come through. While I like to use wild greens, chard, beet greens, green orach, and lambsquarters will also work just fine, alone or in combination. **CONTINUED**

8 ounces nettle leaves, more if at all possible (a plastic vegetable bag, filled)

1 tablespoon butter or olive oil

1 cup sliced onion or scallions

1 small potato, thinly sliced, or 2 tablespoons white rice

6 cups wild spinach (lambsquarters) or chard leaves, removed from the stems and chopped

1 big handful parsley leaves, coarsely chopped

Sea salt and freshly ground pepper

Cream or crème fraîche

1 teaspoon lightly toasted nigella seeds or black sesame seeds

Bring plenty of water to a boil. Using tongs, plunge the nettles into a bowl of cold water and swish them back and forth to rinse them of any dust, then drop them into the boiling water and leave for 2 minutes. Pull them out, drain them, and then coarsely chop them. Discard any large stems. Reserve 6 cups of the water for the soup. (Any extra can go right into the garden.)

Melt the butter in a wide soup pot and add the onion and potato or rice. Cook over medium heat, stirring occasionally, until the onion is translucent, about 5 minutes. Add the wild spinach or chard, parsley, 1½ teaspoons of salt, and the 6 cups of reserved blanching water from the nettles. Bring to a boil, add the nettles, then lower the heat and simmer until the potato or rice is completely soft, 15 to 20 minutes.

Purée the soup until perfectly smooth, then return it to the stove. (If the nettles were stemmy, pass the soup through a food mill or sieve.) Season with more salt, if needed, and with pepper. Swirl a teaspoon of cream into each bowl, then garnish with black sesame seeds or nigella seeds scattered over the surface.

ROUGH-CUT OATS WITH DRIED CHERRIES, RAISINS, AND TOASTED ALMONDS

Makes 2 big bowls; V if butter is omitted, GF

If you're going to have hot cereal for breakfast, this is a good way to go—it's sustaining. The bulkier the oats are, I've noticed, the more unlikely I am to be starving by eleven. Steel-cut oats are a good choice if you don't want to be ravenous a few hours after having breakfast, but they do take longer to cook than the thick-cut rolled oats called for here.

I like the sweetness of raisins or currants or other dried fruits, but I love the look of plump sour cherries and their surprising flavor, so I use a combination. (Plus I bought so many sour cherries in Turkey that I have a lot of them to work my way through.) The almonds are toasted and scattered over the top. A pat of butter might also be slipped into the surface of the cereal, but it can be skipped if it's not on your menu. Sea salt is on the table. Neither my husband nor I put milk on our cereal, but if you do, go right ahead.

I use organic thick-cut oats, which cook in about two parts water to one part oats, plus a little extra liquid, as needed. If you use another type of rolled oat, follow the directions, if any are given. Most cereals have a 3:1 ratio, and if you find your oats too thick at 2:1, you can always add more liquid.

On a trip around the Island of Mull and beyond on a very small Scottish fishing boat, our chef confessed that the two things he was really fearful of making wrong were shortbread and porridge, two very Scottish foods. He was a well-trained chef, but Irish, and not invested in the absolute styles of these dishes. He made the (oat) porridge using a mixture of milk and water, plus sugar and salt. Cereal made that way has a very distinctive flavor, one that is easy to like. And his shortbread? It was divine!

1 cup thick-cut rolled oats	Butter
2 cups water	¼ cup slivered toasted almonds
½ teaspoon salt	Flaky sea salt (optional)
2 to 3 tablespoons raisins and dried cherries, mixed	Milk, if you like

Put the oats, water, and salt in a small saucepan and bring to a boil. Give a stir, add the fruit, and cook over medium-low heat until the water is absorbed and the oats have lost their raw taste, about 6 minutes. Turn off the heat, cover the pan, and let stand for another 5 minutes.

Divide between two bowls, add a slice of butter to each, if using, and cover with the toasted almonds. Serve with flaky salt or with milk.

OLIVE OIL, ALMOND, AND BLOOD ORANGE CAKE

Makes one 9-inch cake

When I was pastry chef at Café Escalera in Santa Fe, we couldn't give olive oil cake away. Actually, we could, but if the words "olive oil" were on the menu, no one would order it until they had tasted it gratis. That's no longer true, of course. I believe the olive oil barrier has been broken when it comes to desserts.

Even after many years, I still absolutely love the olive oil cake from my dessert book and *The New Vegetarian Cooking for Everyone*. It's one I make for birthdays, as it's high and light and fine of crumb and never fails to honor the birthday person. This is a somewhat smaller cake, a variation I worked out for the Greek resort Costa Navarino. It was made with their rich, green olive oil and was intended to be served with their unusual olive spoon sweets. But this cake is also lovely with a fruit. I'd definitely consider sliced mangoes, an orange compote, softly whipped cream flavored with orange flower water, fine apricot preserves in winter, sliced nectarines in lemon verbena syrup (page 184) in summer, or rhubarb compote (page 211) in spring.

The cake is moist, rich, and complex with the flavors of robust olive oil, blood orange, and crackling sugared almonds. If blood oranges aren't available, use navel oranges or tangerines. CONTINUED

1 cup all-purpose flour or, if available,
Sonoran wheat flour

1 cup almond meal or finely grated almonds

1 teaspoon baking powder

½ teaspoon sea salt

2 egg whites

1 cup sugar

2 large eggs plus the 2 yolks from above

Finely grated zest of 2 blood oranges

½ cup blood orange juice

½ cup Greek or other full-bodied
olive oil, such as Spanish Arbequina

¼ teaspoon almond extract

⅓ cup sliced almonds tossed with
1 tablespoon sugar

Powdered sugar, to serve (optional)

Put a rack in the center of the oven, then heat the oven to 350°F. Rub a 9-inch springform pan with butter, then dust the sides and bottom well with flour or sugar. Cut a 9-inch circle of parchment and lay it in the pan.

Combine the flour, ground almonds, baking powder, and salt in a bowl with a whisk.

Whisk the egg whites in an electric mixer until foamy, then add ¼ cup of the sugar and whisk at higher speed until the whites are shiny and firm but not dry or stiff. Scrape the whites into a bowl.

Without rinsing the mixing bowl, add the whole eggs, the 2 yolks, the remaining sugar, and the orange zest. Return it to the machine and, using the whisk attachment, beat the eggs with the sugar and orange zest on medium-high speed until pale and thick, several minutes. Turn the speed to low and add the olive oil, followed by the juice and almond extract.

With the machine still on low, add the flour mixture by the heaping spoonful until all is incorporated. Remove the bowl, then run a wide rubber scraper around the bowl, making sure all the dry ingredients have been combined. Fold the beaten egg whites into the batter, pour it into the prepared pan, and sprinkle the almond-sugar mixture over the surface, making a ring of nuts in the center.

Bake on the center rack until firm, browned, and pulling away from the sides of the pan, 50 to 60 minutes. A cake tester should come out clean. Let the cake cool in the pan, then run a knife around the sides. Transfer to a cake plate. Dust with powdered sugar before serving, if desired.

EASY PINK ONION PICKLES

Makes about 1 cup; V, GF

These quick-to-make pickled onions can become a cheerful addition to a sandwich, a garnish to a black bean and pepper salad, and, in fact, a lively element in salads of all kinds. I've probably included them in one form or another in every book I've written, because they're just so useful, pretty, quick to make, and good to eat. And if you live with someone who doesn't favor raw onions, these are an excellent replacement as the vinegar seems to draw out whatever is problematic.

I love to use the tiny red onion "babies" that I find from time to time at the farmers' market. They make a good size ring that isn't overly large, plus you don't need to make a lot at once. One small onion will yield more than enough pickled onion rings for any occasion.

I always make these by eye, not by a recipe; and in fact, I've changed my approach over the years. I used to pour boiling water over the sliced onions, then put them in a mixture of vinegar and water. Now, it pretty much goes like this:

Choose a firm, smallish red onion. Peel it, leaving it whole. Slice it crosswise into rounds, making them as thin as possible. (A sharp knife is an effective tool for thin slicing—and for slicing raw onions in a way that will, if not prevent, at least subdue tears.) Put the onion rings into a bowl and pour over white vinegar, such as rice wine vinegar or champagne vinegar. (A red vinegar will make the onions not so bright.) They needn't be completely covered, especially if you're using an expensive vinegar that you're loath to run out of. Toss the onion rings in the vinegar. If you wish, add some black peppercorns, bay leaves, or a small dried red chile or two. Put the bowl in the refrigerator for at least 10 minutes, within which time the onions will become a wild color of pink and their hot flavor will be somewhat tamed. That's it.

If you don't use them all at once, put the leftovers in a covered container and return it to the refrigerator. They will become even more suffused with color, but it will be less bright. Over a few days the onions will get softer as well, but they'll stay useable for a week or so. They simply become something rather different than they were on the first day.

CARAMELIZED ONIONS WITH VINEGAR AND CLOVES

Serves 4 to 6; V, GF

If I ask people what they like, or don't like, about cooking, I get different answers. For some, it's the shopping they enjoy (or dread). For others, it's the planning. Some abhor cleaning up or resent the time it takes to make a dish; others don't mind having hot soapy water in the sink for those dirty pots and pans, and still others enjoy the break cooking offers from the rest of their lives. Personally, I have a lot of likes, but I especially enjoy those dishes that need a long slow session over low heat, like these onions. You don't usually have to stay by them, which is perfect for a person who is doing lots of different things. I can go into the garden or my office; I can bring the rest of the meal together, or I can read. I check in on them now and then and give a stir or fiddle with the heat. And when they're done, I'm so glad to have them.

Why? Because caramelized onions can go everywhere! They are good with pasta (page 180), in a frittata (page 178), on toast with more vegetables, or on grilled meats. Crushed walnuts, rosemary and sage, and aged salty, nutty cheeses go hand in hand with caramelized onions. It does take a while for the onions to achieve that golden color, but you don't need to be peering at them. In fact, adding a lid produces the moisture that keeps them from burning.

The clove and vinegar are not usually added to caramelized onion, but I think that both provide a good and unusual twist. Onions are sweet, and they want the sharpness and zing of these two ingredients. When it comes to amounts, a scale might be useful. Sometimes just two (large) onions work out to be 1½ pounds. And one last thing, onions cooked in a dark pan, like a cast-iron skillet, will brown more quickly than those cooked in a stainless steel pan.

Originally this was the filling for a frittata but when I started thinking about all the places I use these onions, I decided to feature them by themselves. Once you have them, you will for sure find ways to use them.

1½ pounds white or yellow onions	Sea salt and freshly ground pepper
1½ tablespoons olive oil	⅛ teaspoon ground cloves
1 to 2 tablespoons sherry vinegar	

Peel the onions and halve them lengthwise, then cut each half into thirds or quarters. Slice each piece crosswise about ¼ inch thick. (Do this if you're using the onions in a frittata—the even slices will keep it looking nice when you cut into it. If this isn't important, just slice the halves into long pieces.)

Warm the olive oil in a 10-inch skillet, add the onions, and cook over medium heat, stirring occasionally until they begin to color. Reduce the heat to medium-low, cover the pan, and continue to cook, stirring occasionally, until they've started to color, about 20 minutes. Remove the lid and stir frequently, keeping an active eye on them to make sure they don't burn.

When they're limp and caramel colored, raise the heat, add the vinegar and let it reduce. Season with ¾ teaspoon of salt, lots of freshly ground pepper, and the cloves. Taste, and if you want a little more vinegar, add it—carefully. Sherry vinegar is strong. You can use the onions right away or refrigerate for several days.

CARAMELIZED ONION FRITTATA
WITH SHERRY VINEGAR

Makes 2 thin frittatas or 1 larger, thicker one; GF

Frittatas with caramelized onions have long been a favorite of mine. What makes them special is the wash of melted butter and vinegar sauce spooned over the finished dish. It's made in the pan in just a few seconds. This recipe calls for half the onion mixture on page 176 in a three-egg frittata. You can serve it whole or cut it into squares, pile it on crackers or bread, and serve as an appetizer.

3 eggs	5 teaspoons butter
Sea salt and freshly ground pepper	Parmigiano-Reggiano, for grating
1 tablespoon chopped parsley	1½ tablespoons sherry vinegar
Half-recipe Caramelized Onions with Vinegar and Cloves (page 176)	

Whisk the eggs with a few pinches of salt and some freshly ground pepper, then stir in the parsley and the caramelized onions. Heat your broiler.

Melt 2 teaspoons of the butter in a 10-inch skillet until it's sizzling, then add the eggs and lower the heat. Cook the eggs, covered, until they are set and golden on the bottom, about 6 minutes for a thin frittata, longer for a thick one.

Grate a little of the cheese over the top, then slide the pan under the broiler to finish cooking. The top should be light gold and firm. Loosen the frittata and tilt it onto a plate, then return the pan to the stove and raise the heat.

Add the remaining butter to the pan and when it begins to foam, add the sherry vinegar. Slide the pan back and forth to emulsify the two. Stand back! The vinegar fumes are strong. When you have a sauce, pour it over the frittata and serve.

6 New Mexican or Anaheim chiles, or 4 poblanos, or 3 Big Jims

2 teaspoons coriander seeds

2 tablespoons sunflower seed oil or other vegetable oil

1 large onion, diced

2 pounds potatoes, a mixture of russets and other varieties, or all russets, scrubbed and chopped into 1½-inch chunks

1 large clove garlic, chopped

Sea salt and freshly ground pepper

6 cups water, vegetable stock, or chicken stock

A big handful of cilantro

½ cup sour cream

Roast the chiles over an open flame until the skins are bubbly and partially charred, then put them in a bowl, cover with a plate, and set aside to steam while you prepare the potatoes. Toast the coriander seeds in a dry skillet until they are fragrant and the color starts to dull; cool on a plate and then grind to a powder in a spice mill.

Heat the oil in a wide soup pot and add the onion, potatoes, garlic, and ground coriander. Turn to coat with the oil, then cook over medium heat, stirring occasionally, until the potatoes are golden in places, about 8 minutes. Meanwhile, slip the skins off the chiles, scrape out the seeds, and chop the flesh in large pieces. Add the chiles to the potatoes along with 1 teaspoon of salt and the water. Give a stir, bring to a boil, then lower the heat to a simmer. Cover the pot and cook until the potatoes are completely softened; the time will vary according to how large they are, but probably about 25 minutes. Taste for salt and season with pepper. If you want to thicken the stew, mash some of the potatoes right in the pot.

Bring a small amount of water to a boil, submerge the cilantro in it for a few seconds, then drain and rinse under cold water. Chop it finely, then stir it into the sour cream. Add a dollop to each bowl. If using either of the cheeses mentioned in the headnote, add them just as you serve the soup.

RED CHILE AND POSOLE WITH BLUE CORN TORTILLA CHIPS AND AVOCADO

Serves 4 as a main dish or 6 more modestly; GF

Today it's hard to remember that there was a time when posole wasn't part of my culinary life, but until I first visited New Mexico, I had never even heard of it. Mostly in this state it's cooked with beef or pork; but I simmer the lime-treated corn only with onion, oregano, and some dried chiles, and its flavor is ample. Once corn is treated with lime to dissolve the outer skin, it changes, possessing a different and much bigger flavor than, say, sweet corn. Posole truly works well as a vegetarian dish—as well as a meaty stew.

It's quite a job to treat the corn kernels with lime, then slough off the outer layer, then rinse the corn, so usually a farmer makes enough to freeze or dry so that there's a supply that will last for a while. Of course, for most people, getting posole is a matter of going to the store, where you can buy it dried or frozen. Canned hominy, which is already cooked, is another version, though it's harder to find in the Southwest than in other parts of the country—and it's not the same (or quite as good) as cooking your own.

A bowl of posole may be simple fare, depending on the garnishes, but whether dried or frozen it does take a while to cook—just how long isn't easy to say with accuracy. Knowing the timing is mostly a matter of getting used to a particular brand.

Frozen posole comes in two-pound bags, which is plenty for a party. I usually cook a pound at a time, which makes six servings, returning the rest of the bag to the freezer for another time.

In general, guajillo chiles are milder, but if you and your friends want more fire, plan to use medium or hot New Mexican chile pods.

1 pound frozen posole, defrosted	2 quarts water
1 onion, finely diced	Sea salt
2 plump garlic cloves, peeled and smashed to a paste with 1 teaspoon salt	Ground red chile, to taste
	1 avocado, diced
3 dried red New Mexican chile pods or guajillo chiles, stemmed and seeds shaken out	Sour cream
	Blue corn tortilla chips
1 teaspoon dried Mexican oregano	Coarsely chopped cilantro sprigs

Put the posole in a soup pot with the onion, garlic, dried chile, oregano, and water. Keep the chile pods in large pieces, as you'll be fishing them out later to purée. Bring to a boil, then lower the heat and simmer, partially covered, until the posole is tender and many of the kernels have opened up or flowered, 1½ to 2 hours. (This flowering gives posole another name: popcorn soup.) Season with 2 teaspoons of salt about halfway through.

When the posole is tender, remove the chile pods and purée them with some of the cooking liquid, then return the purée to the posole. Taste again for salt. If you want it hotter, you might want to add some ground chile to taste.

Ladle the posole into bowls with some of the broth. Make a heap of avocado in each bowl and add a spoonful of sour cream, a few blue corn tortilla chips, and a cluster of cilantro leaves.

QUINCE BRAISED IN HONEY AND WINE

Serves 4 to 6; GF

This dessert is stunning and simple to prepare given that the skins stay on the quinces, plus you leave in the core and simply eat around it. The skins disappear into softness, and the seed sections are handsome. The secret with this—and all quince dishes—is to cook it long enough for the quince to turn rosy pink and become utterly tender and succulent. That's when they become magnificent.

For honey, I reach for what I have in the cupboard, but honey from fall flowers would be wonderful. They usually produce darker, more complex honeys that are not as delicate as those made from spring flowers, and go well with this fruit.

Allow two or three ½-inch rounds per person, which is essentially one large quince. Use any pieces that aren't quite presentable in apple or pear tarts, compotes, ice cream, or other desserts. Serve these quinces warm, with honey ice cream, crème fraîche blended with a little honey, or something else that's cold and creamy.

4 to 6 ripe, fragrant quinces (about 2 pounds)

2 cinnamon sticks

½ cup honey (see headnote)

½ cup dessert wine, such as Ouady's orange muscat or Navarro's late harvest Riesling

2 tablespoons butter, cut into small pieces

Honey ice cream or crème fraîche, to serve

Heat the oven to 400°F. Select a wide, shallow dish, like a round gratin dish, that will comfortably hold the quince slices in a single layer, with some doubling up if need be.

Rub the fuzz off of each quince, rinse, and then slice crosswise into rounds about ½ inch wide or a little wider. Leave the skins on.

Loosely arrange the rounds of fruit in the roomy baking dish. Tuck in the cinnamon sticks, drizzle over the honey, pour in the wine, dot with the butter, and then cover with foil. Bake for 25 minutes, then remove the foil and bake 20 minutes more. Check the fruit, turn the slices over and slosh the juices around, and then return to the oven and bake until gorgeously burnished and tender when pierced with a paring knife. In all, this should take about an hour or an hour plus fifteen minutes or so. In the end, the juices will have cooked down to a thick, dark syrup.

Serve warm or at room temperature, alone or with honey ice cream or crème fraîche. Be sure to spoon any syrup that remains over the fruit.

QUINOA AND BUTTERMILK PANCAKES

Makes about twelve 4-inch cakes

I make pancakes often and I almost never use a recipe. I simply break an egg in a bowl, whisk in buttermilk, vanilla, oil, and salt, then stir in flour, and that's about it. The flour is often a local cornmeal mixed with wheat flour, semolina, spelt, or other flours. I never add sweetener, as that will come later in the form of jam of syrup. But I do stir in any leftover cooked grain I might have, not only quinoa, but rice, or cooked corn.

When you add cooked grains to pancakes, you get more interesting cakes, ones with texture and, in this case, extra protein as well. And yet the cakes are as light as can be. They're delicious with warm maple syrup and a spoonful of sour cream or yogurt.

These could be savory cakes as well: take out the vanilla and add a little grated cheese to the batter, serve with some salsa on top, and you have another dish altogether.

1 large egg

1¼ cups buttermilk

3 to 5 tablespoons melted butter or coconut oil

¼ teaspoon sea salt

1 teaspoon vanilla

¾ cup white whole-wheat flour, spelt, quinoa, or another favorite flour

1 teaspoon baking powder

½ teaspoon baking soda

½ to 1 cup cooked quinoa

Whisk the egg with the buttermilk, melted butter, salt, and vanilla together in a large bowl. Whisk in the flour(s) along with the baking powder and soda, then stir in as much quinoa as you have. The batter can take quite a bit—at least a cup.

Heat a skillet over medium heat. When it's hot, drop in the batter ¼ cup at a time to make cakes. Cook until holes appear all over the tops of the cakes, then turn them, and cook for another minute or so. Then serve.

QUINOA SOUP WITH SPINACH, CORN, FETA, AND CILANTRO

Serves 4; GF

I found this recipe in a cookbook by Felipe Rojas-Lombardi ages ago, and since I simply couldn't imagine it, I had to try it, and I'm so glad that I did. It's been a staple in our house for a long time. I once demonstrated this recipe at a food conference where I went from a bag of groceries to a finished dish in less than 30 minutes, ending up with a light meal. I'm still amazed at how easily and quickly this comes together.

The resulting dish is light, despite the quinoa, corn, and potatoes; it's perfect for occasions when we want a dish that doesn't wallop us over the head with its bigness, times when we want nourishment but not heaviness, and that's what this soup offers. Still, if you find yourself thinking about using chicken stock in place of the quinoa cooking water for a richer flavor, by all means do.

Today I make it pretty much the same way I always have, although I include a bit of red quinoa with the white. If it's corn season, I add the kernels from an ear or two or three (this can be leftover grilled corn) during the last few minutes. Knowing that many people reach for a bag of small spinach leaves rather than a bunch (which I prefer), I have used the small leaves with success, as long as I clip off the stems with kitchen scissors. I also don't put in the egg that was called for originally; it clouds the soup, and most Americans get plenty of protein without it. Quinoa, of course, doesn't need 1½ quarts of water to cook in, but the cooking water becomes the broth for the soup, so don't discard it.

¾ cup white quinoa, mixed with ¼ cup red, well rinsed

Sea salt and freshly ground pepper

1½ quarts water

2 tablespoons olive oil

1 plump garlic clove, chopped

1 jalapeño, seeded and finely diced

2 teaspoons toasted ground cumin seeds

8 ounces potatoes, any variety, scrubbed and diced into ¼-inch cubes

1 bunch of scallions, including an inch of the greens, thinly sliced in rounds

⅓ cup finely chopped cilantro leaves and/or stems, plus a handful of cilantro leaves, coarsely chopped, to finish

3 cups spinach leaves, left whole if small, rolled and sliced if full size

Kernels from 2 to 3 ears corn

4 ounces feta cheese, cut into small cubes (you'll have a cup or more)

Put the rinsed quinoa and the water in a pot with 1½ teaspoons of salt. Bring to a boil, then lower the heat and simmer for 15 minutes. When the quinoa is done, drain it, but be sure to save the liquid. Measure and add water, if need be, to make 6 cups.

Heat the oil in a soup pot over medium heat. Add the garlic and jalapeño and cook for about 30 seconds, giving them a few quick stirs. Add the cumin, a teaspoon of salt, and the potatoes. Cook for a few minutes, stirring frequently, without letting the garlic brown. Add the quinoa water, half the scallions, and the finely chopped cilantro. Simmer until the potatoes are tender, about 15 minutes. Add the cooked quinoa, spinach leaves, remaining scallions, and corn. Simmer a few minutes more and then turn off the heat.

At this point you can serve the soup, seasoning it with pepper and adding feta and the chopped cilantro to each bowl. The soup will have plenty of broth at this stage. As it sits, the quinoa will continue to draw in the liquid, making a thicker dish. I've actually enjoyed this for supper or breakfast the next day. The flavors will have developed more, too.

SEARED RADICCHIO DRAPED WITH MOZZARELLA

Serves 2 to 4; GF

Seared radicchio seems to magically sweeten in the pan while retaining some of its bitter bite. It also gives up its gorgeous purple-red coloration for brown, but so be it. I first had seared radicchio draped with oozing fresh mozzarella cheese in an Italian restaurant in Santa Monica. The waiter was very reluctant to serve this special to me because he was sure I wouldn't like the bitterness of the radicchio. Customers had been returning this special all week. I think he was pleased that nothing remained on the plate when he came to get it. The dish was served with a few drops of good balsamic vinegar, and so is my version here. Use your very best aged balsamic.

Reversing that pattern, I started using chopped seared radicchio over a simple white pizza. Then I discovered that Gorgonzola is another fine partner. The seared vegetable is also marvelous without the cheese. I've used it to lend balance to the naturally sweet flavors of a winter squash soup. Or was it a winter squash risotto? Probably that, too! You get the idea. If you're attracted to its unusual combination of flavors—bitterness, sweetness, and nuttiness all at once—you will no doubt find many uses for this vegetable. Radicchio is a chicory, so keep in mind that escarole and other chicories can be seared—or grilled—as well.

1 large head radicchio

Olive oil

Sea salt and freshly ground pepper

1 (4-ounce) ball fresh mozzarella, cut into thin rounds, or crumbled Gorgonzola

Best balsamic vinegar

Cut the radicchio into wedges about 1½ inches across, keeping the root ends intact. Brush each wedge with olive oil and season well with salt and pepper.

Heat a cast-iron skillet or grill pan over medium-high heat. When it's good and hot, add the radicchio. Press down on the wedges to ensure contact, lower the heat to medium, and cook until browned, about 5 minutes. Turn and cook on the second side. Press down on the wedges again to open the leaves. The red will turn brownish, and the leaves will probably get crisp in places.

Drape (or dot) the radicchio with the cheese, then put a lid on the pan and cook just until the cheese is meltingly soft, after 2 or 3 minutes. Season with pepper, add a few drops of fine balsamic vinegar, arrange on a platter, and serve.

SHREDDED RADICCHIO WITH
A GARLICKY DRESSING

Serves 4; V, GF

I included a version of this salad in *Vegetable Literacy*, in which the radicchio is tossed with hard-cooked egg, toasted bread crumbs, parsley, and a dressing of walnut oil laced with shallots and a sherry vinegar. I love this recipe. Such a salad can easily be a whole meal for me in winter, and it often is. However, there finally did come a time when, lacking all those tasty additions but happening to have a head of radicchio and some garlic, I made the dish, but far more simply. I offer thanks to a snowstorm that prevented a trip to town and forced me to improvise such a minimal but good, strong salad. Of course you can amplify it with the additions already mentioned—parsley, lightly toasted walnuts, and hard-cooked eggs.

Note that you will be subject to garlic breath, so be sure to eat it with those who don't mind. And if you really like garlic, use more. I used a single plump clove from a hard-neck garlic, and it was plenty.

Walnut oil is exceptionally good with any of the chicories. It is nutty and warm, an excellent foil for the bitterness that can be even in winter radicchio, which is generally made sweeter with the cold. But a rich, full olive oil works wonderfully as well. What does matter is to slice the radicchio very thinly, as thinly as possible. It's a dense vegetable, and the thin slicing makes it that much more enjoyable to eat.

Since you might well be making this in winter, your garlic may already be forming a green sprout within. If so, just remove it with the tip of a small knife. It's impossible to mash.

1 round head radicchio

1 plump clove garlic

Sea salt and freshly ground pepper

1 tablespoon aged sherry vinegar or rich red wine vinegar

3 tablespoons walnut oil or best olive oil, or more to taste,

Quarter the radicchio head, then slice it either crosswise or lengthwise, as thinly as possible. Put it in a shallow salad bowl and toss to break up any clumps.

Smash the garlic clove in a mortar with ¼ teaspoon of salt until smooth. This takes very little time, so forgo the garlic press. You want the garlic to be creamy, not broken into little pieces, which is what a press yields. When smooth, add the vinegar and then the oil. Whisk everything together so that it's well emulsified. (You might want to transfer the dressing to a small, lidded jar and give it a shake.)

Pour it over the radicchio and toss well. Taste a strand for salt and add more if desired. Grind pepper over all and toss again.

RHUBARB-RASPBERRY COMPOTE

Serves 4 or more; V, GF

Rhubarb keeps producing pretty much all summer, so strawberries aren't the only fruit you might pair with it. Personally, I prefer raspberries. If you live where soft fruits may not be available or affordable, use frozen. I use organic frozen raspberries, put the broken pieces in with the rhubarb while it's cooking for flavor, then add a cup of the whole berries once it's done but still hot. They thaw as the rhubarb cools. The black pepper is warm and spicy, as surprising as it is good.

A pound of rhubarb doesn't make a lot of compote, but there are many ways you can use it. You can spoon it over yogurt or ice cream, make it into a fool by folding it into whipped cream (or crème fraiche), have it for breakfast on toast spread with mascarpone, spoon it over cottage cheese or whip it up with buttermilk to make a smoothie. Somehow, it just seems to evaporate in our kitchen.

1 pound or more, red rhubarb, the ends trimmed	2 cloves
½ cup maple sugar or organic white sugar	1 cup whole raspberries, fresh or frozen, plus broken or smashed fruit
Zest and juice of 1 orange	Black pepper, freshly ground

Slice the rhubarb stalks on the diagonal ½-inch thick or a little thicker, and put them in a bowl with the sugar, orange zest, and juice. Toss well and let stand for a good hour or more. (This draws out the juices, but skip this step and just go ahead and cook it if that works better for your schedule.)

Slide the macerated rhubarb into a shallow pan and set it over medium-high heat. Once the juice has come out and begins to boil, add the cloves, lower the heat, and simmer gently until the rhubarb is tender. If you have little broken pieces of frozen raspberries or somewhat smashed fresh ones, add them now.

Once the rhubarb is tender but hopefully still holding its shape, turn off the heat and fold in the raspberries. Chill, then add a bit of ground pepper over the top. It should keep well, refrigerated, for about a week.

BROWN RICE PORRIDGE WITH NUT BUTTER AND CHIA SEEDS

Serves 4; V, GF

When it's cold out and our bodies cry out for something warm (besides coffee, that is), brown rice cereal, or porridge, is often what's for breakfast in our house. (I use Bob's Red Mill brown rice farina, which is ground finer than grits.) I nearly always add a spoonful of nut butter for protein. It can be peanut, almond, cashew, or sunflower seed butter—whatever you prefer. The nut butter softens in the hot cereal but not completely so that you get random and unexpected mouthfuls of its goodness. If there's leftover brown rice lurking in the fridge, I might stir some of that into the cereal as well, for texture. Or I'll scatter chia seeds over the top; sometimes I grind them, but more often than not I'm reaching into the jar and scattering them whole over the cereal.

I don't put milk on my cereal, mainly out of a habit cultivated for some twenty years in the Zen community, where we were partial to sesame salt instead. Sesame salt, or *gomasio*, is crunchy, toasty, and good, and I'm happy to use it here as well. You can use milk, if you're inclined. It's cereal, it's morning—I think people should do whatever they like.

1 cup uncooked brown rice cereal	4 heaping tablespoons nut butter
4 cups water	Chia seeds
1 teaspoon sea salt	Milk, if desired

Combine the cereal, water, and salt in a 2-quart saucepan and bring to a boil over medium heat. Stir frequently because brown rice cereal has a tendency to clump and thicken quickly and unevenly. Once it has thickened and no longer tastes raw, cover the pan, turn off the heat, and let it stand for 10 minutes. If it seems too thick, by all means stir in extra water or milk to thin it to a consistency you like. I have found the cereal itself to be a little inconsistent, so you may want to play with it a little to get the texture right.

Divide among bowls, stir a tablespoon of nut butter into each, and cover with chia seeds. Pour over a little milk.

YELLOW COCONUT RICE WITH SCALLIONS AND BLACK SESAME SEEDS

Serves 4 to 6; V, GF

Turmeric and saffron threads make this rice the most delectable color, while green scallions and black sesame seeds add to the drama and texture of the dish. If we truly eat with our eyes, you'll be full without taking a bite. I considered omitting the saffron threads to make this more affordable, and you can leave them out if you wish, but they really do add to the flavor and appearance of this dish.

If you can find it—it's now become difficult to find—use medium- or short-grain rice. Don't rinse it, and follow the suggested ratios of water to rice on the package (the amount of liquid might be different from what's given here). Both hold together so that you can make this ahead of time, press it into a pan, then cut it into shapes and brown them in coconut oil. If you're using a long-grain rice such as basmati or jasmine rice, the long grains won't stick to themselves. It will look as if they do, but when you go to cut and fry the pieces, they'll fall apart and you'll end up making fried rice—which, I must say, is really good, especially when you include gently sautéed soft tofu. Generally, if making this with long-grain rice, I serve it right from the pot it's cooked in.

I especially enjoy this rice with the Collards Simmered in Coconut Milk with Shallots (page 97) and the Golden Tofu with Orange and Yellow Peppers (page 242). Going in another direction altogether, I also like it with cumin-flavored black beans and pickled red onions. CONTINUED

1 can coconut milk plus water to make
2½ cups liquid (3 cups liquid total
if you're using basmati rice)

2 pinches of saffron threads

½ teaspoon turmeric

1½ cups medium- or short-grain rice

Sea salt and freshly ground pepper

5 slender scallions, including the greens,
thinly sliced

2 tablespoons toasted black sesame seeds

Coconut oil, if frying

Bring the coconut milk and water to a boil with the saffron and turmeric. Add the rice and 1 teaspoon of salt, cover the pan, and cook over low heat until the rice is done, in about 20 minutes.

Using a fork, gently toss in the scallions, season with pepper, then turn the rice into a 9 by 12-inch pan. Scatter the sesame seeds over the rice, then place plastic wrap or waxed paper over it and press firmly. Refrigerate until well chilled. (If you used a long-grain rice, plan to serve it from the pan it was cooked in.)

When ready to eat, cut the pressed rice into diamonds or other shapes and brown them in coconut oil.

BAKED RICOTTA INFUSED WITH THYME

Serves 4 to 6; GF

Since we live in the country, we can't really send those we've invited over for a glass of wine to their homes fueled only by alcohol. I feel strongly about offering them food, but food that's easy to put together, and this is often the spur-of-the-moment appetizer I'll make. It takes no time at all to put together—in fact, less time than the oven will take to heat, which is why I sometimes use my toaster oven.

I bake ricotta in a shallow Spanish earthenware dish so that the ricotta is no more than half an inch thick. If there's liquid on top when I open a tub, I pour it off. Formerly, I simply adorned the ricotta with crisscrossed branches of thyme, which you have to remove when serving. Now I tend to infuse the ricotta with fresh thyme leaves as well. But here are some other ideas:

- Lay small tips or branches of rosemary on the surface of the cheese (rosemary is strong).

- Scatter bread crumbs moistened in olive oil over the cheese to crisp and bake (or crisp the bread crumbs beforehand and add them when you serve the cheese).

- Enhance the surface with red pepper flakes, black pepper, or fresh or fried sage leaves.

- Serve the warm baked ricotta with crostini, roasted peppers, olives, or tapenade, a relish of cherry tomatoes, or the like.

When baked until golden and firm, the cheese can be cut into pieces (I like diamond shapes). It will be firm but tender and will still possess the ricotta's delicate flavor. Leftovers will look dry and hopeless, but they regain their supple tenderness when added to a soup or a pasta dish—becoming in fact, little dumplings. I assure you, none will be wasted.

Even though this is written as a recipe, I'll just go ahead and bake whatever I have. A whole pint of ricotta makes quite a bit, especially if you have other goodies to go along with it. One cup baked in a smallish dish should be plenty for four to six servings. CONTINUED

Olive oil	Coarsely ground pepper
1 cup ricotta	Red pepper flakes (optional)
8 sprigs thyme, plus 1 teaspoon or more plucked leaves	

Heat the oven or toaster oven to 375°F. Lightly oil a 2- to 3-cup, shallow baking dish. Pour off any liquid that may have risen around the cheese, then mix the ricotta with the plucked thyme leaves. Spread it evenly in the prepared dish. Drizzle the surface with more olive oil, arrange the thyme sprigs over the surface, and season with freshly cracked pepper. Bake, uncovered, until the top is golden and the sides start to pull away from the dish, 30 to 45 minutes, or longer if the layer of cheese is thicker. Let cool for 10 minutes, then pluck off the thyme sprigs, cut into squares or diamonds, and serve.

ROMESCO SAUCE

Makes 1½ cups; V

I first encountered this sauce on a trip to Spain and started making it when I got back to Santa Fe. I have been enthusiastic about it ever since. It's a sauce I often make in classes, because it's just so good and versatile. It happens to be vegan, but that's not why it's good. It also happens to have lots of good proteins and phytonutrients, but that's also not why it's good, either. It's rich, dynamic, and a bit zesty, with good sherry vinegar and plenty of garlic. It's an enticing mixture of hazelnuts, olive oil, tomato, and roasted peppers (among other ingredients), along with the aforementioned garlic and vinegar. You'll have no problem finding ways to use this up.

My favorite uses? Spread on garlic rubbed toast; over grilled leeks or onions; mounded on roasted fingerling potatoes or cauliflower or stirred into a potato-saffron stew. Really, it's good on just about everything.

What's different today? The recipe I originally used asked for fresh roma tomatoes, but they appear in the garden or market for only a very short time each year, and this is a sauce that's welcome year-round, and especially when the weather is cool. Supermarket romas are among the most disappointing of fruits: they look so red and promising, but they have no flavor at all. So now I use tomato paste. As a slapdash sort of cook, I've learned it's easy to err through excess, so here the paste is not heaped, but measured and tasted—it is so concentrated that if you're not careful, you'll end up with a pretty good tomato sauce.

I also have given up the almond-hazelnut mixture in favor of hazelnuts alone, because I enjoy their subtle and unusual flavor. Once roasted, they tease you—guess what we are? Almonds are a bit bland, but if you can't eat hazelnuts for some reason or can't get them, go for almonds: toast them first to bring out their flavor. And lastly, I can't help but make this with smoked paprika.

1 slice country-style white bread

Olive oil to fry the bread

Sea salt

½ cup hazelnuts, toasted and skins rubbed off as much as is easily possible

3 cloves garlic

1½ teaspoons ground red chile or pepper flakes

1 tablespoon tomato paste, plus a bit more as needed

1 tablespoon chopped parsley

1 teaspoon regular or smoked paprika

2 red bell peppers, roasted, peeled, and seeded (these can be jarred)

¼ cup sherry vinegar

½ cup best olive oil

Fry the bread in olive oil until golden and crisp. When cool, grind it with the hazelnuts and garlic in a food processor until fairly fine. Add the ground chile, tomato paste, parsley, paprika, and bell peppers, and process until smooth. With the machine running, gradually pour in the vinegar and then the olive oil. Taste and make sure the sauce has plenty of piquancy and enough salt. If you feel it needs a little more tomato paste, add it no more than a teaspoon at a time.

Roasted Fingerling Potatoes to Serve with Romesco Sauce

Here's a good little accompaniment to the romesco sauce. If you're serving them as an appetizer, two or three small fingerling potatoes should be enough. If you're serving them for dinner, make more.

Heat the oven to 400°F. Wash the potatoes, halve those that are especially large, and then toss them in olive oil with a few pinches of sea salt to coat lightly. If you wish, add sprigs of rosemary and/or bay leaves as well. Put them in a single layer in a lightly oiled baking dish or sheet pan and bake until tender when pierced with a knife, 25 minutes or so, depending on their size.

CHOPPED SALAD WITH TOASTED SEEDS AND MARJORAM-MINT DRESSING

Serves 1 or 2; GF

A chopped salad needn't necessarily be chopped. Some vegetables, like radishes, look more appealing sliced in paper-thin rounds. But what's important, besides the colorful variety that summer offers, is that the vegetables be easy to eat, together, in a single bite. It may be more attractive to arrange long, whole carrots or round radishes in their entirety, but then, how do you eat them? Think this out as you work.

Here are some ideas for what to use and how to cut it. As for exact amounts, you might want to allow as much as two cups of vegetables per person for a meal, less as a first course. Also, you can certainly include vegetables that aren't mentioned here, depending on your likes and the season—peas, asparagus tips, cauliflower florets, beets, seared shishito peppers, chopped Belgian endive leaves, purslane, salad turnips, and so forth. I sometimes include little cubes of ricotta salata or feta cheese along with pitted green olives or capers for more zing. Because most of the vegetables are raw and firm, those that aren't dressed can be bagged and used the next day—though not so much the tomatoes and avocado—best to do those fresh each time.

The Dressing

2 tablespoons red wine vinegar

¼ teaspoon sea salt

1 heaping tablespoon chopped marjoram

2 heaping teaspoons chopped mint leaves

⅓ cup or more best olive oil

⅓ cup diced feta or ricotta salata cheese

A trio of different-colored carrots (orange, red, and yellow), peeled and thinly sliced

1 cucumber, skin left on if not waxed, seeded and diced

Several radishes, one color or several, sliced in thin rounds

1 celery stalk, including the pale green leaves, sliced crosswise

1 sweet pepper or pimento, diced (any sweet pepper would be fine)

1 small fresh onion, sliced in rounds and tossed in vinegar to sweeten

3 tablespoons roasted sunflower seeds or pepitas (pumpkin seeds)

12 small tomatoes, different varieties (or just one variety), halved or quartered

1 small avocado, halved and diced

Sea salt and freshly ground pepper

TO MAKE THE DRESSING Put the vinegar in a bowl with the salt and let stand a few minutes. Add the herbs and then whisk in the oil. Stir in the cheese.

After you've cut all the vegetables into attractive pieces, put them in a bowl, minus the tomatoes and avocado.

Toss the vegetables with salt and pepper to taste and then with as much dressing as you need to dress the salad. Pour the remainder in a covered jar and use the following day.

Scatter the tomatoes, avocados, and pepitas over the surface and gently wiggle them into the rest of the salad.

SEA GREENS WITH CUCUMBERS, GINGER, AND SESAME

Serves 2; V, GF

I know that *seaweed* is the usual word, but we're so down on weeds that I prefer to use the term *sea greens*. I'm crazy for sea greens—all kinds—and I especially like this salad of mixed sea greens with ginger, sesame oil dressing, and cucumbers; or with roasted peanut oil and a garnish of roasted peanuts. You can buy a package of mixed greens and easily have this done in ten minutes. These premixed sea vegetables are very expensive and there's just a cup of them, but they practically double in size so it might be worth a splurge when you don't feel like assembling your own mix or you simply don't have any. You can also extend them with a handful of wakame or dulce.

You may wonder if Japanese seaweed is safe to eat since Fukishima; I've read quite a bit on the subject, and the consensus is that they're pretty much fine. But there are those who say they're not fine at all. You'll have to decide for yourself whether to use Pacific greens or find greens from the Atlantic.

1 cup dried mixed sea greens (about 20 grams)

1 scant teaspoon freshly grated ginger

1 tablespoon roasted sesame oil or roasted peanut oil

1 tablespoon rice vinegar

1 tablespoon soy sauce

1 tablespoon mirin or sugar

A 6-inch length of cucumber

Toasted sesame seeds or roasted peanuts

Put the dried sea greens in a bowl and cover generously with warm water. Leave them for 10 minutes while you make the dressing.

Combine the ginger, sesame or peanut oil, rice vinegar, soy, and mirin in a bowl or jar and shake to combine. Drain the sea greens, put them in a bowl, and toss with all but a tablespoon of the dressing.

Remove strips of the cucumber peel and then slice it on a mandoline into rounds. Toss them with the remaining dressing and arrange them on a plate. Taste the sea greens—they should be salty enough but that will depend on the soy sauce you used. Add more if need be. Toss and then arrange over the cucumbers. Garnish with the toasted sesame seeds (or the roasted peanuts).

SUMMER SQUASHES WITH HERB BLOSSOMS, BASIL, PINE NUTS, AND PARMIGIANO-REGGIANO

Serves 4; GF

Perhaps this is true for you, too: you go to the farmers' market and you come home with all these different kinds of squashes: pattypans; round zucchini; white, golden, pale green, and black ones; a pretty yellow Zephyr squash or two with their green tips; and so on. Maybe you were prudent and you only bought a few of each kind, so now you need to put them together in one dish. If you love their characteristic looks and personalities, you'll want to keep them intact when you cut them. Here's what I might do: I cut Zephyr squash lengthwise to preserve their yellow bodies and green tips. Cut crosswise, they could be anything. I also cut other zucchini lengthwise, unless they're Costata Romanesco, which has a flowerlike appearance if cut crosswise because of the ribs that run down the body of the squash. Pattypans and round zucchini look good cut from stem end to flower end so that you capture the bulges. Should you have a few crookneck squash, cut them lengthwise and try to capture the curve of their neck. Cut them all the same thickness and they'll cook in the same amount of time regardless of their different shapes.

One of my longtime favorite ways with summer squash is to fry them slowly in olive oil until golden and soft, then toss them with herbs and their blossoms. But I also like this much lighter way of preparing them, especially if the rest of the meal is going to be substantial.

When making this at the photo shoot, I used the purple blossoms of anise hyssop, Thai basil and chives as well as the basil leaves. Of course there are other alternatives—marjoram would be delicious, as would dill or mint along with the basil. You could omit the cheese altogether or use other kinds, such as spoonfuls of smooth ricotta, small spheres of mozzarella, crumbled feta cheese, and so forth. CONTINUED

1 pound or more mixed summer squash

Best olive oil

Sea salt and freshly ground pepper

Parmigiano-Reggiano or other cheese (see headnote)

¼ cup pine nuts, toasted in a dry skillet until golden

Herb blossoms, if available

10 large green or opal basil leaves, torn into pieces

Slice the different summer squash as suggested above, then steam them or simmer in salted water until tender. When the squash is done, arrange it on a platter, cut sides facing up. Drizzle olive oil over it and season with salt and pepper. Grate a veil of Parmigiano-Reggiano over the squash or slice it thinly as shown here, add the pine nuts, blossoms, and basil, and serve.

JAPANESE SWEET POTATO SOUP WITH GINGER, SMOKED SALT, AND AGED BALSAMIC VINEGAR

Serves 2 to 3; V, GF

I love the Asian varieties of sweet potatoes such as Hannah and Kotobuki. They're sweet, but not achingly so like reddish-orange Garnets and Jewels, and their flavor is akin to chestnut. They behave a little differently in other ways, too. The skins can be bitter, so you might choose to peel them. The flesh discolors when you cut it, so you might put cut pieces in water as you work.

In *Vegetable Literacy*, I made this soup with ghee, rosemary, and thyme, which are not usual seasonings for sweet potatoes. In the end, even though I didn't include any ginger in hopes of changing the flavor profile altogether, I could have sworn I tasted it. So here is a gingery version with an unusual finish of smoked salt and a true, aged balsamic vinegar. The soup is creamy textured and the color of ivory. It, along with its rosemary-infused predecessor, is one of my cold weather favorites.

2 tablespoons coconut oil

1 onion, sliced

3 tablespoons chopped peeled ginger

1 rounded tablespoon nutritional yeast (optional)

1 pound Hannah or Kotobuki or other Asian sweet potato variety, peeled and cut into chunks

Sea salt and freshly ground pepper

1 can full-fat coconut milk plus enough water to make 4 cups

Smoked salt

Aged balsamic vinegar

Melt 1½ tablespoons of the coconut oil in a soup pot. When it's hot, add the onion, ginger, and nutritional yeast. Give a stir and let everything cook over medium heat for a minute or two. Then add the sweet potatoes and 1 teaspoon of salt. Again, give a stir and lower the heat. Cook, stirring occasionally, for about 10 minutes, and then add the liquid. Bring to a boil and then lower the heat and simmer, covered, for 25 minutes. Let cool slightly, then purée, leaving a little texture if you wish or making it super smooth. Don't overpurée it, though, or the texture will be a little gummy.

Just before serving, heat the soup and stir in the final ½ tablespoon of coconut oil. Ladle into bowls or soup plates and add some pepper, a few pinches of smoked salt, and, finally, a few drops of the balsamic vinegar.

SWEET POTATO (OR PUMPKIN) PUDDING WITH SILKY PERSIMMON PURÉE

Serves 6

If I have any family traditions, persimmon pudding is one. I try to uphold our family's past, but some years I have to skip it, persimmons being hard to find where I live. Instead I turn to sweet potatoes for this tender pudding or, failing that, a purée of a really good winter squash or pumpkin. The sweet potato is more luscious, dark, and moist; the pumpkin or squash, yields a lighter-colored dish, as shown in the picture. All are finished with a persimmon purée and softly whipped cream.

I like to make my pudding with coconut sugar and coconut milk. It is of course divine served warm, but it's also fine to serve it at room temperature, which you might if you've baked your pudding in a bowl that leaves many inches at the top. If that's the case, let it cool before you turn it out onto a plate so that it won't crack or break when it drops.

For steaming, you will need a bowl or pudding mold with a 6- to 8-cup capacity.

The Pudding
½ cup unsalted butter or coconut oil

1 cup orange sweet potato purée

¾ cup coconut sugar

1 egg

2 teaspoons vanilla

½ cup coconut milk

⅜ teaspoon salt

1 cup all-purpose or white whole-wheat flour

1 teaspoon baking soda

1 rounded teaspoon cinnamon

The Whipped Cream
1 cup whipping cream (or less)

1 teaspoon vanilla

1 tablespoon honey or powdered sugar, to taste (optional)

2 to 4 tablespoons brandy (optional)

The Silky Persimmon Purée
1 large, soft Hachiya persimmon

1 tablespoon honey or maple sugar, to taste

1 teaspoon fresh lemon juice, to taste

A pinch of sea salt

FOR THE PUDDING Select a bowl for your pudding. It can be made of crockery, metal, or glass. Make sure it fits in a second pan when covered with a lid. Place a small inverted bowl (or the lid of a canning jar or a small tuna fish can with both ends removed) in the pan for your mold to sit on so that it's perched over the heat and not sitting on the pan itself. **CONTINUED**

Melt the butter or oil. Generously brush some of it over the pudding bowl and set it on the inverted bowl or canning jar lid. Bring a teakettle of water to a boil.

Combine the sweet potato with the remaining melted butter, sugar, egg, vanilla, coconut milk, and salt. Purée, or whisk together. Mix the dry ingredients together and then whisk them into the wet ingredients.

Pour the batter into the pudding bowl and cover it tightly with plastic wrap. Add the boiling water so that it comes up two-thirds the height of the bowl. Then cover the pan and simmer for 1½ hours. When the pudding is done, a cake tester inserted will come out clean. Remove the pudding from the water, let it cool some (or thoroughly if the bowl is large), then invert it onto a serving plate. If you're not ready to serve, leave the mold resting on the pudding so that it will retain its heat. Whip the cream and make the persimmon purée.

FOR THE WHIPPED CREAM Gently whip the cream until it barely holds soft peaks. Whisk in the vanilla and honey and brandy, if using. Don't let the cream get hard. You want soft drifts.

FOR THE PERSIMMON PURÉE Halve the persimmon and remove any seeds. Set aside a few persimmon chunks, then purée the rest until smooth. Stir in the honey or sugar, lemon juice, and a pinch of salt. Taste and add more sugar or lemon juice, if desired. Makes about 1 cup.

To serve, dust the pudding with powdered sugar. Make the plate festive with holly or pine or whatever winter greens you wish. Slice into pieces and spoon over the persimmon puree and a spoonful of the cream.

SWEET POTATO AND COCONUT-MILK CURRY WITH PANEER

Serves 4; GF

This recipe is good, simple, and virtually effortless to make; it features cubes of the Indian cheese paneer, which actually looks a lot like cubes of tofu. I like it with paneer or tofu, so I give you the choice. Paneer has a simple, delicate dairy flavor, not unlike ricotta although it is firm rather than soft. I'm able to buy it at a market where it's sold frozen and already cut into cubes. I just use it directly from the freezer.

Another change from the original recipe has to do with the tomatoes. Roma tomatoes are so awful except in summer (when they might be local) that I wanted to replace them with another vegetable, one that I'd prefer to eat in the winter when this braise appeals. Hence I use sweet potatoes, previously steamed, which I always have on hand, just like I have steamed beets on hand in the summer. Any variety of sweet potato will be good, but I particularly like the small Asian sweet potatoes with purple skin and pale chestnut-colored flesh, as well as orange-fleshed Jewels with darker red skin. Why not use both together? Whichever you choose, buy organic, scrub them well, and leave the skins on. Steam them until they're almost completely tender, even a day or two ahead of time.

Tamarind gives the dish welcome tartness but darkens the color to a rusty ochre rather than the yellow you might expect in a curry. However, slices of red jalapeño or whole Thai chiles, scallions, coarsely ground pepper or red pepper flakes, plus a sprinkling of black sesame seeds and a cluster of fresh cilantro leaves, pick everything up in terms of both color and flavor. A good, strong Japanese soy or Chinese mushroom soy sauce provides a rich, round seasoning and can be added at the table to taste.

I love this braise served over rice with plenty of sauce, perhaps a spoonful of chutney, and, almost for sure, some toasted cashews.

4 ounces cubed paneer or 1-pound carton (more or less) soft tofu

1 (15-ounce) can full-fat coconut milk

2 teaspoons light brown cane sugar or coconut sugar

Sea salt

1 tablespoon ground coriander seed

2 teaspoons curry powder

A scant ½ teaspoon turmeric

1 large clove garlic, crushed or minced

2 teaspoons grated ginger

1 teaspoon tamarind paste, or more, to taste

About 1½ pounds steamed sweet potatoes, halved lengthwise and cut diagonally into two-bite chunks

4 scallions, including the firm greens, sliced on the diagonal

1 red or green jalapeño, cut into narrow strips

Freshly ground pepper or red pepper flakes

A small handful of chopped cilantro

Toasted black sesame seeds

Soy sauce

If you're using frozen paneer, take it from the freezer to begin thawing; it will finish cooking in the sauce. If you're using tofu, drain it and then cut it into 1-inch cubes. There's no need to blot the tofu dry, as it won't be fried, though you can cook it in a nonstick skillet until it turns golden in its own fat.

Empty the coconut milk into a 10-inch skillet and add the sugar, ½ teaspoon of salt, coriander, curry, turmeric, garlic, and ginger. (If the coconut milk seems especially thick, swish out the can with half its volume of water and pour it into the pan.) Bring to a simmer for a few minutes and then add the sweet potatoes, paneer or tofu, and chile. Add the tamarind paste in dabs here and there, especially if it's very thick and stiff. It will soon soften, and you can swirl it about in the finished sauce. Lower the heat and simmer until everything is thoroughly warmed through, about 10 minutes. Taste for salt.

Garnish with the slivered scallions, freshly ground pepper or pepper flakes, cilantro, and toasted sesame seeds. Serve with soy sauce on the table so that each person can add it to his or her own taste.

PAN-GRIDDLED SWEET POTATOES
WITH MISO-GINGER SAUCE

Serves 4; V, GF

I think of this miso-ginger sauce as a universal sauce because it's so good on so many things—tofu, tempeh, winter squash, and napa cabbage salads, for starters. And it's a great dressing for sweet potatoes, even those that are super sweet, like Jewel and Garnet varieties. If I can suggest a menu, I'd add some spicy Asian greens for a side or some stir-fried bok choy, and maybe some soba noodles or brown or black rice. Not surprisingly, the sauce is good on them, too.

4 sweet potatoes (about 6 ounces each), scrubbed

1 clove garlic, chopped

A 1-inch knob of fresh ginger, peeled and grated

A few pinches of sugar or 2 teaspoons mirin

1 heaping tablespoon white miso

1 tablespoon light sesame oil, plus more for the pan

1 tablespoon toasted sesame oil

1 tablespoon unseasoned rice wine vinegar

1 tablespoon water

2 teaspoons toasted black sesame seeds

Steam the sweet potatoes until tender, 30 to 40 minutes, depending on their size. While they're cooking, make the sauce: pound the garlic and ginger in a mortar until very smooth and then add the sugar, miso, vinegar, sesame oils, and water.

When the sweet potatoes are tender, halve them lengthwise and score the tops in a crisscross pattern with a small knife. Brown them, cut side down, in a pan or a ridged skillet in a little light sesame oil. Their natural sugars will caramelize and turn an appetizing golden brown.

Arrange the sweet potatoes on plates or a platter and spoon the sauce over them. Garnish with the sesame seeds and serve alone or with any accompaniment you like.

TOFU AND CILANTRO SALAD WITH ROASTED PEANUTS

Serves 4; V, GF

This is definitely for cilantro lovers. If that's not you—and there are those who loathe this herb—please go to another recipe. But if cilantro has your name on it, and you happen to grow it or find huge bolting bunches at a farmers' market, consider using the little green buds that form after the blooms. They are delicious to bite on, a mysterious combination of cilantro and coriander, yet not quite either. They're also pretty scattered over the finished dish, as are the cilantro blossoms.

I learned this recipe from Bruce Cost many years ago, but now when I make it, I use less oil, and instead of frying the peanuts, I use salty blister peanuts, which are crisp and crunchy and not at all greasy. This is a product that was not easy to find, if at all, when I first made this dish.

1-pound carton (more or less) firm tofu, drained and pressed on a clean towel to remove most of the water

1 teaspoon sugar

Sea salt

Roasted peanut oil

1 very large bunch of cilantro, most of the stems removed

½ cup blister peanuts

1½ tablespoons soy sauce

Red pepper flakes

2 teaspoons roasted peanut oil or roasted sesame oil

Cilantro buds and flowers, if available

Cut the tofu into cubes somewhat smaller than ½ inch. Set a good nonstick pan or cast-iron skillet over medium-high heat. When it's hot, add the tofu and cook, turning it occasionally, until golden on all sides. Turn off the heat and toss the tofu with the sugar, some salt, and a teaspoon of the roasted peanut oil.

Give the cilantro a good rinse. Bring a quart of water to a boil. Add the cilantro and push it under the surface, then immediately pour it into a colander and cool it under cold running water. Squeeze out the excess moisture and chop finely by hand or in a small food processor.

Add the peanuts and chopped cilantro to the tofu, along with 2 tablespoons of the roasted peanut oil and the soy sauce. Toss well, taste, add more soy or salt if needed, and give a good dash of pepper flakes. Garnish with any coriander buds and cilantro blossoms you might have.

TOFU TRIANGLES WITH RED ONIONS AND TENDER GREENS

Serves 4; V, GF

This is a take-off on my Tofu Bachelor Sandwich with caramelized onions, mustard, and horseradish. You can still put all of this between bread with those condiments, but you can also put it on a plate for a weeknight dinner. When a neighbor gave me an armload of mixed greens from his greenhouse, I knew they'd be delicious wilted into sautéed red onions, and they were. The onions and greens were also good served on top of a bowl of polenta the next day. In fact, you could have all three items on a single plate and be a happy camper.

You'll want firm tofu that's strong enough not to fall apart in the skillet, but not extra-firm, which, to me, is a bit too dense. (See my tofu notes on page 25.) You might use just one type of green (such as spinach) or a mixture (such as tender turnip greens, young kale, beet greens, broccoli raab, and so forth). The exact kind or amount isn't crucial, but they should be very young and tender, and you'll want several big handfuls of leaves.

1 large red onion, sliced about ¼ inch thick

Olive oil

Sea salt and freshly ground pepper

8 ounces (more or less) tender, very young greens, such as spinach

Apple cider or sherry vinegar

1-pound (more or less) carton firm tofu, drained

2 tablespoons Worcestershire sauce or a little tamari

Sautéed red peppers, to serve (optional)

Cooked polenta, to serve (optional)

Peel and slice the onion. Warm 1 tablespoon of olive oil in a wide, deep skillet. Add the onion, give a stir, and start cooking over fairly high heat, stirring occasionally. As the onion slices begin to get some color, season with salt and pepper, lower the heat, and continue cooking until they've softened, after about 15 minutes in all.

While the onion is cooking, slice any long stems off the greens. When the onion is done, add the greens to the pan and cook until they're tender; this will take more time the more mature they are. Taste for salt and add a teaspoon or two of vinegar, to taste.

Slice the tofu diagonally into eight pieces, slightly less than ½ inch thick. Set the pieces on paper towels to drain, briefly. Don't worry about the tofu getting really dry. It will dry as it cooks.

Heat a cast-iron skillet that's wide enough to hold all the tofu. Brush the pan with a little oil and add the tofu. Season well with salt and pepper. Cook over medium-high heat until golden, about 3 minutes, then turn. Brush the Worcestershire sauce or tamari over the surface and turn the tofu once. Continue frying until the sauce is absorbed and the tofu is laced with fine glaze. Turn off the heat.

To serve, mound the onion and greens mixture on four plates, and lay two slices of tofu on top of each mound. Serve with a mound of polenta or with sautéed red peppers. Both add color, substance, and flavor.

GOLDEN TOFU WITH ORANGE AND YELLOW PEPPERS

Makes 4 good-sized portions; V, GF

This braise has made something of a departure from its original form in *This Can't Be Tofu!*, with the emphasis settling more on the orange and yellow peppers and on good-tasting tomatoes in their season. But of course, red peppers are also so good, and green peppers, with their somewhat more tart flavor, are good as well, though sharper. I've made this both with and without coconut milk. If you've set aside some coconut cream or a little extra coconut milk from another dish, go ahead and add it to make a sauce. If you don't have it but you have pretty much everything else, don't worry about it and just use water.

For tofu, I use either medium or firm tofu from an Asian market. It is not as dense as many American brands and comes out delicate and almost quivery, especially the softer tofu. If you are using that extra-firm American tofu, it's sturdy enough that you can toss it in curry powder (using twice as much) before browning it.

Yes, the ingredient list looks formidable, but it moves right along. It's only the vegetables, really, that need dicing and chopping. The tofu takes but a moment to turn into cubes.

This tofu braise is excellent served with the equally golden Yellow Coconut Rice with Scallions and Black Sesame Seeds (see page 213), whether it's formed into cakes and browned or served fresh from the pot.

1-pound carton (more or less) medium or firm tofu, preferably an Asian brand	1 jalapeño seeded, stemmed, and cut into lengthwise strips
Coconut oil	1 heaping tablespoon diced ginger
Sea salt	3 plump garlic cloves, slivered
½ teaspoon curry powder	1 teaspoon ground roasted cumin
Juice of 1 lime	2 teaspoons ground, roasted coriander
1 large orange pepper	¼ teaspoon turmeric
1 large yellow pepper	½ cup coconut milk or water, or more
3 or 4 ripe, good roma tomatoes	A handful of coarsely chopped cilantro leaves
1 onion, diced into ½-inch squares	

First drain the tofu, then cut it into large, irregular cubes. Heat an 10-inch nonstick skillet. If you like, you can add a teaspoon or so of oil for flavor, but the tofu will brown without it. Add the tofu to the pan and cook over medium-high heat, shuffling the pan back and forth and turning the pieces so that all are eventually golden. When they are handsomely colored, season them with several pinches of salt and scatter over the curry powder. Add a squeeze of lime and set aside.

Slice the bell peppers lengthwise into sixths, then cut into large, irregular pieces that are visually bold yet comfortable to eat. Halve the tomatoes lengthwise, scoop out the seeds and juice, and then cut them into a small dice, slightly less than ½ inch cubed.

Heat 2 tablespoons of the oil in a pan with fairly high sides over medium-high heat. When hot, add the onion, stir it about, and cook for 5 to 7 minutes, or until softened. Next add the peppers, jalapeño, garlic, ginger, coriander, and turmeric. Cook until the peppers have softened some, then season with a teaspoon of salt. If you feel the pan has become too dry, add the ½ cup of water or coconut milk to prevent burning. This will also produce a little sauce.

Finally, add the tofu and the tomatoes. Gently turn so that all the ingredients are amalgamated but not broken, then serve, showered with the cilantro.

TOMATO AND RED PEPPER TART
IN A YEASTED CRUST

Makes one 10- or 11-inch tart

A savory jam of sweet late-summer vegetables makes for a very succulent tart. A bit of time is involved since you're doing it all from scratch, so think of this as a special offering at the table and, by all means, wait until produce is at its best. Late summer is the time to make this, when sweet plump peppers are in the market and roma tomatoes have a chance of actually being good. Winter? Don't bother.

The time involved in making the filling will give a yeasted dough time to rise; so start the dough first, unless you wish to make the filling hours ahead of time. A yeast-risen dough allows you to use olive oil, and it's easy to make. Such doughs are angelic to handle plus they end up with golden, sculpted surfaces. However, you must roll it very thin if you don't want a big doughy crust at the end.

An egg contributes to the strength and suppleness of the dough, but if you don't eat eggs, you can replace it with 3 tablespoons of water and 1 tablespoon of oil. As for flour, use whatever mixture of flour appeals to you—rye, toasted barley, quinoa, or spelt flour might go into a mix along with wheat flour or a gluten-free mixture.

You will have dough left over. It's hard to make less, but you can refrigerate it and use it later for impromptu dinner rolls or a pizza crust. CONTINUED

The Yeasted Dough

1 package (2¼ teaspoons) active dry yeast

½ teaspoon sugar

½ cup warm water

3 tablespoons olive oil

1 egg, lightly beaten

⅜ teaspoon salt

1¾ cups all-purpose flour, white whole-wheat flour, or a mixture, including spelt, rye, or other flours

The Tart Filling

2 tablespoons olive oil

2 large red onions, finely diced

2 plump garlic cloves, minced or pounded to a paste

1½ pounds ripe roma or other paste tomatoes, peeled, seeded, and chopped

3 large red bell peppers, roasted and peeled; 2 diced, 1 cut into thin strips

A good pinch of saffron threads, if possible

¼ teaspoon aniseed

Sea salt and freshly ground pepper

2 tablespoons chopped basil

16 Niçoise olives, pitted

TO MAKE THE YEASTED DOUGH Dissolve the yeast and sugar in the water and let stand until it's bubbly, about 10 minutes. Whisk the oil, egg, and salt together with the proofed yeast, then stir in the flour. When the dough is too stiff to work with a spoon, turn it onto a lightly floured counter and knead until smooth and elastic, about 4 minutes. Add flour to keep it from sticking, but aim to keep the dough on the wet and tacky side. (If you live in a very dry climate, your flour will be extra dry and you may not be able to use entire amount called for.) Set the dough in an oiled bowl and turn it over to coat, cover with a towel or a shower cap and let rise until doubled in bulk, 45 minutes to an hour, depending on how warm your kitchen is.

Turn the dough out. Roll it out into a thin circle (or other shape appropriate to the pan you're using) and line a tart shell with it. If you're not ready to fill the tart just then, put in the refrigerator so that it doesn't continue to rise.

TO MAKE THE TART FILLING Warm the oil over medium heat in a wide skillet, add the onions, and cook until soft, about 15 minutes, stirring occasionally. Add the garlic, tomatoes, and diced peppers along with the crumbled saffron threads and aniseed. Season with ½ teaspoon of salt and a little pepper. Cook for 30 minutes, stirring occasionally, especially toward the end. It should be quite thick. Taste for salt and stir in the basil.

Heat the oven to 400°F. Set the tart shell on a baking sheet. Add the filling to the shell and smooth it out. Use the pepper strips to make a crisscross design over the top. Place the olives in the spaces formed by the peppers. Bake for 35 minutes. Carefully unmold the tart onto a platter and serve warm or at room temperature.

SWEET-TART SUN GOLD TOMATO SOUP WITH AVOCADO RELISH

Makes 4 small portions; V, GF

Long before we had Sun Gold tomatoes and the plethora of heirlooms and sun-ripened tomatoes that can now be bought or grown and picked at home, I published a different chilled tomato soup in my second book, *The Savory Way*. It was based on a can of chilled tomato juice, probably the best possibility at that time. Actually, it is quite good with the avocado, lime, and sour cream, and if you don't have access to any good tomatoes, you might consider using canned (preferably organic) tomato juice. It's of course, super-fast.

The tiny supersweet Sun Gold tomatoes have been appearing at the market for at least the past fifteen years, but people are still over the moon about them. Is it their sweetness? Their cuteness? The fact that you buy these orange-gold spheres tucked in bright green pint baskets? It could be all of the above, but I suspect that it's mostly their sweetness that people like. "They are like candy!" shoppers say. I like them too, and always grow them, although I find that their sweetness can be a bit overwhelming, which is why there is vinegar in this soup.

I first had Sun Gold tomatoes in a chilled soup at Casa Blanca restaurant in Cambridge, Massachusetts, where Anna Sortun was cooking before she opened her own restaurant. She tempered their sweetness with a bit of Chardonnay vinegar, making, in effect, a sweet-tart soup. I further soften the flavors by including a fine dice of avocado, but today I don't always include the serrano chile that I did originally. It's just somehow too much.

You don't need a lot of this soup—it's intense. Less than a half-cup is enough for a stimulating, eye-opening start to a summer meal on a hot day. You might decide to amplify it, however, by including a few spoonfuls of cooked black quinoa, black rice, or smoky freekeh. **CONTINUED**

2 pints Sun Gold tomatoes

2 shallots, finely diced and divided

Sea salt and freshly ground pepper

2 to 3 tablespoons Chardonnay vinegar or champagne vinegar

1 firm avocado, diced into small pieces

2 tablespoons best olive oil

1 tablespoon slivered basil leaves, marjoram, or cilantro

Pluck and discard the stems from the tomatoes and then rinse them. Put them in a heavy saucepan with a tight-fitting lid with half of the shallots, ½ teaspoon of salt, and 1 cup of water. Cook over medium-high heat, keeping one ear inclined to the pot. Once you hear the tomatoes popping, take a peek to make sure there's sufficient moisture in the pan so the tomatoes don't scorch. If the skins are slow to pop and give up the tomato juice, add a few extra tablespoons of water as a precaution. Once the tomatoes release their juices, lower the heat and cook gently for 25 minutes.

Run the tomatoes through a food mill. You'll have about 2 cups of thick purée. Chill well, then taste for salt.

Just before serving, combine the remaining shallots in a bowl with the vinegar, avocado, olive oil, and herbs. Season with a pinch or two of salt and some pepper. Spoon the soup into small cups or bowls, divide the shallot-avocado mixture among them, and serve.

THREE TOMATO SAUCES

V, GF

Here are three very simple sauces you can make with canned or fresh tomatoes. These are not long-cooking nor are they seasoned heavily with vegetables and herbs. They are just very basic, tomato-based sauces to pull together without a fuss.

A Sauce Made with Canned Tomatoes

2 tablespoons olive oil

1 clove garlic, crushed

1 (15-ounce) can organic diced tomatoes or Italian plum tomatoes, diced

A few pinches of dried or a teaspoon fresh oregano or marjoram

1 teaspoon tomato paste, or more, to taste

Sea salt and freshly ground pepper

Heat the oil in a sturdy skillet with the garlic. When you can smell the garlic, add the tomatoes with their juices and cook over a lively heat, smashing them against the pan to break up some of the chunks. Add the herbs and stir in the tomato paste to fortify the sauce. Season to taste with salt and pepper. Leave chunky or purée, as you like.

A Sauce Made with Fresh Tomatoes

When the tomatoes are coming on strong, whether I have five or fifty, I make this the same way. Paste tomatoes naturally make a thicker sauce as they are drier fleshed, but I often mix varieties, which is another way of saying, I use what I have.

Cut the tomatoes in half or in chunks and put them in a heavy pan with a few tablespoons of water. Cover the pot, turn the heat to medium-high, and cook until they're broken down and have given up their juice. This might take about 25 minutes. (Usually I'm doing this late at night, so I turn off the heat and go to bed, leaving them on the stove to cool, though you can do this all as one step.) Pass the tomatoes through a food mill.

If you have a very watery, thin sauce, return the pot to the heat and simmer until some of the water has cooked away and it is has more body. If it seems thick enough already, go ahead and season it with salt to taste. At this point, you can season it with garlic, fresh herbs, or whatever appeals. If you've made a lot of sauce and are doing so over a period of weeks, decant it into zip-lock bags and freeze it. I find that a two-cup portion is fine for most recipes. I don't season it until I'm cooking a particular dish; then I add the appropriate fat, herb, garlic, and so on, for what I'm making.

An Oven-Roasted Tomato Sauce

A 30-pound box of big, gorgeous Astina tomatoes arrived in the mail, sent by farmers Anthony and Carol Boutard of Gaston, Oregon. In subsequent emails about making sauce from fresh tomatoes was Carol's brief description of how she makes hers. I tried it and really liked the results, which were thick and sweet.

Take your tomatoes, however many you have, and slice them in half. Put them in a spacious baking dish and bake at 225°F for about 12 hours, or until they have broken down completely.

As they cook they will release a liquid, which you can pour off and save to use as the basis for a soup. Don't be surprised if it's a bit gelatinous.

When the tomatoes are soft and mushy, pass them through a food mill. You'll end up with a thick, luscious sauce plus the tomato water to use in a soup. You can season the sauce later, assuming you have enough to can or freeze, to go with whatever dish you're making.

TOMATO AND ROASTED CAULIFLOWER CURRY WITH PANEER

Serves 4 to 6; V, GF

This is a relatively new dish for me and one I find myself making frequently. Of course, changes are bound to occur with recipes you make often, and this version incorporates those extras. For example, I now toss the cauliflower florets in melted coconut oil or ghee with turmeric, black pepper, and salt before roasting it. The roasted cauliflower is irresistible on its own, but the turmeric and pepper add another layer of flavor to the dish. (The cauliflower is also very good with a curry mayonnaise, like the one on page 100.)

Another change is that instead of canned diced tomatoes, I use a very simple sauce of the summer's tomatoes, cooked, passed through a food mill, then reduced a bit (see page 250). I freeze it in zip-lock bags to use over the winter. A cup, more or less, will be ample. It lacks the chunks of diced tomatoes, but, as my husband says, "Somehow this is extra-good!" Indeed, the sauce *is* richer and denser.

I often add a half-cup or more of cubed paneer during the last ten minutes. This mild, Indian cheese offers another texture, and its delicacy is enjoyable against the flavors of the rest of the dish.

Serve it over toasted-then-simmered quinoa or white, brown, or black rice, garnished with cilantro and a quarter lime on the side for those who find it wants a little extra acid. CONTINUED

The Cauliflower

2 tablespoons coconut oil or ghee

1 cauliflower, cut into large florets
(1½ pounds is not too large for six)

¾ teaspoon turmeric

1 teaspoon peppercorns, ground

¾ teaspoon salt

The Tomato Base

1½ tablespoons coconut oil or ghee

1 teaspoon cumin seeds

1 bay leaf

1 plump garlic clove, pounded into a paste
with a pinch of salt or finely minced

2 teaspoons grated or finely minced ginger

1 large onion, very finely diced

1 tablespoon ground coriander

1 teaspoon garam masala

½ teaspoon turmeric

2 small red chiles, sliced lengthwise up to
the stem, seeds removed for less heat

About 1 cup cooked, puréed tomatoes
(see headnote) or 1 (15-ounce) can diced
tomatoes with their juices

Sea salt

About ½ cup cubed paneer (optional)

¼ cup minced cilantro

¼ lime per person

Heat the oven to 425°F.

TO PREPARE THE CAULIFLOWER Melt the coconut oil or ghee in a wide pan, then add the cauliflower. Turn it in the melted fat, then add the rest of the ingredients and toss all together. Roast for 20 minutes, turning at least once, until golden. Remove and set aside until needed.

TO MAKE THE TOMATO BASE Melt the oil or ghee in a shallow braising pan. When it's hot, add the cumin seeds and bay leaf. Allow the seeds to sizzle, then add the garlic and ginger and stir them about the pan for 20 to 30 seconds. Reduce the heat to medium and add the onion. Cook, stirring occasionally, until the onion has begun to color and soften, 8 to 10 minutes.

Stir in the coriander, garam masala, turmeric, and chiles, and then add the tomato and 1 cup of water. Scrape up any darkened bits on the bottom of the pan, add ½ teaspoon of salt, and simmer, covered, for 5 minutes. Add the cauliflower pieces to the pan, cover again, and reduce the heat to low. Cook gently until the cauliflower is done and the flavors are well amalgamated, after 10 to 15 minutes, adding the paneer during the last ten minutes. (It's fine to submerge or turn the cauliflower florets in the tomato, and to do this an hour or more in advance of serving.)

Spoon the dish over cooked quinoa or rice, shower the cilantro over it, and add a chunk of lime to the side of each serving.

ROASTED TOMATOES AND FINGERLING POTATOES WITH THYME, OLIVES, AND CAPERS

Serves 4; V, GF

This is, with some changes, an old recipe that we used to make at Greens, based on one I had found in Salvador Dali's *Les Diners de Gala*. The amount of oil I used then is really just too much, and certainly no cheese is needed, as I originally suggested. Once again, when vegetarian cooking was new in America, cheese was what we turned to to make the dishes feel substantial.

I wanted to include it in this collection as a summer dish because we have so many kinds of potatoes available today, among them many varieties of fingerlings. My favorite fingerling is one with exceptional melting yellow flesh—La Ratte. But I would happily use Rose Finn Apple or any other golden-fleshed fingerling potato. Why summer? Because that's when the potato harvest comes in and when potatoes are close to divine—and also because tomatoes are finally good and in season as well. Avoid using low-acid yellow or orange tomatoes here.

If you're inclined to make this in the winter with storage potatoes, they're fine, but winter tomatoes are not. Just leave them out and be sure to finish with a splash of vinegar. Herbs and garlic are also plentiful in summer, and the garlic cloves are firm and free of sprouts. Originally I made this with lemon thyme, but I can't seem to grow it where I live, at least thus far, so a little lemon peel adds its zest. You might prefer to flavor this dish with torn basil leaves or marjoram, and both would be excellent.

Serve this warm or at room temperature with some spicy salad greens or, if you're inclined, a grilled grass-finished steak. CONTINUED

1 pound fingerling potatoes, more or less the same size

Sea salt and freshly ground pepper

3 good-sized ripe tomatoes

2 tablespoons olive oil

1 large red or yellow onion, sliced about ¼ inch thick

¼ teaspoon dried thyme

½ teaspoon toasted fennel seeds

4 thin strips of lemon zest (removed with a vegetable peeler, then slivered)

3 cloves garlic, peeled and thinly sliced

½ cup olives (Niçoise, kalamata, or your favorite), pitted and halved

2 tablespoons capers

12 thyme branches

Red wine vinegar or 1 lemon, quartered

Heat the oven to 400°F.

Wash the potatoes, then slice them in half lengthwise. If any are a lot larger than the rest, slice them in thirds so that the pieces are more or less the same size. Bring 6 cups of water to a boil. Add 1 tablespoon of salt, then the potatoes. When the boil returns, cook for 4 minutes, then scoop the potatoes out and set them aside in a strainer.

Drop the tomatoes into the same pot for about 10 seconds, then remove them to a bowl of water and peel off the skins. Halve them crosswise and gently squeeze out the seeds, then cut the walls into large pieces. Finely chop the cores.

Warm half the olive oil in a skillet set over medium-high heat. When it's hot, add the onions along with the dried thyme and fennel seeds. Cook, tossing them in the pan, until they begin to soften in color, after about 5 minutes. Turn off the heat, add the lemon zest, and season with salt and pepper.

Lightly oil an 8-cup gratin dish. Spread half the onions, the minced tomato cores, and half of the larger pieces of tomato, garlic, olives, capers, and thyme branches in the dish. Cover with the potatoes and the remaining tomatoes and tuck in the remaining slivers of garlic. Season with salt and pepper. Cover the potatoes with the remaining onions and wiggle in the rest of the thyme, olive, and capers. Drizzle a little oil over the potatoes, cover with foil, and bake for 25 minutes. Remove the foil and bake another 10 minutes, or until the potatoes are done. Put out vinegar or lemon quarters for those who wish a little more acid.

A ROUGH-AND-READY TURNIP SOUP, REFINED

Serves 3 to 4; GF

Transformations are bound to happen if you stray from your kitchen. A rough and chunky turnip soup came about because I put the soup vegetables on to cook, then rushed outside to clean up my garden. When I came in most of the liquid had simmered away, leaving a rustic looking potage. I actually liked its looks and taste and have stayed with it, albeit more intentionally, over the years. But I also like this more refined version, which requires that you stay closer to, if not actually by, your soup. And if I do that, I'm more likely to serve it to others.

Although there were some promising elements for a quick stock, I didn't bother to make one, and I don't for this version either. There's plenty of flavor from the vegetables alone. Just try to use organic potatoes so that you can safely leave the skins on. They give color, texture, and other good qualities to the soup.

This is a late fall–winter soup, when there are most likely no turnip greens to add, although broccoli raab could stand in for some, simmered until tender, then chopped and stirred in at the finish. Originally I made this with leeks, which I recommend if you have access to them. But just use an onion if leeks aren't available. The funny thing is that when I made this soup for a party, I overheard some guests speculating that it was leek and potato soup, never suspecting turnips lurking behind the scents of rosemary and thyme, and the absence of leeks!

During the past few years, Japanese salad turnips, Hakurei turnips, have become popular. They're mild, delicious raw, and needn't be peeled. In our farmers' market, these little gems have nearly replaced the more common and aggressive-tasting turnips with their thick skin and purple top. But it's the latter type that is my preference for this soup. They have character. Look for them.

1 large onion, coarsely chopped,
or 3 leeks, the white parts, finely sliced

2 russet potatoes
(enough for 3 cups chopped)

3 hefty purple-topped turnips
(enough for 4 cups chopped)

1½ tablespoons butter

2 bushy thyme sprigs

A 5-inch branch of rosemary or a heaping
teaspoon of finely chopped leaves

1 bay leaf

5½ cups water

Sea salt and freshly ground pepper

¼ cup cream (optional)

Chop or slice the onion or leeks. (Be sure to wash the leeks well.) Scrub the potatoes, quarter them lengthwise, and chop them. Peel the turnips, then cut them into chunks about the same size as the potatoes.

Melt the butter in a soup pot and add the herbs. Let them sizzle a bit to flavor the butter, then add the onion, potatoes, and turnips. Give them a toss and cook for 5 minutes or so over medium heat, then add the water and 1½ teaspoons of salt. Bring to a boil, then simmer until the vegetables are tender, 25 to 30 minutes.

Purée about two-thirds of the soup. Break up the chunks of remaining vegetables with a potato masher, then pour the puréed soup back into the pot. Pour in the cream and swirl it around. Taste for salt and season with pepper.

BRAISED SUMMER VEGETABLES

Makes 6 generous servings; V, GF

This is the kind of dish I'm apt to make throughout the summer, which means it changes as different vegetables come into season or finish, and as different vegetables appear in seed catalogues, farmers' markets, and the garden. When I first started making this, we didn't have the variety of vegetables that we have today. I'm especially thinking of carrots, which now come in all shades from white to pale yellow, rich yellow, orange, and scarlet. A mixture of those alone would be so pretty. And while big onions are fine, whole shallots or cipollini onions would be even better. Tomatoes can be so many shapes, colors, and sizes, from tiny sweet Sun Golds or Black Cherries— added at the very end—to big, meaty heirlooms peeled and seeded, their walls neatly sliced. Peppers could be bells, pimentos, Corno di Toro, or other kinds of big chiles. The squash, too, could be many different varieties and types. But to me, it's the shelling beans that are the signature of this dish, be they fava beans, fresh black-eyed peas, or cannellini beans, a handful or a mound. They're simmered separately and added to the rest of the dish once it's more or less done cooking. They will look far more dramatic before they are cooked, but they add a special texture to the dish.

Whatever the particulars of your garden or market, this dish more or less cooks itself. In the end, the vegetables will be tender-soft, the flavors big and aromatic. As for amounts, these are merely suggestions. You may not have any of one vegetable but lots of another, so adjust accordingly. Serve it with a sauce, such as the marjoram sauce on page 152, a basil purée or pesto, or a homemade garlic mayonnaise. This version is finished with simmered, peeled fava beans and small tomatoes, halved. CONTINUED

12 small carrots, different colors, scrubbed or peeled

Olive oil

2 bay leaves

5 thyme sprigs

10 shallots or small cipollini onions, peeled and left whole

4 plump garlic cloves, peeled and halved

Sea salt and freshly ground pepper

1 pound fingerling potatoes, halved lengthwise

8 ounces fresh green or yellow beans, stems cut off (the tips can stay), cut into 3-inch lengths

1 pound or more tomatoes, different colors and/or varieties, peeled, seed, and cut neatly into large pieces, juices reserved, cores minced

Sweet peppers (1 bell, or 1 Corno di Toro, or 2 pimento), sliced into 1-inch strips or pieces

4 small summer squash, halved and cut diagonally into large chunks

1 to 2 pounds fresh shell beans, shelled

If the carrots are large, halve them and cut them into 3- or 4-inch pieces.

Warm 3 tablespoons of oil and the bay leaves in a heated Dutch oven with a lid. When fragrant, add four of the thyme sprigs, the shallots or onions, and three of the garlic cloves. After a minute or so, add the carrots, as they take longest to cook. Season with salt and pepper.

Cover the pan while you prepare the rest of the vegetables. Cut them into large, neat pieces. Lay the potatoes over the onions and carrots. Next add the green beans, followed by the tomato slices and their minced cores, the pepper strips, and the summer squash. Season each layer with salt and pepper. Pour the reserved tomato juice through a strainer over the vegetables. Cover and cook gently until the vegetables are very tender, about 40 minutes. A good tight lid will ensure that there's plenty of fragrant juice, but if the pot seems dry at any point, add a few tablespoons of water or white wine.

While the vegetables are cooking, simmer the shell beans in water to cover with the remaining thyme sprig and garlic clove, and a little olive oil. When the beans are tender, after 30 minutes or so, depending on the bean and its maturity, season them with salt, then add them to the pot, with some of their cooking water if more liquid is needed.

Serve the vegetables in shallow bowls and drizzle your chosen sauce over them. Offer hunks of good bread to mop up the juices.

WALNUT NUGGET COOKIES

Makes about 35 bite-sized cookies

I'm always in search of a "dry, cookie-like thing"—a quote from Richard Olney's *Simple French Food*—to serve with fruit compotes or afternoon coffee. (I especially like these served with the figs roasted in olive oil and honey on page 116.) This recipe works well in both capacities. I chose it for this collection because not only do I like it, it uses little sugar (half as much as is usually called for in a cookie dough) and includes plenty of walnuts. I see this as a winter confection as much as a cookie, and I tend to make it when walnuts are fresh and new. The dough, which now includes a pinch of cinnamon and white whole-wheat flour, is on the dry side, but it can be rolled into balls. When the cookies first come out of the oven, they are very delicate and will crumble easily, but as they cool they become firm and durable.

1 cup fresh walnut meat, plus extra pieces to finish the cookies

7 tablespoons butter

1 tablespoon walnut oil

¼ cup white sugar

¼ cup light brown sugar

⅛ teaspoon sea salt

½ teaspoon cinnamon

1½ teaspoons vanilla

1¼ cups white whole-wheat flour or all-purpose flour

Powdered sugar

Heat the oven to 350°F. Line two sheet pans with parchment paper.

Break up the nuts in a small food processor until they resemble coarse sand. Watch carefully—it's easy to end up with walnut butter. If that happens, though, simply use it along with the bits and pieces.

Cream the butter with the oil until soft and well blended, then add the sugars, salt, and cinnamon. When well combined, add the vanilla and then the ground walnuts. With the mixer on low, add the flour bit by bit until it's all incorporated.

Roll teaspoon-sized lumps of the dough between the palms of your hands to make small spheres. Place each one on a paper-lined pan. You should have between 30 and 35 in all. Insert a piece of walnut into each ball of dough, then bake for 15 minutes. The flour is a little dark, so it's hard to tell when they're browned, but 15 minutes will be enough time.

Let the cookies cool on the pans, then dust them with powdered sugar and remove to a serving plate. Again, they harden as they cool.

WINTER SQUASH BRAISED IN PEAR OR APPLE CIDER

Serves 4; GF

Squash, apples, and pears make a comfortable and seasonal pairing in this dish, in a soup, or wherever you might join them.

When I first started making this dish, hard cider was a rarity. Now both apple and pear ciders are everywhere, and cider is my preference here because it's generally not as sweet as the juice, and it has the zip that comes from fermentation. However, if you can't find it, don't overlook some of the very good fresh and unfiltered apple juices that can be found in the farmers' market; they're good, too, and I've used both. If I'm using juice, a little apple cider vinegar added at the end sharpens everything, giving it focus and keeping sweetness at bay. If I'm using cider and the dish is a little tart, I drizzle a bit of very good balsamic vinegar over each serving to add both sweetness and acidity.

Here, the squash drinks up the juice and emerges succulent, still a bit firm, and lightly glazed. It can serve as the backbone of a great little fall supper, spooned, perhaps over a bowl of black quinoa alongside a pile of braised greens and a smattering of toasted almonds—all simple foods that more or less cook themselves.

In the original recipe, I suggested using delicata squash because it's easy to peel, but you don't really need to peel it all; the skins will soften. However I far prefer butternut squash, because it's more dense and filling. When you use just the neck end of the butternut, there are no cavities for seeds, no curves to deal with, and you can get good substantial pieces. (As for the seed-filled bulbous end, scrape out the seeds, steam it, then enjoy.)

I've made a few other changes. I use rosemary, which brings together the sweet and savory notes without being overwhelming, but not lots of it—it's strong. A small amount of good balsamic vinegar helps here; really, just a few drops. I've switched to a combination of olive oil and butter, and sometimes I include a few pieces of finely sliced peeled ginger, which seems to be the perfect seasoning.

1 butternut squash with a 6-inch neck	1 (12-ounce) bottle apple or pear cider
2 teaspoons butter	Sea salt and freshly ground pepper
2 teaspoons olive oil	True balsamic vinegar or unfiltered apple cider vinegar, to taste
2 teaspoons finely chopped rosemary	

With a whack of the knife, separate the stem end of the squash from the rounded blossom end. Peel the stem end (which is the bulk of the squash), then dice it into ½-inch chunks. They will be uneven, and that's fine.

Melt the butter with the olive oil in an 8-inch-wide pan with straight 2-inch sides and a lid. Add the rosemary and cook over medium heat for 2 to 3 minutes to flavor the butter. Add the squash and cider and bring to a boil. Add ½ teaspoon of salt, turn the squash to mix in the salt, and simmer, covered, until the squash is tender, by which time the juice will have reduced enough to provide a glaze for the squash. This can take about 40 minutes. If need be, raise the heat to quickly reduce the remaining cider. Sprinkle over a few drops of balsamic vinegar. Taste for both vinegar and salt, then season with pepper and serve.

WINTER SQUASH AND CARAMELIZED ONION SOUP WITH EIGHT FINISHES

Makes 4 to 6; V, GF

Squash soup is so enormously versatile that I found it impossible to choose just one of mine for this book. I've decided to provide you with a very basic recipe that uses roasted squash so that you can use any of the interesting winter squashes that might be available but that aren't as easy to use as butternut. Sadly, there are some excellent squashes that just don't get used because people find dealing with their tough, warty skins either intimidating or too time-consuming. But you can always bake a squash whole if you can't manage to slice it in half first. Once it softens, cut it in half and turn it so that the cut side is facing down on the sheet pan and bake until it's soft and the cut surface has browned.

The slowly caramelizing onions will add depth of flavor to the soup. You can also make a simple quick stock with the seeds and fibers from the squash cavity, as well as the skin and a few other ingredients if you wish, but this will add an extra 25 minutes or so to your time. Still, it's worth it.

One two-pound squash, which is a fairly small specimen, yields about three cups of cooked flesh. One cup of cooked squash requires about two cups of liquid in a soup. You might wish to use a larger squash and make more soup. And if you end up with extra cooked squash, it's quite good browned in a small skillet in olive oil or butter, seasoned well with salt and pepper and sage leaves, and possibly covered with thick slices of Gruyère cheese, goat's milk Gouda, or blue cheese. CONTINUED

1 (2-pound) winter squash or larger

Olive oil

A few parsley stems

2 medium onions, thinly sliced

½ cup white wine

5½ cups quick vegetable stock (below) or water

Sea salt and freshly ground pepper

One of the Eight Finishes (opposite)

Heat the oven to 375°F. Slice the squash in half lengthwise and brush with olive oil. Set it cut side down on a parchment-covered sheet pan and bake until soft and yielding when pressed with a finger, about an hour depending on variety and size.

While the squash is roasting, warm 2 tablespoons of olive oil in a wide pan. When it's hot, add the onions and give them a stir. Cook over high heat for a few minutes, then reduce the heat to medium and cover the pan. Stir every so often. As the onions wilt, they will eventually color. After about 20 minutes, add the wine and give a stir. Cover again and continue cooking. Eventually the wine will cook away, but continue cooking until the onions are a rich caramel color; then turn off the heat.

When the squash is done, scoop out the seeds and fibers that cling to them and remove the flesh from the skins. If you want to make a quick stock, simmer these elements—the seeds, fibers, and skin—with 6½ cups of water, some parsley stems and a few slices of onion for about 25 minutes.

Add the squash flesh to the caramelized onions, then add the stock or water and 1 rounded teaspoon salt. Simmer together for 20 minutes, covered, then purée in a blender until smooth as many squashes are fibrous. Taste for salt and season with pepper. Return the soup to the pot and finish using any of the following ideas.

The Eight Finishes

1. Drizzle a few drops of true balsamic vinegar into each bowl and add pepper and a small sprinkle of finely minced parsley.

2. Drizzle a good teaspoon or more of your best olive oil in each bowl and grate Parmigiano-Reggiano over it, along with freshly ground pepper.

3. Stir a few tablespoons of cream into the soup, leaving it streaky, and serve with plenty of freshly ground pepper. You might also add some cooked rice to the soup.

4. A sprinkling of berbere (page 151) would be a good source of heat and complexity, whether as a powder or mixed with olive oil and drizzled over the top. Or, for another source of heat and spice, stir a slice or spoonful of the smoky-spicy butter on page 64 into each bowl.

5. Garnish the soup with red pepper flakes, ground red chile, and plenty of fresh mint.

6. Serve with crumbles of blue cheese in the soup, black pepper, and a tad of butter. Or make blue cheese–covered crostini and serve one or two alongside or actually floating in each bowl of soup.

7. Fried sage leaves, finely minced rosemary needles, and vibrant parsley are all good herbs to use with winter squash, alone or with crumbled blue cheese.

8. Sear radicchio (see page 206), then chop it and use it to garnish a soup along with a few drops of balsamic vinegar.

NATIVE WILD RICE AND CELERY ROOT SOUP

Serves 4

This pretty vegetable and wild rice soup derives its stock from the rice-cooking water itself. Its flavor is clean, the color golden-green and fragrant, "Like the water it grows in," a friend from Minnesota observed when we were cooking hand-harvested native wild rice.

Authentic wild rice is quite different than the hybridized versions most of us are familiar with. Not that the shiny black grains aren't tasty, but you might want to try the real thing. The grains are gray and brown and have a subtle parched taste. You can find it online, or, if you can, visit a farmers' market in Minnesota.

When you cut the vegetables, make sure the pieces fit in a soup spoon, especially if you tend to cut things large; otherwise they're just too awkward to eat.

¾ cup wild rice, preferably native wild rice

6 cups water

Sea salt and freshly ground pepper

1 onion, sliced, or 1 large leek, chopped and rinsed well

1 celery root, peeled and diced into cubes

1 or 2 carrots, cut diced into small pieces

1 small russet potato, peeled and cut into cubes

2 celery stalks, peeled and finely diced

2 tablespoons butter

2 tablespoons flour

½ cup cream or milk

A few tablespoons minced celery or parsley leaves

Rinse the rice, then add it to the pot with the 6 cups water and 1 teaspoon salt. Bring to a boil, then lower the heat and simmer, covered, until the grains have started to burst and are pleasantly edible, about 30 minutes. Pour off the liquid and set it aside to use in the soup. Cover the pot and set the rice aside to steam.

Peel, trim, and cut the vegetables. Melt the butter, add the vegetables, and give them a stir. Cook over medium heat for several minutes, then add 1 teaspoon of salt and the flour. Add the reserved rice cooking liquid plus water to make 7 cups. Simmer until all the vegetables are tender, about 20 minutes. Purée a cup or two of the vegetables and return them to the pot. Add the rice and stir in the cream. Taste for salt, season with pepper, and serve with a generous sprinkling of celery leaves.

YOGURT, CUMIN, AND GREEN HERB SAUCE

Makes 1 cup; GF

Put together dill, basil, and cilantro, and you have a flavor you might not be able to imagine. I'm exceedingly fond of this combination, whether in a salad, a cold soup, or this sauce.

The first time I met him, writer Clifford Wright made a similar sauce, which he served over lentils. I was famished and thought it was the best thing I had ever eaten, which speaks both to Cliff's skill as a cook and to the power of hunger. That sauce was made with yogurt, cayenne, and dill. This one is a little more complex with the larger range of herbs, plus cumin and a drizzle of olive oil to finish.

There are many places I'd use this sauce: spooned over freekeh or lentils; with beets; stirred into a soup (maybe lentil or carrot); added to cooked spinach or chard; spooned over sliced tomatoes or a zucchini skillet cake; and so on. It's one of those sauces that, if you have it on hand, you'll find yourself using it everywhere. And of course, you can make it simpler by focusing on one herb or leaving out the pepper flakes.

1 plump garlic clove, pounded to a paste with ¼ teaspoon sea salt

¾ cup thick yogurt

¼ cup sour cream

½ teaspoon ground roasted cumin

About 1 generous cup of herbs with their stems removed: equal amounts dill, basil, and cilantro

Sea salt and freshly ground pepper

Best olive oil

Sumac or red pepper flakes

After you've pounded the garlic to a paste with the salt, put it in a bowl with the yogurt and sour cream. Stir in the cumin. Chop the herbs finely and stir them into the yogurt–sour cream mixture. Taste and add more of any particular herb if you want more of its flavor. Season with more salt, if needed, and freshly ground pepper.

Scrape the sauce into a bowl and drizzle a little olive oil over it just before serving, then sprinkle with sumac or pepper flakes.

ZUCCHINI CAKE, TWO WAYS

Serves 4

Although I'm very fond of them, I had considered leaving these little vegetable pancakes out of the book until a friend mentioned that her husband makes them often for himself (the Cheddar version), and that he loves them! That did it; we weren't the only ones who like these little cakes.

I've approached these little zucchini cakes so many different ways, and finally come up with this method for dealing with the squash and for two flavor variations, although there can be plenty more. I love the version with dill and feta cheese, but I also like the one that features a good sharp Cheddar and fresh oregano. These I serve with fresh hot salsa and a spoonful of sour cream. With the other, I might include a dollop of the yogurt and herb sauce on page 273 or the marjoram sauce on page 152.

These cakes go so well with different herbs, cheeses, and sauces, plus they're versatile in other ways, as well. For example, having what amounted to a cup of slivered spinach leaves, I added them to the zucchini during the last few minutes it was cooking and they fit in fine. I suspect that's true with lots of other vegetables you might have in small amounts.

You can go from start to finish in 30 minutes even with the slicing and chopping. They can be made small, for an appetizer, or larger, using about ½ cup of batter, for a single, larger serving

Keep your eyes open for a variety of zucchini called Costata Romanesco. *Costata* means "ribs" and the squash in fact do have raised ridges, like ribs, running down their length. They are exceptionally meaty and not as watery as most zucchini. When you slice them, the pieces will look like flowers with their scalloped edges. This is the only zucchini I grow. It's so good that it's worth putting up with the squash bugs. CONTINUED

Zucchini Cakes with Cheddar, Oregano, and Tomatilla Salsa

1 pound zucchini, Costata Romanesco, if possible

1 tablespoon butter, olive oil, or some of each

Sea salt and freshly milled pepper

2 large eggs, beaten

1 large shallot or about 3 tablespoons finely sliced scallions

½ to 1 cup bread crumbs

¼ cup chopped oregano or marjoram

3 tablespoons chopped parsley or cilantro

½ cup or more grated Cheddar cheese

Olive oil or butter for cooking the cakes

Tomatilla salsa or another favorite salsa

Sour cream or yogurt

Thinly slice the zucchini on a mandoline or by hand. Heat a wide skillet with the olive oil or butter. Add the zucchini, toss it with a scant teaspoon of salt, and cook over medium-low heat, turning every few minutes, until it's golden in places and starting to dry out. While it's cooking and as you chop the herbs, add a few pinches to the squash. In all, this should take about 25 minutes at most.

Meanwhile whisk the eggs with ½ cup bread crumbs, add the shallot, remaining herbs, and cheddar. Stir in the cooked zucchini and season with pepper.

To test the consistency and seasoning of the batter, heat a little olive oil or butter in a small skillet, drop in a tablespoon of batter and cook over medium heat until golden and crisp, then turn and cook the other side. Taste it. You'll be able to judge the salt level and make other adjustments, such as adding more bread crumbs, if it seems too wet.

When you're about ready to eat, cook the batter, making your cakes the size you want, in olive oil or butter. Cook over medium heat and don't rush. After a few minutes, when the bottom is set, turn the cake over and cook the second side. When done, serve them with salsa plus sour cream or yogurt.

Zucchini Pancakes with Feta and Dill

Proceed as directed in the previous recipe, but when making the batter, substitute ½ cup chopped dill for the oregano, use feta cheese in place of the Cheddar, and include the zest of 1 lemon.

Serve these cakes with a spoonful of your favorite yogurt sauce and a fresh dill sprig. If you have dill flowers, use them to garnish the cakes as well. They're very good with Yogurt, Cumin, and Green Herb Sauce (page 273), which includes dill.

ACKNOWLEDGEMENTS

A book never comes into being without a great many people. I'm fortunate to have the opportunity to say thank you to at least some of the people who made *In My Kitchen* possible.

My heartfelt thanks to Jenny Wapner, editor of clear-eyed wisdom, consummate patience, and the determination to make the best possible book. She has been a support from beginning to end. Every author should be so fortunate to have such an editor. And along with Jenny, a big thank-you to my lively agent, Sharon Bowers, who, whether in Dublin or New York, shepherded *In My Kitchen* from beginning to end.

Thank you to many people at Ten Speed for their involvement and friendship—especially, Michele Crim, Daniel Wikey, Kristin Casemore, Aaron Wehner, Hannah Rahill, and Allison Renzulli. You have all been supportive when support was needed—and you're so good at what you do! Also among the Ten Speed crew is Ashley Lima, to whom I am indebted for her beautiful book design (and her patience with me).

Erin Scott, Lillian Kang, and Veronica Vallejo contributed their handsome photographs, styling talents, and cooking skills. All were a joy to work with day after day in a situation that is often simultaneously fraught with boredom and tension, despite which we had a good time while making a beautiful book. My gratitude also goes to Sandy Simon and Robert Brady for their beautiful ceramics, to Ann Hatch for sharing her fine olive oil, and to my brother Michael for the same.

At home in New Mexico many people lent a hand in one way or another—Dan Welch, Tanya Young, Scott Diffrient, Tim Willms, Nancy Ranney, Jannine Cassobel, and the farmers at the Santa Fe and Eldorado Farmers' Markets for their beautiful produce. Thank you also to Ellen Zachos for pointing out local wild edibles I had overlooked—in my own back yard, even! And a very special thanks to Jane and Steve Darland of Monticello, New Mexico, for introducing me to their amazing and life-changing balsamic vinegar.

Because I often ask myself what could be better than to cook with a curious dog at your side and a hungry husband at the table, I once again want to say how grateful I am to Patrick McFarlin, for patiently standing by, whether waiting for dinner or the tomatoes to ripen. He has for the past 26 years been an unfailing support in all my endeavors, enriched my life with his beautiful paintings, and returned the joy to cooking when it had faltered.

And finally big love to my little brown dog, Dante, the ultimate enthusiastic kitchen companion who is always parked by my feet while I'm cooking, his eyes and nose following my every move, his little squeaks and squeals voicing requests for a taste of whatever I'm cutting up, which he generally doesn't like but has to know about anyway. He does, however, like sweet potatoes and beets.

INDEX

A

Almonds
  Chard and Saffron Flan in an
    Almond Crust with Spring
    Greens, 88–91
  Dates with Almond Paste or
    Marzipan, 104
  Figs with Toasted Almonds and
    Anise Seed, 103–4
  Olive Oil, Almond, and Blood
    Orange Cake, 173–74
  Rough-Cut Oats with Dried
    Cherries, Raisins, and
    Almonds, 170–71
Anise Seed Shortbread with
  Star Anise Impressions, 37
Apple Cider, Winter Squash
  Braised in, 266–68
Artichoke and Scallion Sauté over
  Garlic-Rubbed Toast, 29–30
Arugula
  Golden Beets with Mâche,
    Pickled Shallots, and Purple
    Orach, 47–48
  Improvised Platter
    Salad, An, 189–91
  Roasted Asparagus and Arugula
    with Hard-Cooked Eggs and
    Walnuts, 33–34
Asparagus, Roasted, and Arugula
  with Hard-Cooked Eggs
  and Walnuts, 33–34
Avocados
  Black Rice with Mixed Beets,
    Their Greens, Avocado, Feta,
    and Pomegranate Seeds, 54–55
  Chopped Salad with Toasted
    Seeds and Marjoram-Mint
    Dressing, 220–21
  Citrus and Avocado with Lime-
    Cumin Vinaigrette, 95–96
  Masa Crêpes with Chard, Black
    Beans, Avocado, and Pickled
    Onions, 156–57
  Red Chile and Posole with Blue
    Corn Tortilla Chips and
    Avocado, 198–99
  Sweet-Tart Sun Gold Tomato Soup
    with Avocado Relish, 247–48

B

Balsamic vinegar, 12, 21
Beans
  Black-Eyed Peas with Yogurt-
    Tahini Sauce and Three
    Green Herbs, 53
  Braised Summer
    Vegetables, 260–63
  cooking, 9
  Green, Yellow, or Purple Beans
    with Sun Gold Tomatoes
    and Opal Basil, 38–41
  heirloom, 10
  Improvised Platter
    Salad, An, 189–91
  Masa Crêpes with Chard,
    Black Beans, Avocado,
    and Pickled Onions, 156–57
  Potato and Chickpea Stew with
    Sautéed Spinach, 192–94
  Rio Zape Beans with Smoked
    Chile, 42–43
  See also Chickpeas
Beets
  Black Rice with Mixed Beets,
    Their Greens, Avocado, Feta,
    and Pomegranate Seeds, 54–55
  Golden Beets with Mâche,
    Pickled Shallots, and Purple
    Orach, 47–48
  Thick Marjoram Sauce for Beets
    (and Other Vegetables), 152–53
Berbere, 151
Berries
  Berries Scented with Rose
    Geranium Leaves and
    Flowers, 49–50
  Rhubarb-Raspberry Compote, 211
Black-Eyed Peas with
  Yogurt-Tahini Sauce
  and Three Green Herbs, 53
Bread
  Artichoke and Scallion Sauté over
    Garlic-Rubbed Toast, 29–30
  Breakfast Bread with Rosemary
    and Lemon, 56–58
  Herb-Laced Fritters Made
    with Good Stale Bread
    and Ricotta, 128–31
  Savoy Cabbage, Leek, and
    Mushroom Braise on Toast with
    Horseradish Cream, 69–70
  Scrambled Eggs Smothered with
    Crispy Bread Crumbs, 107
Breakfast Bread with Rosemary
  and Lemon, 56–58
Broccoli
  Broccoli with Roasted Peppers,
    Feta, Olives, and Herbs, 59–61
  Curry Mayonnaise for Roasted
    Cauliflower or Steamed
    Broccoli, 100
Buckwheat Waffles, Yeasted, 62–63
Bulgur and Green Lentil Salad
  with Chickpeas and Preserved
  Lemon, 67–68
Butter, Smoky-Spicy, for Three
  Orange Vegetables, 64–65

C

Cabbage
  Citrus and Avocado with Lime-
    Cumin Vinaigrette, 95–96
  Savoy Cabbage, Leek, and
    Mushroom Braise on Toast with
    Horseradish Cream, 69–70
  Warm Cabbage Salad with
    Togarashi Tofu Crisps, 73–75
Cakes
  Olive Oil, Almond, and Blood
    Orange Cake, 173–74
  Zucchini Cakes with Cheddar,
    Oregano, and Tomatillo
    Salsa, 275–76
  Zucchini Pancakes with Feta
    and Dill, 275, 277
Carrots
  Braised Summer
    Vegetables, 260–63
  Carrot Soup with Zesty Relish
    or Smoky-Spicy Butter, 76–77
  Chopped Salad with Toasted
    Seeds and Marjoram-Mint
    Dressing, 220–21
  Smoky-Spicy Butter for Three
    Orange Vegetables, 64–65

Cauliflower
  Cauliflower and Sweet Peppers,
    Saffron, Parsley, and
    Olives, 80–81
  Curry Mayonnaise for Roasted
    Cauliflower or Steamed
    Broccoli, 100
  Roasted Cauliflower with
    Romesco Sauce and a Shower
    of Parsley, 82
  Tomato and Roasted Cauliflower
    Curry with Paneer, 252–54
Celery root
  Celery Root and Potato Mash
    with Truffle Salt, 85
  Native Wild Rice and Celery
    Root Soup, 272
Cereal
  Brown Rice Cereal with Nut
    Butter and Chia Seeds, 212
  Rough-Cut Oats with Dried
    Cherries, Raisins, and
    Almonds, 170–71
Chard
  Chard and Saffron Flan in an
    Almond Crust with Spring
    Greens, 88–91
  Chard Stems with Lemon, 87
  Masa Crêpes with Chard, Black
    Beans, Avocado, and Pickled
    Onions, 156–57
  Silky Braised Chard and
    Cilantro, 86
  Stinging Nettle Soup with
    Nigella Seeds, 167–68
  Trouchia (Failed-to-Catch-a-
    Trout Frittata), 122–23
Cheese
  Baked Ricotta Infused with
    Thyme, 215–17
  Black Rice with Mixed Beets,
    Their Greens, Avocado, Feta,
    and Pomegranate Seeds, 54–55
  Broccoli with Roasted Peppers,
    Feta, Olives, and Herbs, 59–61
  Cheese Soufflé, A, 92–93
  Eggplant Gratin with a Golden
    Dome of Saffron-Ricotta
    Custard, 108–11
  Herb-Laced Fritters Made
    with Good Stale Bread and
    Ricotta, 128–31

Kale and Quinoa Gratin, 140–43
Masa Crêpes with Chard,
  Black Beans, Avocado, and
  Pickled Onions, 156–57
Pasta with Gorgonzola, 181–83
Quinoa Soup with Spinach, Corn,
  Feta, and Cilantro, 204–5
Seared Radicchio Draped with
  Mozzarella, 206
Smoky Pimento Cheese
  on Cucumbers, 188
Summer Squashes with
  Herb Blossoms, Basil,
  Pine Nuts, and Parmigiano-
  Reggiano, 223–24
Sweet Potato and Coconut-Milk
  Curry with Paneer, 234–35
Tomato and Roasted Cauliflower
  Curry with Paneer, 252–54
Trouchia (Failed-to-Catch-a-
  Trout Frittata), 122–23
Warm Feta with Toasted Sesame
  Seeds, 118–19
Zucchini Cakes with Cheddar,
  Oregano, and Tomatillo
  Salsa, 275–76
Zucchini Pancakes with Feta
  and Dill, 275, 277
Cherries, Dried, Rough-Cut Oats
  with Raisins, Almonds,
  and, 170–71
Chickpeas
  Bulgur and Green Lentil Salad
    with Chickpeas and Preserved
    Lemon, 67–68
  Hummus Worth Making, 132–33
  Potato and Chickpea Stew with
    Sautéed Spinach, 192–94
Children, enlisting help of, 18
Chiles
  Potato and Green Chile
    Stew, 195–97
  Red Chile and Posole with
    Blue Corn Tortilla Chips
    and Avocado, 198–99
  Rio Zape Beans with Smoked
    Chile, 42–43
Chopped Salad with Toasted
  Seeds and Marjoram-Mint
  Dressing, 220–21
Cilantro
  Quinoa Soup with Spinach, Corn,
    Feta, and Cilantro, 204–5

Silky Braised Chard and
  Cilantro, 86
Tofu and Cilantro Salad with
  Roasted Peanuts, 238
Citrus and Avocado with
  Lime-Cumin Vinaigrette, 95–96
Coconut milk
  Collards Simmered in Coconut
    Milk with Shallots, 97
  Golden Tofu with Orange and
    Yellow Peppers, 242–43
  Japanese Sweet Potato Soup with
    Ginger, Smoked Salt, and
    Aged Balsamic Vinegar, 228
  Sweet Potato and Coconut-Milk
    Curry with Paneer, 234–35
  Yellow Coconut Rice with
    Scallions and Black Sesame
    Seeds, 213–14
Collards Simmered in Coconut
  Milk with Shallots, 97
Cookies, Walnut Nugget, 265
Corn
  Corn, Shitake Mushrooms,
    and Sage with Millet, 98–99
  Quinoa Soup with Spinach, Corn,
    Feta, and Cilantro, 204–5
  Red Chile and Posole with
    Blue Corn Tortilla Chips
    and Avocado, 198–99
Crêpes, Masa, with Chard,
  Black Beans, Avocado,
  and Pickled Onions, 156–57
Cucumbers
  Chopped Salad with Toasted
    Seeds and Marjoram-Mint
    Dressing, 220–21
  Quick Cucumber Pickles, 101
  Sea Greens with Cucumbers,
    Ginger, and Sesame, 222
  Smoky Pimento Cheese on
    Cucumbers, 188
Curries
  Sweet Potato and Coconut-Milk
    Curry with Paneer, 234–35
  Tomato and Roasted Cauliflower
    Curry with Paneer, 252–54
Curry Mayonnaise for Roasted
  Cauliflower or Steamed
  Broccoli, 100

D

Dates
  Dates with Almond Paste
    or Marzipan, 104
  Dried Fruits with Fennel,
    Sesame Seeds, and Orange
    Flower Water, 102
Desserts
  Berries Scented with Rose
    Geranium Leaves and
    Flowers, 49–50
  Dates with Almond Paste
    or Marzipan, 104
  Dried Fruits with Fennel,
    Sesame Seeds, and Orange
    Flower Water, 102
  Figs with Toasted Almonds
    and Anise Seed, 103–4
  Mission Figs Roasted with Olive
    Oil, Honey, and Thyme, 116
  Olive Oil, Almond, and Blood
    Orange Cake, 173–74
  Quince Braised in Honey and
    Wine, 202
  Sweet Potato (or Pumpkin)
    Pudding with Silky
    Persimmon Purée, 229–32
  Walnut Nugget Cookies, 265
Dressings
  Lime-Cumin Vinaigrette, 96
  Marjoram-Mint Dressing, 221

E

Eggplant
  Eggplant Gratin with a Golden
    Dome of Saffron-Ricotta
    Custard, 108–11
  Roasted Eggplant on the
    Stove, 114
  Roasted Eggplant with Dill,
    Yogurt, and Walnuts, 114–15
Eggs, 21
  Caramelized Onion Frittata with
    Sherry Vinegar, 178
  Cheese Soufflé, A, 92–93
  Egg Salad for Spring with
    Tarragon, Lovage, and
    Chives, 105
  Improvised Platter Salad,
    An, 189–91
  Roasted Asparagus and Arugula
    with Hard-Cooked Eggs and
    Walnuts, 33–34

Scrambled Eggs Smothered with
    Crispy Bread Crumbs, 107
  Trouchia (Failed-to-Catch-a-
    Trout Frittata), 122–23

F

Fats, 8–9
Fennel Salad, Shaved, with
    Fennel Blossoms, Fronds,
    and Pistachios, 121
Feta
  Black Rice with Mixed Beets,
    Their Greens, Avocado, Feta,
    and Pomegranate Seeds, 54–55
  Broccoli with Roasted Peppers,
    Feta, Olives, and Herbs, 59–61
  Masa Crêpes with Chard, Black
    Beans, Avocado, and Pickled
    Onions, 156–57
  Quinoa Soup with Spinach,
    Corn, Feta, and Cilantro,
    204–5
  Warm Feta with Toasted Sesame
    Seeds, 118–19
  Zucchini Pancakes with Feta
    and Dill, 275, 277
Figs
  Dried Fruits with Fennel,
    Sesame Seeds, and Orange
    Flower Water, 102
  Figs with Toasted Almonds and
    Anise Seed, 103–4
  Mission Figs Roasted with Olive
    Oil, Honey, and Thyme, 116
Flan, Chard and Saffron, in an
    Almond Crust with Spring
    Greens, 88–91
Flour, 21–22
Frittatas
  Caramelized Onion Frittata
    with Sherry Vinegar, 178
  Trouchia (Failed-to-Catch-a-
    Trout Frittata), 122–23
Fritters, Herb-Laced, Made with
    Good Stale Bread and
    Ricotta, 128–31
Fruits
  Dried Fruits with Fennel,
    Sesame Seeds, and Orange
    Flower Water, 102
  organic, 24
  See also individual fruits

G

Gardening, 7
Garlic, 22
GMOs, 24
Goat cheese
  Cheese Soufflé, A, 92–93
Gorgonzola, Pasta with, 181–83
Gouda
  Kale and Quinoa Gratin, 140–43
  Trouchia (Failed-to-Catch-a-
    Trout Frittata), 122–23
Grains, 9–10. See also individual
    grains
Gratins
  Eggplant Gratin with a Golden
    Dome of Saffron-Ricotta
    Custard, 108–11
  Kale and Quinoa Gratin, 140–43
Greens
  Black Rice with Mixed Beets,
    Their Greens, Avocado, Feta,
    and Pomegranate Seeds, 54–55
  Chard and Saffron Flan in an
    Almond Crust with Spring
    Greens, 88–91
  Citrus and Avocado with Lime
    Cumin Vinaigrette, 95–96
  Herb (and Wild Green)
    Salad, 124–27
  Improvised Platter Salad,
    An, 189–91
  Tofu Triangles with Red Onions
    and Tender Greens, 240–41
  See also individual greens
Gruyère
  Kale and Quinoa Gratin, 140–43
  Trouchia (Failed-to-Catch-a-
    Trout Frittata), 122–23

H

Hazelnuts
  Romesco Sauce, 218–19
Herbs
  growing, 7
  Herb-Laced Fritters Made
    with Good Stale Bread
    and Ricotta, 128–31
  Herb (and Wild Green)
    Salad, 124–27
  Yogurt, Cumin, and Green
    Herb Sauce, 273
Holidays, 19

Horseradish Sauce, 70
Hummus Worth Making, 132–33

J

Japanese Sweet Potato Soup
with Ginger, Smoked Salt, and
Aged Balsamic Vinegar, 228
Jerusalem Artichoke Soup, Roasted,
with Sunflower Sprouts and
Seeds, 134–37

K

Kale
Hearty Lentil Minestrone with
Kale, 144–45
Kale and Quinoa Gratin, 140–43
Kale and Walnut Pesto with
Roasted or Seared Winter
Squash, 138–39
Knives, 7–8

L

Leek, Savoy Cabbage, and
Mushroom Braise on Toast
with Horseradish Cream, 69–70
Lentils
Bulgur and Green Lentil Salad
with Chickpeas and Preserved
Lemon, 67–68
Green Lentils with Yogurt,
Sorrel, and Parsley Sauce, 146
Hearty Lentil Minestrone with
Kale, 144–45
Red Lentil Soup with Berbere,
149–50
Lettuce
Citrus and Avocado with Lime-
Cumin Vinaigrette, 95–96
Herb (and Wild Green) Salad,
124–27
Improvised Platter Salad,
An, 189–91
Lime-Cumin Vinaigrette, 96

M

Mâche, Golden Beets with
Pickled Shallots, Purple
Orach, and, 47–48
Marjoram
Marjoram-Mint Dressing, 221

Thick Marjoram Sauce for Beets
(and Other Vegetables), 152–53
Marzipan, Dates with Almond
Paste or, 104
Masa Crêpes with Chard, Black
Beans, Avocado, and Pickled
Onions, 156–57
Mayonnaise, Curry, for Roasted
Cauliflower or Steamed
Broccoli, 100
Menu planning, 13–14, 17–18
Millet, Corn, Shiitake
Mushrooms, and Sage
with, 98–99
Minestrone, Hearty Lentil, with
Kale, 144–45
Miso-Ginger Sauce, 237
Mozzarella, Seared Radicchio
Draped with, 206
Mushrooms
Corn, Shiitake Mushrooms, and
Sage with Millet, 98–99
Dried Porcini, Fresh Mushroom,
and Whole Tomato Ragout
with Seared Polenta, 163–64
Mushroom Soup for
Company, 161–62
Savoy Cabbage, Leek, and
Mushroom Braise on
Toast with Horseradish
Cream, 69–70

N

Nectarines in Lemon Verbena
Syrup, White Peaches or, 184
Nettle Soup, Stinging, with Nigella
Seeds, 167–68
Nuts, 9. *See also individual nuts*

O

Oats, Rough-Cut, with Dried
Cherries, Raisins, and
Almonds, 170–71
Olive oil, 22, 24
Olive Oil, Almond, and
Blood Orange Cake, 173–74
Olives
Broccoli with Roasted Peppers,
Feta, Olives, and Herbs, 59–61
Cauliflower and Sweet
Peppers, Saffron, Parsley,
and Olives, 80–81

Marjoram in a Thick, Green
Sauce for Beets (and Other
Vegetables), 152–53
Roasted Pepper and Tomato Salad
with Basil and Capers, 186–87
Roasted Tomatoes and Fingerling
Potatoes with Thyme, Olives,
and Capers, 255–57
Tomato and Red Pepper Tart in
a Yeasted Crust, 245–46
Onions
Caramelized Onion Frittata with
Sherry Vinegar, 178
Caramelized Onions with
Vinegar and Cloves, 176–77
Easy Pink Onion Pickles, 175
Pasta with Caramelized Onions
and Crushed Roasted
Walnuts, 180
Winter Squash and Caramelized
Onion Soup with Eight
Finishes, 269–71
Oranges
Citrus and Avocado with Lime-
Cumin Vinaigrette, 95–96
Olive Oil, Almond, and Blood
Orange Cake, 173–74
Organic agriculture, 24

P

Pancakes
Quinoa and Buttermilk
Pancakes, 203
Zucchini Cakes with Cheddar,
Oregano, and Tomatillo
Salsa, 275–76
Zucchini Pancakes with Feta
and Dill, 275, 277
Paneer
Sweet Potato and Coconut-Milk
Curry with Paneer, 234–35
Tomato and Roasted Cauliflower
Curry with Paneer, 252–54
Pasta
Hearty Lentil Minestrone with
Kale, 144–45
Pasta with Caramelized Onions
and Crushed Roasted
Walnuts, 180
Pasta with Gorgonzola, 181–83
Peaches, White, or Nectarines in
Lemon Verbena Syrup, 184

Peanuts, Roasted, Tofu and
    Cilantro Salad with, 238
Pear Cider, Winter Squash
    Braised in, 266–68
Pepper, 24
Peppers
    Braised Summer
        Vegetables, 260–63
    Broccoli with Roasted Peppers,
        Feta, Olives, and Herbs, 59–61
    Cauliflower and Sweet Peppers,
        Saffron, Parsley, and
        Olives, 80–81
    Chopped Salad with Toasted
        Seeds and Marjoram-Mint
        Dressing, 220–21
    Golden Tofu with Orange and
        Yellow Peppers, 242–43
    Potato and Chickpea Stew with
        Sautéed Spinach, 192–94
    Roasted Pepper and Tomato
        Salad with Basil and
        Capers, 186–87
    Romesco Sauce, 218–19
    Smoky Pimento Cheese
        on Cucumbers, 188
    Tomato and Red Pepper Tart
        in a Yeasted Crust, 245–46
    See also Chiles
Persimmon Purée, Silky, Sweet
    Potato (or Pumpkin) Pudding
    with, 229–32
Pesticides, 8, 24
Pesto, Kale and Walnut, with
    Roasted or Seared Winter
    Squash, 138–39
Pickles
    Easy Pink Onion Pickles, 175
    Quick Cucumber Pickles, 101
Pimento Cheese, Smoky, on
    Cucumbers, 188
Pine Nuts
    Breakfast Bread with Rosemary
        and Lemon, 56–58
    Marjoram in a Thick, Green
        Sauce for Beets (and Other
        Vegetables), 152–53
    Summer Squashes with Herb
        Blossoms, Basil, Pine Nuts, and
        Parmigiano-Reggiano, 223–24
Pistachios
    Citrus and Avocado with Lime-
        Cumin Vinaigrette, 95–96

Shaved Fennel Salad with Fennel
    Blossoms, Fronds,
    and Pistachios, 121
Platter Salad, An Improvised, 189–91
Polenta, Seared, Dried Porcini,
    Fresh Mushroom, and Whole
    Tomato Ragout with, 163–64
Pomegranate Seeds, Black Rice
    with Mixed Beets, Their
    Greens, Avocado, Feta,
    and, 54–55
Posole, Red Chile and, with
    Blue Corn Tortilla Chips
    and Avocado, 198–99
Potatoes
    Braised Summer
        Vegetables, 260–63
    Celery Root and Potato Mash
        with Truffle Salt, 85
    Improvised Platter
        Salad, An, 189–91
    Potato and Chickpea Stew with
        Sautéed Spinach, 192–94
    Potato and Green Chile
        Stew, 195–97
    Quinoa Soup with Spinach, Corn,
        Feta, and Cilantro, 204–5
    Roasted Fingerling Potatoes, 219
    Roasted Tomatoes and Fingerling
        Potatoes with Thyme, Olives,
        and Capers, 255–57
    Roasted Jerusalem Artichoke
        Soup with Sunflower Sprouts
        and Seeds, 134–37
    Rough-and-Ready Soup, Refined,
        A, 258–59
Presentation, 14
Pudding, Sweet Potato
    (or Pumpkin), with Silky
    Persimmon Purée, 229–32

Q
Quince Braised in Honey
    and Wine, 202
Quinoa
    Kale and Quinoa Gratin, 140–43
    Quinoa and Buttermilk
        Pancakes, 203
    Quinoa Soup with Spinach, Corn,
        Feta, and Cilantro, 204–5

R
Radicchio
    Citrus and Avocado with Lime-
        Cumin Vinaigrette, 95–96
    Seared Radicchio Draped with
        Mozzarella, 206
    Shredded Radicchio with a
        Garlicky Dressing, 208–9
Raisins
    Dried Fruits with Fennel,
        Sesame Seeds, and Orange
        Flower Water, 102
    Rough-Cut Oats with Dried
        Cherries, Raisins, and
        Almonds, 170–71
Rhubarb-Raspberry Compote, 211
Rice
    Black Rice with Mixed Beets,
        Their Greens, Avocado, Feta,
        and Pomegranate Seeds, 54–55
    Brown Rice Cereal with Nut
        Butter and Chia Seeds, 212
    Yellow Coconut Rice with
        Scallions and Black Sesame
        Seeds, 213–14
Ricotta
    Baked Ricotta Infused with
        Thyme, 215–17
    Eggplant Gratin with a Golden
        Dome of Saffron-Ricotta
        Custard, 108–11
    Herb-Laced Fritters Made
        with Good Stale Bread
        and Ricotta, 128–31
Romesco Sauce, 218–19

S
Salads
    Black Rice with Mixed Beets,
        Their Greens, Avocado, Feta,
        and Pomegranate Seeds, 54–55
    Broccoli with Roasted Peppers,
        Feta, Olives, and Herbs, 59–61
    Bulgur and Green Lentil Salad
        with Chickpeas and Preserved
        Lemon, 67–68
    Chard and Saffron Flan in an
        Almond Crust with Spring
        Greens, 88–91
    Chopped Salad with Toasted
        Seeds and Marjoram Mint
        Dressing, 220–21

Salads, continued
    Citrus and Avocado with Lime-
        Cumin Vinaigrette, 95–96
    Egg Salad for Spring with
        Tarragon, Lovage, and
        Chives, 105
    Golden Beets with Mâche,
        Pickled Shallots, and Purple
        Orach, 47–48
    Herb (and Wild Green)
        Salad, 124–27
    Improvised Platter
        Salad, An, 189–91
    Roasted Asparagus and Arugula
        with Hard-Cooked Eggs and
        Walnuts, 33–34
    Roasted Pepper and Tomato
        Salad with Basil and
        Capers, 186–87
    Shaved Fennel Salad with
        Fennel Blossoms, Fronds,
        and Pistachios, 121
    Shredded Radicchio with a
        Garlicky Dressing, 208–9
    Tofu and Cilantro Salad with
        Roasted Peanuts, 238
    Warm Cabbage Salad with
        Togarashi Tofu Crisps, 73–75
Salt, 24
Sauces
    Horseradish Sauce, 70
    Kale and Walnut Pesto, 138–39
    Marjoram in a Thick, Green
        Sauce for Beets (and Other
        Vegetables), 152–53
    Miso-Ginger Sauce, 237
    Oven-Roasted Tomato Sauce,
        An, 251
    Romesco Sauce, 218–19
    Sauce Made with Canned
        Tomatoes, A, 250
    Sauce Made with Fresh
        Tomatoes, A, 250
    Yogurt, Cumin, and Green Herb
        Sauce, 273
    Yogurt, Sorrel, and Parsley
        Sauce, 146
    Yogurt-Tahini Sauce, 53
Scallions
    Artichoke and Scallion Sauté over
        Garlic-Rubbed Toast, 29–30
    Yellow Coconut Rice with
        Scallions and Black Sesame
        Seeds, 213–14

Sea Greens with Cucumbers,
    Ginger, and Sesame, 222
Sesame seeds
    Dried Fruits with Fennel,
        Sesame Seeds, and Orange
        Flower Water, 102
    Sea Greens with Cucumbers,
        Ginger, and Sesame, 222
    Warm Feta with Toasted Sesame
        Seeds, 118–19
    Yellow Coconut Rice with
        Scallions and Black Sesame
        Seeds, 213–14
Shallots
    Collards Simmered in Coconut
        Milk with Shallots, 97
    Golden Beets with Mâche,
        Pickled Shallots, and Purple
        Orach, 47–48
Shortbread, Anise Seed,
        Imprinted with Star Anise, 37
Soufflé, A Cheese, 92–93
Soups
    Carrot Soup with Zesty Relish
        or Smoky-Spicy Butter, 76–77
    Hearty Lentil Minestrone with
        Kale, 144–45
    Japanese Sweet Potato Soup with
        Ginger, Smoked Salt, and
        Aged Balsamic Vinegar, 228
    Mushroom Soup for Company,
        161–62
    Native Wild Rice and Celery
        Root Soup, 272
    Quinoa Soup with Spinach,
        Corn, Feta, and Cilantro,
        204–5
    Red Lentil Soup with Berbere,
        149–50
    Rough-and-Ready Soup, Refined,
        A, 258–59
    Stinging Nettle Soup with
        Nigella Seeds, 167–68
    Sweet-Tart Sun Gold Tomato
        Soup with Avocado Relish,
        247–48
    Winter Squash and Caramelized
        Onion Soup with Eight
        Finishes, 269–71
Soy sauce, 24
Special occasions, 19
Spinach
    Potato and Chickpea Stew with
        Sautéed Spinach, 192–94

Quinoa Soup with Spinach, Corn,
    Feta, and Cilantro, 204–5
Stinging Nettle Soup with
    Nigella Seeds, 167–68
Tofu Triangles with Red Onions
    and Tender Greens, 240–41
Squash, summer
    Braised Summer
        Vegetables, 260–63
    Summer Squashes with
        Herb Blossoms, Basil,
        Pine Nuts, and Parmigiano-
        Reggiano, 223–24
    Zucchini Cakes with Cheddar,
        Oregano, and Tomatillo
        Salsa, 275–76
    Zucchini Pancakes with Feta
        and Dill, 275, 277
Squash, winter
    roasted, 139
    Smoky-Spicy Butter for Three
        Orange Vegetables, 64–65
    Winter Squash and Caramelized
        Onion Soup with Eight
        Finishes, 269–71
    Winter Squash Braised in Pear
        or Apple Cider, 266–68
Stinging Nettle Soup with Nigella
    Seeds, 167–68
Stocks, 12–13
Sweet potatoes
    Japanese Sweet Potato Soup with
        Ginger, Smoked Salt, and
        Aged Balsamic Vinegar, 228
    Pan-Griddled Sweet Potatoes
        with Miso-Ginger Sauce, 237
    Smoky-Spicy Butter for Three
        Orange Vegetables, 64–65
    Sweet Potato and Coconut-Milk
        Curry with Paneer, 234–35
    Sweet Potato (or Pumpkin)
        Pudding with Silky
        Persimmon Purée, 229–32

T

Tart, Tomato and Red Pepper,
    in a Yeasted Crust, 245–46
Tofu, 25
    Golden Tofu with Orange and
        Yellow Peppers, 242–43
    Sweet Potato and Coconut-Milk
        Curry with Paneer, 234–35

PASTA WITH CARAMELIZED ONIONS AND CRUSHED ROASTED WALNUTS

Serves 4

Caramelized onions are just so, so good. It's always a treat to have some on hand to toss with pasta or spread over hot toast rubbed with garlic and brushed with olive oil, finished with a thin slice of hard cheese. In the past I've made this dish with long strands of spaghetti, but because I've chosen to cut the onions into smaller pieces so that they'll work well in a frittata, I use a smaller, dried pasta, such as shells or snails. They are the perfect size for the onions.

If this is a winter supper and there's nothing much green yet to eat (and we've had enough romaine salads), I'm inclined to serve this piled over or nestled around beet greens or chard doused with a spoonful of fine olive oil. I always like to grate a hunk of good Parmigiano-Reggiano over this pasta, but I have to say that an aged Gouda or a good blue cheese are also worth considering. And if there are only two of you at home, it's easy to make half this amount and use the remaining onions in another dish, like the onion frittata on page 178. That's what we do. Or we double up, as here, for company. If you have the onions made already, this dish is a snap. If not, you need to plan for the 40 minutes or so that it takes to make them, though most of that time does not demand much from you.

Caramelized Onions with Vinegar and Cloves (page 176)	5 cups dried pasta shapes, such as snails or shells
2 heaping teaspoons finely chopped fresh rosemary	½ cup finely chopped toasted walnuts
Sea salt and freshly ground pepper	Parmigiano-Reggiano, aged Gouda, or crumbled blue cheese

If you haven't made the onions already, begin them first. If they're already cooked, heat them with the rosemary.

Bring plenty of water to a boil for the pasta. Add lots of salt and then the pasta, and cook until it's as done as you like. Taste as it cooks after 10 minutes or so. (The exact time is difficult to give. Water doesn't boil as hot at 7,000 feet as it does at sea level.)

Scoop the pasta into a bowl and toss with the hot onions and the walnuts. Taste for salt and season with pepper. Serve with the cheese grated over the top.

PASTA WITH GORGONZOLA

Serves 2

Roseanna, my neighbor in Rome, frequently made this dish (with fresh pasta) for her husband when he came home for lunch. Lunch at home? Fresh pasta? On an ordinary weekday? That, to us, seems extraordinary!

Dried or fresh, this pasta is extraordinary, too, especially if you love blue cheese and cream. Plus there's a secret ease to its preparation: a bowl warms on top of the heating pasta water, and the heat melts the butter, softens the cheese, and spreads the flavor of the garlic throughout both. Cooked pasta goes in, is tossed, and served. That's it.

This past holiday season, as I stood staring at an unused chunk of Gorgonzola, some very good butter, and the remains of a half-pint carton of cream, I realized that I hadn't made this in years. Of course, I hadn't. It's super rich, filled with dairy, and made with white pasta that probably has no virtue other than its blandness or delicacy, depending. I decided to make it. It was the end of the holiday season, and we had had a chaste vegetarian Christmas. So I used up all those rich and creamy odds and ends, and we had a small portion each plus a salad. It was so insanely good, I plan to do it again next year. Although I have cut the portions of everything down in this version, it is still rich. Follow it with a good green salad.

This dish was originally in *The Savory Way*, which I wrote after returning from a year in Rome and moving to, of all places, Flagstaff, Arizona. At that time, I had to bring back the cheese (along with olive oil and good pasta) when making emergency food trips to the Bay Area. Now you can probably find those ingredients not only in Flagstaff, but pretty much anywhere. CONTINUED

6 ounces dried pasta, whatever shape you like best, or fettuccine

1 clove garlic, thinly sliced

4 ounces Gorgonzola, crumbled in large pieces

2 tablespoons of your best butter, cut in pieces

2 to 4 tablespoons cream

Sea salt and freshly ground pepper

Parmigiano-Reggiano, to grate over all

Bring a large pot of water to a boil for the pasta. While it is heating, set a bowl large enough to hold the cooked pasta over the pot and add the garlic, cheese, butter, and cream. As the water heats, everything will become warm and soft.

Remove the bowl when the water comes to a boil. Add plenty of salt to the pot, then the pasta, and give it stir. Cook until the pasta is as done as you like it, then scoop it out and add it directly to the bowl. The heat of the pasta will melt any lumps of cheese that haven't melted yet. Toss everything together with freshly cracked pepper, and transfer to warm pasta plates. Grate a little Parmigiano-Reggiano over each plate and serve.

WHITE PEACHES OR NECTARINES
IN LEMON VERBENA SYRUP

Serves 6; V, GF

I adore both peaches and nectarines, especially white ones, when the fruits are properly ripe and juicy and not green or hard the way they so often are. You don't really need to do anything but enjoy them, but if you wish to, you can make this compote, flavored with lemon verbena leaves and serve it by itself or with ice cream. I have also made a version where I use both lemon verbena and culinary lavender, but I think in the end I'm partial to the lemon verbena. In northern New Mexico, it has to be planted each summer; it just won't winter over nor will it become very tall, as it does in Texas and other warmer climes. But it's worth giving it a try each year, and happily I've discovered that even dried leaves (hopefully not more than a year old) will swell up nicely and yield their flavor. If you prefer lavender, by all means use it.

This compote is a simple one that you can easily make more complex with the addition of a few small fragrant strawberries, a handful of raspberries, or other berries.

3 to 4 tablespoons sugar	**1 cup water**
1 small handful of fresh lemon verbena leaves, or 12 dried	**6 medium to large ripe white peaches or nectarines**

Combine the sugar and lemon verbena in a small saucepan with the water and bring it to a boil. Stir to dissolve the sugar, lower the heat, and simmer for 4 minutes. Turn off the heat and let steep for at least 15 minutes for the lemon verbena to yield its flavor.

Bring several quarts of water to a boil. Slide in the peaches, leave for 5 seconds, then remove to a bowl of cool water to stop the cooking. Slip off the skins.

Pour the syrup into the compote dish. Slice the peaches directly into it. If you're including berries, add them now, while the syrup is still warm. Make sure to leave a few of the lemon verbena leaves in with the fruit. Lay a piece of parchment paper or waxed paper directly over the fruit and refrigerate until ready to serve.

ROASTED PEPPER AND TOMATO SALAD WITH BASIL AND CAPERS

Serves 4 to 6; V, GF

What do I like about this dish? The texture: It's silky. The flavor: It's pure summer.

I once made this dish for a magazine and was sent several cartons of vegetables from Holland to use in it. The vegetables looked perfect, but the dish was utterly insipid. Yes, the peppers and tomatoes were organic, and that was good; but they were grown in plastic tunnels and apparently in the absence of those all-important ingredients: the sun and the heat of a dry summer. Peppers and tomatoes simply *need* plenty of heat and sun to be all they can be—then they're amazing. This is a simple but spectacularly satisfying dish, and because it's so simple, the quality of the ingredients matters. A lot. Start by choosing the best, most flavorful vegetables and herbs before you even think about cooking.

The short time the vegetables spend in the oven melds their flavors, transforms them into something bigger than the elements themselves, and releases copious amounts of juice that invites dunking with a hunk of good bread. And as far as its uses go, this can act as a salad, a topping for a last-minute pasta, the filling for a sandwich, the stuff of a summer frittata. Mostly it's a cooked salad, but it needn't be limited to that, for there will be leftovers unless your table is large and full.

4 large bell peppers, red, orange, or yellow

1 or 2 ripe-but-on-the-firm-side yellow or orange tomatoes (about 1¼ pounds)

6 large sprigs Italian parsley

1 tablespoon fresh marjoram or 12 large basil leaves

1 plump clove garlic

2 tablespoons capers

12 Niçoise olives, pitted

3 tablespoons best olive oil, plus extra for the dish

Sea salt and freshly ground pepper

Char the peppers over a charcoal fire or the flames of a gas burner, burning the skin and softening the flesh. If you're using yellow peppers, halve and oil them and then broil them without letting them char so that the skins can be removed but the flesh isn't darkened. Drop the roasted peppers into a bowl, cover, and set them aside while you prepare everything else. Then wipe off the skin, pull out the seeds, and core and cut the peppers into wide strips. Trim any ragged ends and set them aside for another use.

Make an "x" in the blossom ends of the tomatoes and then drop them into boiling water for 10 seconds. Remove them, peel off the loosened skins, then halve them crosswise and gently squeeze out the seeds and juice in a strainer. Cut the walls into wide pieces. Reserve the cores for a soup or sauce. Pour the strained juice over the tomato pieces.

Pull the leaves off the parsley stems. Chop them finely with the basil and garlic, then put in a bowl with the capers, olives, and 3 tablespoons of the oil. Season with ½ teaspoon of salt and some pepper.

Heat the oven to 400°F. Lightly oil an 8-inch diameter earthenware dish. Scatter a third of the tomatoes over the dish, then spoon on some of the sauce that has collected from them. Make a layer of peppers and sauce, follow with more tomatoes, and so on, until everything is used up. If your dish is large, you may only make two layers of tomatoes and peppers. Cover and bake for 20 minutes. Remove from the oven and let cool before serving. Serve at room temperature or chilled.

SMOKY PIMENTO CHEESE ON CUCUMBERS

Makes plenty for 6; GF

Pimento cheese didn't appear in my lexicon until I married a Southerner who reminisced about his mother making it in a grinder clamped to a an old wooden table under the post oak trees. Once we made it, I had to admit that pimento cheese is pretty good; but I've made changes to his mother's recipe. The diced pimentos that come in a tiny jar don't have that much flavor, I've found, so I use roasted pepper instead, either a jarred one or one I've roasted myself. I love the smoke that comes from using a good dash of Pimentón de la Vera (hot or sweet smoked paprika), and I use it generously. And the cheese will be either a white or yellow aged Cheddar, not American cheese. In the end, this is a zestier version than his mom's more traditional one. It makes a great filling for a grilled cheese sandwich (there's enough here for four) or you can mound a small pile on a thickly sliced cucumber and serve it for an appetizer on a summer's eve, when cucumbers are plentiful in the market or garden. Lacking your own, use a long English cucumber from the store.

8 ounces sharp white or yellow Cheddar cheese

⅓ cup diced roasted peppers or roasted pimentos

2 tablespoons mayonnaise, or more

2 teaspoons prepared mustard, or more

1 teaspoon Pimentón de la Vera, or more

Freshly ground pepper

1 scallion, thinly sliced, or 1 tablespoon finely snipped chives

Cucumber as needed, to make 1-inch-thick rounds

Grate the cheese on the large holes of a box grater. Put it in a bowl and stir in the diced peppers, mayonnaise mustard, pimentón, plenty of freshly ground pepper, and scallion. Taste and adjust as needed, adding more mustard, mayonnaise, pimentón, or pepper.

Wash the cucumber and peel off strips of skin, leaving some strips firmly attached. Slice it into thick rounds. If you don't mind being fiddly, scoop out the centers of each slice a bit, then mound a spoonful of cheese on top, pressing slightly into the scooped out area so that it will adhere and not slide off. If you're not inclined to do that, simply mound the cheese on top of the cucumbers. (It will tend to slip a little more.) Or put out bowls of each and let each person assemble his or her cucumbers and cheese.

AN IMPROVISED PLATTER SALAD

Serves 4 as a meal; GF

I also call this dish for joyfully overwhelmed market shoppers. Platter salads are a blessing for those of us who are unable to choose one vegetable over another or who simply can't make up our minds about *what* to focus on when faced with abundance, as is so often the case when the market (or garden) is at its summer peak. I am such a person, and what helps me (aside from the platter) are two maxims: one is that foods in season together taste good together; the other is that botanical families offer a unique coherence of flavor. Keep these thoughts in mind, and the chaos of abundance is bound to turn into success.

Collections of compatible vegetables, cooked or pickled when appropriate, left raw when not, arranged on a large platter, showered with herbs, and bathed with a dressing are always gorgeous to behold. If you wish, you can supplement a platter salad with good farm eggs cooked until firm but still moist in the center or a fine local cheese.

Here is an example of how you might approach putting the market on a platter. First, of course, let the market guide your specific choices. For example, your green beans might be fat romanos, slender filet beans, or curved Sultan's Crescents (or all three); your carrots, French market carrots or larger varieties, sliced; your greens arugula, wild spinach, orach, or frisée (lettuce being finished in the markets). When I first started making platter salads, we didn't have shishito peppers; now, you might sear some and add them to the platter. A sweet onion, thinly sliced, would be lovely, or a red onion, made scarlet and sweet by being tossed in vinegar (see page 175). Cucumbers might be included as well. I'm giving you a very simple platter salad—there could be many more more vegetables in it, in the spirit of the dish. As you can see in the photograph, this particular salad includes a few kinds of radishes and those gorgeous black cherry tomatoes. **CONTINUED**

1 or 2 cloves garlic

Sea salt

1 teaspoon mustard

⅓ cup best olive oil

Aged red wine vinegar

1 heaping tablespoon chopped fresh herbs, such as marjoram, chives, parsley, or lovage

1 pound small fingerling potatoes, such as La Ratte or Rose Finn Apple

1½ pounds green beans, one variety or mixed

Freshly ground pepper

A few handfuls of garden lettuces, arugula, or other greens

1 pound tomatoes, mixed varieties or one kind only, sliced into wedges

4 hard-cooked eggs, halved

Sprigs of purslane

1 small sweet white or red onion, thinly sliced and tossed in a little rice wine vinegar

3 tablespoons capers or a few caper berries

Have ready a large bowl for dressing the vegetables and a platter for arranging them.

To make the dressing, pound the garlic with ½ teaspoon of salt until smooth. Stir in the mustard, olive oil, vinegar, and the chopped herbs.

Put the potatoes in a saucepan and cover them with cold water. Add 1 teaspoon of salt and bring to a boil. Simmer until tender when pierced with a knife, about 25 minutes. When they're done, drain them, slice them in half lengthwise, and toss them with a few tablespoons of the dressing.

While the potatoes are cooking, put on a large pot of water to boil for the green beans. Slice off the stem ends of the beans. If using different varieties of beans, cook each type separately in the boiling water until tender but still a little firm. Scoop them out and put them on a towel to dry briefly, then toss them while still hot with a tablespoon or more of the dressing. Season to taste with salt and pepper and heap them in the center of the platter.

Arrange the greens on the platter. Add mounds of the potatoes around the beans. Tuck the tomatoes and eggs here and there, add sprigs of purslane, then spoon the remaining dressing over all. Finish with the addition of the capers and scatter over the sweet onion. Season with pepper. Serve the salad arranged on the platter and then toss at the table.

POTATO AND CHICKPEA STEW WITH SAUTÉED SPINACH

Serves 4; V, GF

For years I made this stew the same way, but over time I've varied it some. Originally I suggested serving it with romesco sauce—and I still do, especially if you have it on hand. It's the ideal accompaniment, reflective of the stew's ingredients and enhanced with roasted hazelnuts. But you could simply spoon a good Spanish olive oil over the surface along with a flourish of minced parsley and a grinding of pepper. And of course, some sautéed spinach added to each serving is very good, too.

Other changes have to do with the seasoning, the beans, and the tomatoes. I am very partial to both saffron and smoked paprika, both of which are excellent here. I tend to use both, but I don't use them together. One tends to cancel out the other, and if you're going to the expense of using saffron, you don't want to give up its unusual flavor.

As for the beans, chickpeas are very good. But when I haven't had a single chickpea on hand in any form, dried or canned, I've turned to cannellini beans and our native *bolita*, or pink beans. It changes the dish, but perhaps not that much. It's also quite possible to include no legumes at all, but I like them for their contrasting texture and for the protein they offer. A few times, I've included a cup or so of cooked pasta, such as snails or shells. While that might seem redundant to some—pasta with the potatoes—again, the pasta offers another texture, which many enjoy. In late summer I use tomatoes from the garden, but when they're not available, I use diced tomatoes and their juices from a jar.

This is a straightforward, brightly colored dish, but you do have to start by readying the onion, peppers, and potatoes. While they cook, you can prepare the rest of the ingredients. CONTINUED

1 pound fingerling potatoes, or Yellow Finns

2 tablespoons olive oil

1 large onion, finely diced

2 generous pinches saffron or
1 rounded teaspoon smoked paprika

2 large red bell peppers, stemmed,
seeded, and finely diced

1 large yellow bell pepper, stemmed, seeded
and cut into strips a scant 1 inch wide

2 large cloves garlic, thinly sliced

Sea salt and freshly ground pepper

1 heaping teaspoon sweet
or hot (unsmoked) paprika

3 tablespoons chopped parsley

½ cup dry sherry

1½ cups fresh or canned diced tomatoes,
plus their juices

1½ cups or more cooked chickpeas
or other beans

1 to 2 cups liquid (use a combination
of chickpea or bean broth plus
tomato juice or water)

1 bunch spinach, stems removed,
leaves carefully washed

Best olive oil, for finishing the
spinach and serving

Romesco sauce, to serve (optional)

If you're using fingerling potatoes, scrub them and then halve them lengthwise. Round potatoes can be scrubbed and quartered.

Warm a wide skillet or Dutch oven and then add the oil. When it's hot, follow with the onion, saffron threads (if you are using smoked paprika instead of saffron, you'll add it a bit later), diced and sliced peppers, and potatoes. Cook over medium heat, turning the vegetables every now and then with a wide rubber scraper, until the potatoes are tender-firm, 20 to 25 minutes. Cover the pan so that moisture collects and drops onto the vegetables, keeping them from burning. Add the garlic to the pan. Season with 1 teaspoon of salt and plenty of pepper.

Once the potatoes have begun to soften, remove the lid, add the sweet or hot paprika (plus the smoked paprika, if you are using it) and the parsley, along with the sherry. Cook until the juices in the pan have reduced and are thick and syrupy.

Add the tomatoes and chickpeas and enough of the liquid (tomato juice plus broth or water) to cover. Cover and cook over low heat until the potatoes are completely tender, 10 to 20 minutes more. Taste for salt and pepper and add more, if needed.

Drop the wet spinach into a pan (if it's dry, add a little water to the pan) and cook, turning the leaves, until wilted and tender, several minutes. Press out the excess moisture, toss with the good olive oil, and season with salt.

Serve the stew in bowls with the spinach divided among them. If you have romesco sauce on hand, add a dollop. If not, add a little more of your best olive oil to each bowl and serve.

POTATO AND GREEN CHILE STEW

Serves 4; GF

Not only is this a favorite dish of mine, others appear to have made it one of their favorites as well. I think of it as an autumnal stew, one to make when farmers are roasting their chiles at the market and filling the air with that good smell. That's also when the market is rich in potatoes and the weather is turning crisp. But because New Mexicans make it a practice to keep a stash of roasted chiles in the freezer, this can stand in as a hearty winter dish as well.

To me, our roasted northern New Mexican green chiles are the best, but all kinds, really, can be used. A New Mexican green chile stew would for sure have meat in it, but potatoes and chiles are also a timeless combination that overcomes the lack of pork or beef. Add a spoonful of cilantro-laced sour cream and you have a chunky stew that will warm you up any time of year.

For potatoes, I like to use russets because they fall apart and thicken the mixture, but it's also nice to have some big chunks of waxy-fleshed boiling potatoes that hold their shape. So I use both.

I like the simplicity of this stew, but you can add other good things. Fry halloumi cheese in a little oil until golden, then cut it into small pieces and add a few to each bowl. The heat softens the cheese and makes it a rich little surprise. Leftover baked ricotta cheese, which can look so unpromising, will also turn into a tender mouthful when added to a soup. CONTINUED

Tofu and Cilantro Salad with
Roasted Peanuts, 238
Tofu Triangles with Red Onions
and Tender Greens, 240–41
Warm Cabbage Salad with
Togarashi Tofu Crisps, 73–75
Tomatoes
Braised Summer
Vegetables, 260–63
Chopped Salad with Toasted
Seeds and Marjoram-Mint
Dressing, 220–21
Dried Porcini, Fresh
Mushroom, and Whole
Tomato Ragout with Seared
Polenta, 163–64
Eggplant Gratin with a Golden
Dome of Saffron-Ricotta
Custard, 108–11
Golden Tofu with Orange and
Yellow Peppers, 242–43
Green, Yellow, or Purple Beans
with Sun Gold Tomatoes and
Opal Basil, 38–41
Improvised Platter Salad, An,
189–91
Oven-Roasted Tomato Sauce,
An, 251
Potato and Chickpea Stew with
Sautéed Spinach, 192–94
Rio Zape Beans with Smoked
Chile, 42–43
Roasted Tomatoes and Fingerling
Potatoes with Thyme, Olives,
and Capers, 255–57
Roasted Pepper and Tomato
Salad with Basil and
Capers, 186–87
Sauce Made with Canned
Tomatoes, A, 250
Sauce Made with Fresh
Tomatoes, A, 250
Sweet-Tart Sun Gold Tomato
Soup with Avocado
Relish, 247–48
Tomato and Red Pepper Tart
in a Yeasted Crust, 245–46
Tomato and Roasted
Cauliflower Curry with
Paneer, 252–54

Tortilla Chips, Blue Corn,
Red Chile and Posole with
Avocado and, 198–99
Trouchia (Failed-to-Catch-a-Trout
Frittata), 122–23
Turnips
Rough-and-Ready Soup,
Refined, A, 258–59

V

Vegetables
Braised Summer
Vegetables, 260–63
buying, 4, 21
caramelizing, 8
Chopped Salad with Toasted
Seeds and Marjoram-Mint
Dressing, 220–21
growing, 7, 21
Improvised Platter
Salad, An, 189–91
organic, 24
See also individual vegetables
Vegetarian cooking tips, 4, 7–10,
12–14, 17–19
Vinegars, 12, 21

W

Waffles, Yeasted Buckwheat, 62–63
Walnuts
Dried Fruits with Fennel,
Sesame Seeds, and Orange
Flower Water, 102
Kale and Walnut Pesto with
Roasted or Seared Winter
Squash, 138–39
Marjoram in a Thick, Green
Sauce for Beets (and Other
Vegetables), 152–53
Pasta with Caramelized Onions
and Crushed Roasted
Walnuts, 180
Roasted Asparagus and Arugula
with Hard-Cooked Eggs and
Walnuts, 33–34
Roasted Eggplant with Dill,
Yogurt, and Walnuts, 114–15
Walnut Nugget Cookies, 265
Wild Rice, Native, and Celery
Root Soup, 272

Y

Yeast, nutritional, 22
Yogurt
Green Lentils with Yogurt,
Sorrel, and Parsley Sauce, 146
Roasted Eggplant with Dill,
Yogurt, and Walnuts, 114–15
Yogurt, Cumin, and Green
Herb Sauce, 273
Yogurt-Tahini Sauce, 53

Z

Zucchini
Zucchini Cakes with Cheddar,
Oregano, and Tomatillo
Salsa, 275–76
Zucchini Pancakes with Feta
and Dill, 275, 277

Copyright © 2017 by Deborah Madison
Photographs copyright © 2017 by Erin Scott

All rights reserved.
Published in the United States by Ten Speed Press, an imprint of the
Crown Publishing Group, a division of Penguin Random House LLC,
New York.
www.crownpublishing.com
www.tenspeed.com

Ten Speed Press and the Ten Speed Press colophon are registered
trademarks of Penguin Random House LLC.

Library of Congress Cataloging-in-Publication Data is on file
with the publisher.

Hardcover ISBN: 978-0-399-57888-5
eBook ISBN: 978-0-399-57889-2

Printed in China

Design by Ashley Lima
Food styling by Lillian Kang
Assistant food styling by Veronica Vellejo
Prop styling by Christine Wolheim
Additional props provided by Sandy Simon

10 9 8 7 6 5 4 3 2 1

First Edition